The Biblical Seminar
61

PAULINE IMAGES
IN FICTION AND FILM

PAULINE IMAGES
IN FICTION AND FILM

On Reversing the Hermeneutical Flow

Larry J. Kreitzer

Sheffield Academic Press

Copyright © 1999 Sheffield Academic Press

Published by
Sheffield Academic Press Ltd
Mansion House
19 Kingfield Road
Sheffield S11 9AS
England

Typeset by Sheffield Academic Press
and
Printed on acid-free paper in Great Britain
by The Cromwell Press
Trowbridge, Wiltshire

British Library Cataloguing in Publication Data

A catalogue record for this book is available
from the British Library

ISBN 1-85075-933-2

CONTENTS

Foreword   7
Abbreviations   12

INTRODUCTION   17

Chapter 1
ROBINSON CRUSOE: SHIPWRECK, SIN AND SALVATION   31
    1. Paul: The Shipwrecked Apostle   34
    2. Daniel Defoe: The Dissenting Scribbler   40
    3. Shipwreck, Sin and Salvation in *Robinson Crusoe*   48
    4. Shipwreck, Sin and Salvation in Film Interpretations
      of *Robinson Crusoe*   66
    5. Summary   77

Chapter 2
THE PICTURE OF DORIAN GRAY:
LOOKING IN THE MIRROR DARKLY   80
    1. Mirror Imagery in 1 Corinthians 13.12
      and 2 Corinthians 3.18   82
    2. The Writing of *The Picture of Dorian Gray*   86
    3. Mirror Imagery in Wilde's Novel   93
    4. Some Film Interpretations of Wilde's Masterpiece   98
    5. Summary   111

Chapter 3
DRACULA: 'THE BLOOD IS THE LIFE!'   113
    1. The Lord's Supper in Paul's Thought   114
    2. Communion Imagery in Bram Stoker's *Dracula* (1897)   117
    3. Communion Imagery in Some Film Adaptations of *Dracula*   128
    4. Summary   141

Chapter 4
UNCLE TOM'S CABIN: THE LIBERATION OF SLAVERY?   143
    1. 1 Corinthians 7.20-24 and Paul's Attitude to Slavery   145
    2. Harriet Beecher Stowe: The Crusading Pen
       of God Almighty   152
    3. Slavery and Liberation in *Uncle Tom's Cabin*:
       Various Responses to Emancipation   159
    4. Film Adaptations of *Uncle Tom's Cabin*   173
    5. Summary   189

CONCLUSION   192

Bibliography   195
Index of References   232
Index of Authors   235

FOREWORD

When I was on sabbatical in Oxford at Regent's Park College in 1994, I met Larry Kreitzer and we discovered we had a mutual interest in literature and film. In the course of our conversations, he confessed that he had a desire to share with students his fascination for the life and work of Franz Kafka (which had been heightened by his own sabbatical spent in Prague in 1989 during the waning years of the communist regime). I told him that I regularly taught a class in modern fiction at Georgetown College and could very well arrange my syllabus around a 'Kafka week' if he would plan to come to Kentucky the following spring. In April 1995 the visit and the course materialized, to the huge advantage of my undergraduate students who unabashedly exclaimed that the week Dr Kreitzer spent with us discussing Kafka and his fiction (*Metamorphosis*, *In the Penal Colony* and *The Trial*) and the afternoons and evenings we spent together viewing film versions of *The Trial* were among the best experiences they had had in college.

I am delighted to be asked to write this foreword, since I have experienced with my own students over the years the advantage of combining studies of film and literature. Students on both sides of the Atlantic seem to feel that film is their generation's medium. Even if the film versions are not exactly faithful to the books, the very conflict between the two can generate some very stimulating discussions and lead to new insights about the sources.

Two earlier volumes by Larry Kreitzer, *The New Testament in Fiction and Film* (1993) and *The Old Testament in Fiction and Film* (1994) have established his unique interdisciplinary approach to theology, literary criticism and film study. Kreitzer's concept of 'reversing the hermeneutical flow' encourages contemporary cinema audiences to revisit the head waters of the biblical texts from which so many modern films flow.

This new volume, *Pauline Images in Fiction and Film*, encourages theological scholars as well as film buffs to explore with fresh eyes the plights of Robinson Crusoe, Dorian Gray, Count Dracula and Uncle Tom. Kreitzer brings together these four diverse literary characters because the individual texts share values found in biblical sources. The central images in each of the films Larry Kreitzer discusses rework Pauline metaphors, just as the films themselves adapt the original fictions for twentieth-century audiences. The flow thus reverses from film to original fiction to the controlling metaphors found in the Scripture.

Some fictional characters step outside the pages of their fictions to take on lives of their own. At least three of the central fictional characters in the works that Kreitzer chooses for his discussion have that kind of unique energy. Robinson Crusoe is a prime example of just such a character. Kreitzer begins his discussion of Pauline images by showing how Crusoe, the fictional character, and St Paul share the experience of having been shipwrecked which, in each case, becomes a metaphor for their individual spiritual journeys. Kreitzer's meticulously documented discussion of the actual shipwreck of Paul described in Acts and the literary shipwreck of Robinson Crusoe described by Daniel Defoe launches his discussion of film versions of *Robinson Crusoe*. Of several cinematic treatments, Kreitzer focuses on two (although Jack Gold's *Man Friday* [1975], which shifts the narrative perspective from Crusoe to Friday, might have been an equally interesting third example). The two films that Kreitzer chooses for his discussion are *The Adventures of Robinson Crusoe* (1964) directed by Jean Sacha, and *Crusoe* (1988) directed by Caleb Deschanel. The latter is particularly interesting in that it presents Crusoe as a slave trader and introduces into Defoe's original story the tensions surrounding the issue of slavery. This prepares readers of *Pauline Images in Fiction and Film* for the much more complex treatment of slavery found in *Uncle Tom's Cabin* in the last chapter and forges something of a thematic *inclusio* for Kreitzer's book as a whole.

In his analysis of Oscar Wilde's novel *The Picture of Dorian Gray*, and the various film adaptations of it, Kreitzer examines the mirror imagery used by Paul in his letters to the Corinthians as a 'symbol of for self-knowledge'. He explores Wilde's own use of the sphinx as both a reflection of himself and a representation of the enigmatic nature of any mirror reflection. Of approximately a dozen films of this novel, Kreitzer chooses two for his discussion, one British and one American: Albert Lewin's *The Picture of Dorian Gray* (1944) and Glenn Jordan's

The Picture of Dorian Gray (1973). In the 1944 film adaptation the sphinx is used to connect Dorian Gray (or Wilde) with the mirror-like portrait. This subtle linking of riddles, portraits and mirrors reverses the hermeneutical flow to reveal mystical depths to Paul's reference to mirrors and the property of mirrors as reflective of the religious struggle within Dorian Gray. Just as Dorian Gray's portrait mysteriously reflects the depraved nature of his soul although his outer bodily appearance remains beautifully youthful, Paul uses the mirror image to reflect the eternal spiritual dimension of human life.

In more than 100 years since Bram Stoker's novel *Dracula* was published, it has never been out of print. Stoker's vampire is definitely one of those fictional characters who has left his book far behind to roam about the world on his own, fang-bared and neck-seeking, wearing myriad disguises. Kreitzer documents Stoker's six years of careful research prior to writing the novel and summarizes the multitude of critical approaches to it (Freudian and feminist, political and sociological, as well as Marxist). Kreitzer himself, however, maintains that *Dracula* is a 'profoundly theological novel' with a multitude of biblical allusions. He focuses particularly on the crucifixion and communion images in his discussion of the novel. Out of over 200 Dracula and vampire films, Kreitzer selects three for discussion: Francis Ford Coppola's *Bram Stoker's Dracula* (1992), Joel Schumacher's *The Lost Boys* (1987) and Boris Sagal's *The Omega Man* (1971). The last, an adaptation of Richard Matheson's ground-breaking novel *I Am Legend* (1954), which is itself an update of Stoker's book, provides a 'quasi-scientific explanation' of vampirism with a political sub-text. In this version the blood imagery ('the blood is the life!') is presented as blood transfusions with blood serum. Near the end of the film, a saviour-figure dies in a literal fountain filled with blood (evoking the graphic imagery of William Cowper's famous hymn). *The Lost Boys*, a horror comedy set in California, uses the eucharistic concept of drinking blood as a part of youth culture's initiation rite. Kreitzer criticizes Coppola's film *Bram Stoker's Dracula* as being 'barely recognizable' as Stoker's novel, transforming the predatory Dracula's relationship with Mina Harker into a 'tale of lost love' and thereby reducing the book's Gothic horror to romantic sentimentality. The biblical imagery common to all Dracula films draws on Paul's discussion of the Lord's Supper in 1 Corinthians and his improbable celebration of it aboard ship on the way to Rome in Acts 27–28.

For his last work, Kreitzer chooses Harriet Beecher Stowe's best-selling abolitionist novel, *Uncle Tom's Cabin*, to shed light on Paul's controversial passage in 1 Cor. 7.20-24, which raises the question of whether or not Christian slaves should seek their freedom. Stowe's novel highlights the Christian drama of redemption and liberation: both Little Eva's self-sacrifice and Uncle Tom's martyrdom evoke Christ's death. The fictional juxtaposition of George Harris and Uncle Tom dramatizes the conflict that slaves face—whether to submit passively and remain a slave, or choose rebellion and freedom. Insofar as Uncle Tom is the hero of the novel, Kreitzer maintains that Stowe favored the passive approach (but then she would, *wouldn't she?*).

Several theatrical adaptations of *Uncle Tom's Cabin* were produced soon after it was published; many of the extant film versions date from the silent film era. Kreitzer chooses two modern films for his analysis: Geza von Radvany's *Onkel Toms Hütte* (1965) and Stan Lathan's *Uncle Tom's Cabin* (1987) which was a made-for-TV adaptation. *Onkel Toms Hütte*, which exists in French, Italian, German, Serbo-Croat and English versions, takes so many liberties with the novel that it is some-times hard to recognize its classic source. Many of the changes are fac-tually inaccurate as well as anachronistic. The most fundamental change is that in this film Simon Legree's violence causes Tom to become a revolutionary. On his deathbed, Uncle Tom inspires Legree's other slaves to open the levy (thus destroying the crops) and to run away. On the other hand, Harris, the rebellious character in Stowe's novel, is portrayed in a non-violent role, buying his freedom with money he made from inventing the cotton gin (one of the film's more obvious historical inaccuracies). In this movie, Tom's Christian faith is linked to his revolt against Simon Legree's tyranny, a reversal of 'gentle Jesus, meek and mild' if ever there was one. The film even ends with a triumphant singing of 'Joshua fit de Battle of Jericho' by an uncredited Paul Robeson, who himself was familiar with the debilitating effects of racial prejudice and discrimination.

In contrast, Kreitzer praises Stan Lathan's 1987 film, with its all-star cast, as a 'high quality effort which offers a sensitive version of Stowe's novel...' This version pointedly depicts Tom's moral dilemma, although some of the complexities of both Paul the apostle's letters and Harriet Beecher Stowe's novel have been over-simplified and Uncle Tom's name has been changed to 'Tom' in order to avoid the negative connotations of the original, politically incorrect 'Uncle Tom'.

Through these four works of fiction and their many film adaptations, Larry Kreitzer opens the eyes of both moviegoers and readers to a number of complex Pauline ideas and images. Because Kreitzer has chosen books which have introduced fictional characters into the society of popular culture where they live lives altogether independent of their original novels, the understanding of the scriptural images is enhanced as the multitudinous variety of interpretations is presented through films. If you are at all interested in the interface between the Bible, fiction and film, you will find this a stimulating and thought-provoking book. This is biblical hermeneutics at its most fascinating.

Gwen Curry
Professor of English
Georgetown College, Kentucky

ABBREVIATIONS

AAR	*African American Review*
AB	Anchor Bible
ABD	David Noel Freedman (ed.), *The Anchor Bible Dictionary* (New York: Doubleday, 1992)
ABR	*American Benedictine Review*
AI	*American Imago*
AL	*American Literature*
ALH	*American Literary History*
AQ	*American Quarterly*
ATQ	*American Transcendental Quarterly*
BA	*Biblical Archaeologist*
BAFCS	Bruce W. Winter (ed.), *The Book of Acts in its First-Century Setting* (6 vols.; Carlisle: Paternoster Press, 1993–)
BJECS	*British Journal of Eighteenth-Century Studies*
BibRes	*Biblical Research*
BS	Biblical Seminar Series
BS	*Buffalo Studies*
BST	Bible Speaks Today
BUSE	*Boston University Studies in English*
CBQ	*Catholic Biblical Quarterly*
CenR	*The Centennial Review*
CGTC	Cambridge Greek Testament Commentary Series
CL	*Contemporary Literature*
CLAJ	*College Language Association Journal*
CLS	*Comparative Literature Studies*
ClQ	*Classical Quarterly*
CTM	*Concordia Theological Monthly*
DR	*Dalhousie Review*
EC	*Essays in Criticism*
EC	Epworth Commentary Series
ECF	*Eighteenth-Century Fiction*
ECS	*Eighteenth-Century Studies*
EJ	*English Journal*
ECTI	*The Eighteenth Century: Theory and Interpretation*
ELH	*English Literary History*

ELN	*English Language Notes*
ELT	*English Literature in Transition*
EvQ	*Evangelical Quarterly*
FAJWS	*Frontiers: A Journal of Women's Studies*
GR	*Georgia Review*
HLQ	*Huntington Library Quarterly*
HR	*History of Religions*
HT	*History Today*
HTR	*Harvard Theological Review*
IC	Interpretation Commentary Series
IJWS	*International Journal of Women's Studies*
JACult	*Journal of American Culture*
JBL	*Journal of Biblical Literature*
JECS	*Journal of Early Christian Studies*
JEGP	*Journal of English and German Philology*
JELH	*Journal of English Literary History*
JNH	*Journal of Negro History*
JNT	*Journal of Narrative Technique*
JP	*Journal of Psychohistory*
JPFT	*Journal of Popular Film and Television*
JQR	*Jewish Quarterly Review*
JSH	*Journal of Southern History*
JSNTSup	*Journal for the Study of the New Testament*, Supplement Series
JTC	*Journal for Theology and the Church*
JTS	*Journal of Theological Studies*
KPR	*Kentucky Philological Review*
LP	*Literature and Psychology*
LT	*Literature and Theology*
MFS	*Modern Fiction Studies*
MLN	*Modern Language Notes*
MP	*Modern Philology*
MQ	*The Midwest Quarterly*
MR	*Minnesota Review*
NALF	*Negro American Literature Forum*
NCF	*Nineteenth-Century Fiction*
NCL	*Nineteenth-Century Literature*
NEQ	*New England Quarterly*
NHB	*Negro History Bulletin*
NICNT	New International Commentary on the New Testament
NLH	*New Literary History*
NovT	*Novum Testamentum*
NQ	*Notes & Queries*
NR	*New Republic*
NTC	New Testament Commentary Series

NTG	New Testament Guides
NTS	*New Testament Studies*
NWSAJ	*National Women's Studies Association Journal*
NY	*The New Yorker*
PC	Proclamation Commentary Series
PDG	Oscar Wilde, *The Picture of Dorian Gray* (London: Penguin Books, 1985 [1891])
PF	*Philosophy Forum*
PLL	*Papers in Language and Literature*
PMLA	*Publications of the Modern Language Association*
PQ	*Philological Quarterly*
PsyQ	*Psychoanalytic Quarterly*
PSS	*Psychoanalytic Study of Society*
PTT	Playing the Texts
RC	Daniel Defoe, *Robinson Crusoe* (ed. Angus Ross; London: Penguin Books, 1985 [1719])
REL	*Review of English Literature*
RES	*Review of English Studies*
RTR	*Reformed Theological Review*
SAF	*Studies in American Fiction*
SAQ	*South Atlantic Quarterly*
SB	*Studies in Bibliography*
SBLDS	SBL Dissertation Series
SBT	Studies in Biblical Theology
SCH	*Studies in Church History*
SE	*Studia Evangelica I, II, III* (= TU 73 [1959], 87 [1964], 88 [1964], etc.)
SEL	*Studies in English Literature 1500–1900*
SHR	*Southern Humanities Review*
SLI	*Studies in the Literary Imagination*
SN	*Studies in the Novel*
SNTSMS	Society for New Testament Studies Monograph Series
SP	*Studies in Philology*
SPC	Sacra Pagina Commentary Series
TBC	Torch Biblical Commentary
TDNT	Gerhard Kittel and Gerhard Friedrich (eds.), *Theological Dictionary of the New Testament* (trans. Geoffrey W. Bromiley; 10 vols.; Grand Rapids: Eerdmans, 1964–)
TMR	*The Massachusetts Review*
TNTC	Tyndale New Testament Commentaries
TSL	*Tennessee Studies in Literature*
TSLL	*Texas Studies in Literature and Language*
TynBul	*Tyndale Bulletin*
UES	*Unisa English Studies*

UTC	Harriet Beecher Stowe, *Uncle Tom's Cabin, or, Life among the Lowly* (ed. A. Douglas; London: Penguin Books, 1986 [1852])
UTQ	*University of Toronto Quarterly*
VIJ	*Victorian Journal*
VN	*The Victorian Newsletter*
VS	*Victorian Studies*
YR	*Yale Review*
WBC	Word Biblical Commentary
WLWE	*World Literature Written in English*
WS	*Women's Studies*
WUNT	Wissenschaftliche Untersuchungen zum Neuen Testament
YJC	*Yale Journal of Criticism*
ZNW	*Zeitschrift für die neutestamentliche Wissenschaft*

INTRODUCTION

This book is a continuation of the experiment in biblical hermeneutics that I first attempted some five years ago. The aim is to listen to the conversation that takes place between biblical texts, great works of literature and cinematic adaptations of those works of literature. This volume takes as its biblical starting-point the life and ministry of the apostle Paul, with each of the four chapters concentrating on selected passages from the Pauline letters, which in turn are occasionally complemented by passages from the Acts of the Apostles containing additional information about the ministry of Paul. In keeping with the pattern set within my first two volumes in the Biblical Seminar series of Sheffield Academic Press, *The New Testament in Fiction and Film* (1993) and *The Old Testament in Fiction and Film* (1994), I have deliberately chosen works of fiction that have stood the test of time and are commonly acknowledged to be 'classics'. Each of these literary works has also been the subject of at least one film adaptation. As a matter of principle, too, I have included a fictional work written by a woman author (not an easy thing to do since few women writers have had their work successfully translated into film).

The studies begin with an investigation of Daniel Defoe's most famous literary work, his adventure novel *Robinson Crusoe* (1719). There has been something of a revival of interest in Defoe in recent years, as is witnessed by the 1996 Granada TV adaptation of his novel *Moll Flanders* (1722). Yet despite this long overdue attention to one of his most raucous female characters of fiction (and one wonders when a filmed version of *Roxana* will appear to carry on the trend!), it is without doubt that *Robinson Crusoe* remains Defoe's best-loved work. Popular fascination with desert-island experiences continues unabated and has even picked up some women disciples in what has been for a long time a male-dominated territory,[1] as the success of both Lucy Irvine's novel *Castaway* (1983) and Joanna Lumley's 1994 BBC1

1. Saxton (1996) discusses this.

television special, entitled *Girl Friday*, of her nine-day odyssey on a desert island testify. There are even space-age equivalents, which explore the idea of being marooned in a spaceship or alone on a hostile planet in some forgotten corner of the galaxy. Popular fascination with the Robinson Crusoe theme peaked in the 'space-race' of the 1960s and is evidenced by such television cult classics as diverse as *Gilligan's Island* (1964–66) and *Lost in Space* (1965–67). Even Walt Disney Studios ventures an attempt at the genre, as *Lt. Robin Crusoe U.S.N.* (1966), starring Dick Van Dyke in the title role, illustrates. This is a playful, battle-of-the-sexes version of the story, set in the Pacific during World War Two, and chronicles how a stranded US Navy pilot manages to survive life on a tropical island. Crusoe here salvages a wrecked Japanese submarine, befriends a space-chimpanzee named Floyd, and 'tames' an island woman whom he names Wednesday (a character corresponding to Robinson Crusoe's man-servant Friday).

Central to Defoe's story is the account of Robinson's shipwreck on an uninhabited island and how he came to perceive the hand of providence at work in his salvation. The obvious parallel to this is the account of Paul's shipwreck in Acts 27.1-44, together with the brief allusions that the apostle himself makes to his three experiences of shipwreck in 2 Cor. 11.25-26. There are intriguing parallels to Defoe's novel here in that the hero Robinson Crusoe can boast, as Paul does, that he has survived three similar disasters at sea (once when his ship founders at Yarmouth, once when his ship is captured by Moor pirates, and once when he shipwrecks on the island). Similarly, Robinson has his equivalent of Paul's 'day and night spent on the open sea', when the canoe he makes to circle the island is caught up in a swift current which takes him out to sea, and it looks as if he will not be able to get back to land safely.

There is much to be gleaned from a study of how the shipwreck motif is used within *Robinson Crusoe* when compared with the two New Testament writings, although the parallel is very rarely made. In fact, as far as I am aware, the only instance of a recent New Testament commentator even mentioning Defoe's classic tale is I. Howard Marshall's *Acts* (1980a). Marshall calls attention to *Robinson Crusoe* in his explanation of one of the awkwardness of narrative in Luke's account, namely that contained in Acts 27.30. In the verse we read: 'the sailors were seeking to escape from the ship, and had lowered the boat into the sea, under pretence of laying out anchors from the bow.' The difficulty is, of course, that it is unlikely that experienced sailors would do such a thing at night in the middle of a severe storm; rather, they would stay on board, wait out the storm, and try their chances in the morning. So what is going on here? Marshall (1980a: 412) comments:

> Readers of *Robinson Crusoe* will remember a very similar situation in which the ship ran aground in the early morning and the crew took to the boat and all perished except for Crusoe himself who later was able to come back to the ship and commented, 'I saw evidently, that if we had kept on board, we had been all sage—that is to say, we had all got safe on shore.' Defoe's story indicates that men will do foolish things, although it remains possible that the intention of the sailors was misunderstood by the passengers.

Given the tumultuous life that Daniel Defoe lived, with many personal disasters and 'shipwrecks' along the way, it comes as no surprise that his classic is often described as a 'spiritual autobiography'. This is one of the sub-themes which I shall pursue within the study on Defoe's *Robinson Crusoe*.

The description 'spiritual autobiography' has also been applied to Oscar Wilde's *The Picture of Dorian Gray*, which is the subject of the second study pursued within this book.[2]

The talented Irish-born English dandy Oscar Wilde was one of the most controversial figures of the Victorian era. Wilde's life and work has undergone something of a renaissance in recent years, as a full-length feature film and a number of new theatrical productions all serve to illustrate. For example, 1997–98 saw a production of David Hare's *The Judas Kiss* at the Playhouse Theatre in London's fashionable West End (starring the acclaimed Irish actor Liam Neeson), a Broadway production of Moises Kaufmann's *Gross Indecency: The Three Trials of Oscar Wilde*, and a revival of John Gay's *Oscar Wilde: Diversions & Delights* in an off-Broadway production in New York City. Collectively these plays serve to illustrate something of the change of fortune that Wilde's reputation has undergone.

This is in stark contrast to the way that Wilde was treated following his death in November 1900. In fact, he was vilified for some years by the British press, and was even accused of being responsible for some of the follies that characterized the debacle of World War One.[3]

2.   See Cervo (1985: 19) for a discussion of Defoe's *Robinson Crusoe* along these lines.

3.   See Hoare (1997) for more on this subject. The Tory MP Pemberton Billing

My exploration within this study concentrates on Wilde's novel *The Picture of Dorian Gray*, a work which was cited as evidence against Wilde in his public trials for gross indecency. In this regard, the novel is alluded to within Brian Gilbert's recent film on the life of Oscar Wilde, simply entitled *Wilde* (1997), as well as within the earlier effort written and directed by Ken Hughes entitled *The Trials of Oscar Wilde* (1960), which starred Peter Finch in the title role.[4] Gilbert's film stars Stephen Fry as Oscar Wilde, a role which he seems destined, by both looks and temperament, to have played, and one which he carries off with considerable charm and extraordinary talent and sensitivity.[5] Indeed, it is difficult to imagine another contemporary actor who could accomplish what Stephen Fry has managed to achieve within this film. He brings Oscar Wilde to life in an astonishing way; through his performance Wilde becomes a living, breathing, and extremely vulnerable human being who challenges us to reconsider our assumed right to judge another human being simply on the basis of his or her sexuality. A more salient lesson for humanity entering the twenty-first century, with the gauntlet lines of a homophobia and religious intolerance already drawn and established in many quarters, is difficult to conceive. Indeed, one cannot help but wonder how far a double issue on video of Antonia Bird's *Priest* (1995) (a film chronicling the life of a gay Roman Catholic priest in Liverpool) and Brian Gilbert's *Wilde* might go in changing perceptions and advancing the cause of mutual understanding and respect, at least as far as it is applied to the area of human sexual relationships.

The study offered here of Oscar Wilde's *The Picture of Dorian Gray* explores a theme which has had a number of expressions over the

claimed that the British war effort was being undermined by the fact that the German High Command was blackmailing 40,000 British homosexuals. These men, Billing claimed, were well placed within the upper echelons of society and their commitment to the war effort was called into question. Effectively, Wilde (and the moral corruption he was thought to have represented) was being blamed for the fiasco in the trenches of the Western Front!

4.   The film was based upon H. Montgomery Hyde's *The Trials of Oscar Wilde* (first published in 1948). Hyde developed a fascination for Wilde and his life after occupying the same rooms that Wilde did in Magdalene College, Oxford. Hyde's recounting of these traumatic episodes in Wilde's life has also been recently revived in a CSA Telltapes production from 1996 entitled *Great Trials: Oscar Wilde*. The production uses transcripts of the trials and stars Martin Jarvis.

5.   See Fry (1997) for the actor's feelings about his destiny in playing the role.

centuries, but one which has roots that extend to the very beginnings of classical civilization. I speak of the idea of looking at oneself in a mirror, of encountering our reflections and being challenged in some way by them. Within Paul's letters to the church at Corinth there are two specific passages which allude to such imagery, namely 1 Cor. 13.12 and 2 Cor. 3.18. It appears that Paul here relies upon the importance of mirrors within the experience of the Corinthian Christians (Corinth was known as a centre of mirror manufacture in the ancient world), and turns to such mirror imagery in the midst of his writing to them. Although we might feel that in this regard Paul shows himself to be a good contextual theologian, one who is adaptable to the concerns and interests of his own audience, we would be mistaken to think that he is doing something unique. In fact, he is doing nothing more than employing an image that was well established within the ancient world.

The idea of a person being fascinated by a reflection of himself or herself is as old as the myth of Narcissus, and as modern as Walt Disney's versions of fairy-tale classics. In this sense, when the novel's central character Dorian Gray looks into the mirror, and thus looks at himself, he is asking the same question of his soul that the wicked queen does within the fairy-tale *Snow White and the Seven Dwarfs*: 'Mirror, mirror on the wall, who is the fairest one of all?'[6] How accurate are reflections, and what do they reveal about the person's soul, the inner self? It is this deep soul-searching that is magnificently explored within Wilde's novel.

There is little doubt that Wilde's *The Picture of Dorian Gray* offers a rich exploration of many of the myths which are foundational to Western literature, and there is an intriguing connection between *Dorian Gray* and the myth which is the focus of the third chapter within this volume, Bram Stoker's *Dracula* (1897). It has been suggested that Wilde's novel is a creative adaptation of the mythical tradition of vampires which was so prevalent within English nineteenth-century literature (Twitchell 1981: 171-78). At least one biographer of Stoker has gone so far as to argue that the character of Count Dracula is a fictionalization of Oscar Wilde, who, by the time that Stoker began to write the novel in earnest, was known as a figure of some notoriety.[7] Indeed, a number of scholars in the past decade have put forward the

6. Sullivan (1972: 14) describes *The Picture of Dorian Gray* as a version of the classic fairy-tale.

7. Farson (1975: 130, 152) discusses this.

suggestion that Stoker, a fellow Irishman who knew Wilde well and had even rivalled him for the affections of Florence Balcolme (she married Stoker in the end), was himself a closet homosexual. Stoker, so it is contended, was deeply shocked by Wilde's trial for 'gross indecency', and he allegedly wrote *Dracula* in the wake of the public scandal it produced.[8]

In a recent study of *Dracula*, I examined the way in which the apostle Paul expressed the significance of the death of Jesus Christ on the cross, and I compared that with the way in which crucifixion imagery is used within Bram Stoker's novel (Kreitzer 1997). This comparison then led to an exploration of how crucifixion imagery is portrayed within some of the many *Dracula* films which have been produced over the years. I suggested that the portrayal of the crucifixion has undergone something of a reversal of fortunes in most modern films, with the cross moving from being an object of veneration to an object of ridicule, particularly in vampire films that are aimed at the teenage movie-going public. An excellent illustration of this (which I did not mention in the earlier study) is Fran Rubel Kazul's *Buffy the Vampire Slayer* (1992). This film is set in a typical mid-American town and focuses on the trials and tribulations of Buffy, a cheerleader for the local high-school basketball team, who discovers that she is the latest in a long line of female vampire-killers who is now called to rise to her destiny. Predictably, the film panders to many themes commonly associated with teenage angst (boy–girl relationships, sexual awakening, high-school peer-pressure, the preoccupation with personal crises at the cost of the trivialization of world issues, etc.). Not surprisingly, the idea of 'the power of the cross' is employed within the film as a standard vampire image, but what is interesting is the way in which the cross is made fun of in the process. At the climax of the film Buffy (played by Kristy Swanson) faces her arch-enemy the evil vampire Lothos (played by Rutger Hauer), and we have the following exchange:

> Lothos: How are you going to stop me? I am life beyond death, and you are just like the other girls.
>
> Buffy: Well, maybe I'll surprise you! *(She takes out a small crucifix and holds it in front of her.)*
>
> Lothos: This is your defence? Oh, *please!* Your puny faith? *(He reaches out and grabs hold of the crucifix. It bursts into flame.)*

8. Howes (1988) and Schaffer (1994) both address this matter. Schaffer (1994: 406) describes *Dracula* as 'a dreamlike projection of Wilde's traumatic trial'.

Buffy: No! My keen fashion sense! *(She takes out a can of hairspray and sprays it into the burning crucifix, transforming it into a flame-thrower with which she sets Lothos on fire.)*

In the study on Bram Stoker's *Dracula* contained within this book I extend the focus of my earlier investigation and turn from the importance of crucifixion imagery to another motif which is central to both the New Testament and the original novel. The exploration here concerns the extent to which communion imagery, particularly the idea of the sacrificial shedding of blood (or even the *drinking* of, or *transfusion* of blood) is used within the novel. Once again, this is shown to be an important theological motif in *Dracula*, one which is creatively adapted within several of the many Dracula-vampire films which build upon Stoker's imagery. Not least among these are Francis Ford Coppola's film from 1992 entitled *Bram Stoker's Dracula* and Boris Sagal's science-fiction classic *The Omega Man* (1971), both of which are discussed within the study. It goes without saying that Paul's discussion of communion in such texts as 1 Cor. 5.7 and 11.23-26, passages which have been so influential in the life of the Christian church, forms an important backdrop against which all of the eucharistic imagery in *Dracula* and subsequent developments of the vampire myth are to be viewed.

The fourth study within this volume seeks to explore the meaning of two controversial passages from Paul's first letter to the church at Corinth: 1 Cor. 7.20-24 and 1 Corinthians 9. Scholarly investigations into these passages are rightly set against the backdrop of one of the prevailing socio-economic institutions of the Graeco-Roman world—slavery. Steven Spielberg's recent film *Amistad* (1997) has done much to rekindle interest in the crucial place that slavery had within American history. The film powerfully challenges the contemporary audience to consider what events from 1839 can contribute to our understanding of freedom in the present day, particularly on the vexed matter of open rebellion in the face of enslavement (Dalzell 1998; Rosen 1998).

The fourth literary selection is one that is carved out of the controversy over slavery which divided the North and the South in the United States and eventually culminated in the American Civil War (1860–65). I speak, of course, of Harriet Beecher Stowe's classic work *Uncle Tom's Cabin* (1852), perhaps the most influential novel ever to have been written on the theme of slavery. The differences between slavery as it was practised in the first-century Graeco-Roman world and slavery as it was practised in the United States during the nineteenth century are considerable.[9] Even the definition of something as fundamental as 'family' is problematic. The idea of 'the family' as the basis for a good and just society is central to *Uncle Tom's Cabin*, but there is a huge difference between what constituted a 'family' in Roman times and what Harriet Beecher Stowe meant by the term.[10] And if we have difficulty in establishing a connection between the first century and the nineteenth century on something so foundational as 'the family', what are our chances of exploring a social phenomenon as controversial and complex as slavery? As one New Testament scholar (Bartchy 1992: 66) has observed:

> It must be stressed that for the most part knowledge of slavery as practiced in the New World in the 17th–19th centuries has hindered more than helped in achieving an appropriate, historical understanding of social-economic life in the Mediterranean world of the 1st century, knowledge which is absolutely essential for a sound exegesis of those NT texts dealing with slaves and their owners or using slavery-related metaphors.

Yet there is sufficient overlap between the two worlds to suggest that the slavery theme could be profitably explored. Within the ancient world, for example, there are a number of precedents for the kind of passive response to slavery that we see is characteristic of Uncle Tom in Stowe's novel; the Stoic philosopher Epictetus of Hierapolis (c. 60–120 CE) is a classic case in point.[11]

The abolitionist struggle stands as a decisive chapter within American history and has been the subject of many film-makers over the years. Understandably, the interest has also spilled over into the period of post-war reconstruction, and gave opportunity for one of the most significant efforts of a fledgling film industry—D.W. Griffith's *The Birth of a Nation* (1915). This film is commonly regarded as a landmark, an artistic endeavour which perhaps more than any other single work heralded the rise of cinema as a self-conscious art-form. Within the Civil War sequences of Griffith's film we see the tension over the

9.   Finley (1980) addresses the question of how our contemporary presuppositions, including our ideas about the place that race played in the American experience of slavery, influence our interpretation of slavery within the Graeco-Roman world.

10.   The place of slaves within the extended Roman 'family' is the major difference. See the various contributions in Rawson (1986); Saller (1987).

11.   Hudson (1963) discusses parallels between the two figures.

issue of the emancipation of slaves graphically set forth. In one scene, as the Confederate troops march off to do battle against the Yankees and to defend the traditional Southern way of life, we see the slaves of the Cameron family cheering the boys in grey who will protect them against the perils of emancipation.[12] In one sense, *The Birth of a Nation* can be viewed as something of a sequel to Harriet Beecher Stowe's *Uncle Tom's Cabin* in that it chronicles the aftermath of the Civil War for emancipation which Stowe's book did so much to help bring about. There is certainly some truth in President Abraham Lincoln's comment to Stowe (assuming it was ever said) when he greeted her during a visit to the White House in 1863: 'So this is the little lady who started this great big war.'[13] Indeed, one recent study has described the 'unmaking of *Uncle Tom's Cabin* as the making of *The Birth of a Nation*', at least as far as the way in which both gender and race are portrayed in cinema.[14]

In many ways, *Uncle Tom's Cabin* stands as Harriet Beecher Stowe's solitary contribution to world literature. She is rarely remembered for having written anything else, although she followed up her masterpiece with many other novels as well as a host of contributions to journals and magazines. Indeed, probably the only other piece of Stowe's writing which had any sort of a social impact was her decision to publish Lady Byron's account of Lord Byron's life. This was an attempt to reclaim the reputation of Lady Byron (whom Stowe had befriended) and effectively lifted the lid on the poet's incestuous relationship with his half-sister Augusta Leigh (Stowe 1869).[15] The article caused something of a sensation and was not well received in many literary quarters in England. Charles Dickens, for example, changed his mind about Harriet Beecher Stowe and *Uncle Tom's Cabin* as a result of the article in the *Atlantic Quarterly*. He was extremely irritated over public scrutiny of the private lives of England's great literary figures and felt that Stowe had gone too far in the matter and castigated her severely for

12. For more on the film see Nelsen and Nelsen (1970); Carter (1960); Henderson (1972: 141-65); Fiedler (1979: 43-57; 1982: 179-95); Bogle (1997); and the various contributions in Lang (1994).

13. See Wilson (1942: 484-85) for more on this.

14. See Williams (1996: 129) on this controversial point. Riggio (1976) discusses the novels of Thomas Dixon, including *The Clansman* (1905) which served as the inspiration for D.W. Griffith's film.

15. Gerson (1976: 182-90) and Hedrick (1994: 353-79) discuss the matter.

it (Stone 1957). Ironically, controversy over the truth (or not) of Stowe's revelations about the relationship between Lord and Lady Byron was used by Stowe's own critics to undermine the veracity of *Uncle Tom's Cabin* (Wilson 1942: 532-51; Gossett 1985: 356-57). In the end, it is really only because of *Uncle Tom's Cabin* that Harriet Beecher Stowe continues to be read and discussed today, but this novel on its own is enough to justify contemporary interest in her. Anthony Burgess (1980: 122) once described Stowe as the mother of both the literature of the American South, and the modern protest novel; her ability to give birth to two such different children makes any study of *Uncle Tom's Cabin* an intriguing prospect.

Rarely in the course of American history have the rhetorics of both politics and religion been so engaged as they were in the debate over the question of the abolition of slavery. Harriet Beecher Stowe's novel was a major factor in these discussions, giving voice to the feelings of many, especially in the North, for whom the issue was a matter of deep, ethical conviction. In the words of one critic (Bellin 1993: 276-77):

> The novel gathers the threads of a debate which had raged within the churches and consciences of the nation: what was the proper Christian response to slavery?

Without a doubt, *Uncle Tom's Cabin* is at heart a profoundly theological work which attempts to address issues that had long occupied the Christian church. As another critic (Brandstadter 1974: 174) puts it:

> While ostensibly concerned about freeing the slave from his master, *Uncle Tom's Cabin* was even more concerned with freeing Christianity from the sin of slavery.

The novel takes up a stance which occupies the middle ground of this religio-political debate and, at the same time, provides fictional characters who serve on both sides of the discussion. Supremely we see this in the characters of George Harris and Uncle Tom, who represent active revolution and passive resistance respectively. Yet other responses to the question of slavery are also contained within the novel, responses which invite a comparison with the apostle Paul's thought on the subject. Such a comparison is the main intent of the study offered here.

Commenting on Paul's attitude to slavery, the New Testament scholar R.T. France once remarked that through his teaching about equality (in such texts as 1 Cor. 7.22, Gal. 3.28 and Phlm. 16), the apostle 'undercuts the value-system of a slave-owning society and plants a time-bomb which was one day to explode in the abolition of slavery' (France 1986: 17). Perhaps it would not be going too far to suggest that Harriet Beecher Stowe's *Uncle Tom's Cabin* stands as a fictional narration of the detonation of that abolitionist time-bomb. One thing that immediately strikes the reader of *Uncle Tom's Cabin* is the extent to which it is shot through with biblical imagery, allusions and quotations. In some ways it is ironic that Stowe chose to ground her abolitionist message so firmly in Scripture, given the fact that there is ample evidence from the pages of the Bible that supports (or at least does not challenge) the practice of slavery. In the words of the classicist G.E.M. de Ste Croix (1988: 30),

> In the great debate in North America in the eighteenth and nineteenth centuries it seems to me that the pro-slavery propagandists easily had the better of the abolitionists, in so far as both appealed to the supreme authority of the Old and New Testaments.[16]

Much of the discussion of *Uncle Tom's Cabin* will revolve around the different responses that the characters of the book have towards their enslavement. Should they actively resist slavery and fight for their freedom, or should they accept their positions as part of the divine will, their lot in life? The same two basic options are on offer in scholarly interpretations of 1 Cor. 7.21; indeed, the tension can be clearly seen by comparing how two modern versions of the Bible translate the critical phrase at the end of the verse:

> Were you a slave when called? Never mind. But if you can gain your freedom, avail yourself of the opportunity (RSV).

> Were you a slave when called? Do not be concerned about it. Even if you can gain your freedom, make use of your present condition now more than ever (NRSV).

The fact that the NRSV, published in 1989, overturns the more politically acceptable translation of the RSV (the New Testament section of which first appeared in 1946) illustrates the abiding difficulties of getting to the bottom of Paul's exhortation in this passage.

In short, it goes without saying that the practice of slavery presented a huge moral dilemma for people who lived in the United States, both North and South, prior to the American Civil War (1860–65). It also

---

16. See also de Ste Croix (1975).

appears to be the case that slavery presented some difficulties for first-century Christians in Corinth, particularly as both slaves and masters sought to find the proper response to their social situation in light of their newly made Christian commitments. The study on *Uncle Tom's Cabin* attempts to find common ground between these two radically different historical eras, and in so doing to offer some insights about the respective values of active revolt and passive resistance as ways of effecting social change in light of Christian faith.

To conclude, I offer these four studies on Pauline images in fiction and film in the anticipation that they will stimulate further thinking about the process of biblical interpretation in the contemporary world. They serve as additional examples of how the hermeneutical flow can sometimes be creatively reversed, and consequently how we as readers find ourselves enabled to discover new depths and fresh insights about the New Testament materials via classic works of literature and their film adaptations which use those materials. This approach is not without its difficulties, however, and a short comment about the methodology used here is in order.

In a recent article in the journal *Literature and Theology*, Steve Nolan offered a stimulating summary of some of the modern trends in film criticism, including a discussion of my work within this area. In his opinion, my particular approach is caught up in a methodological weakness, one which he feels characterizes biblical studies in general. As Nolan says:

> The weakness is Kreitzer's analytic method. He appears to be suggesting a reader-response approach to the texts, moving from 'facets of our cultural heritage, and then to apply it to our understanding of the NT materials'. Instead, his meticulous investigation of sources and nuances of adaptation reveals the redaction-critical preoccupation with authorial intent of NT scholarship.[17]

In response, I can only plead guilty to the charge. I *do* assume that there is something vital to be gained from an investigation into the circumstances surrounding the production of a piece of literature. I take it for granted that a well-grounded understanding of the author's intent in producing a piece of literature, however difficult that is to determine, can contribute significantly to our appreciation of his or her writing. In short, the 'kill the author' approach to the interpretation of literature

---

17. See Nolan (1998: 8) on this point. The article has a very fine bibliography.

seems to me to be fraught with danger, if not to be a demonstration of folly. At the very least it is an approach which needlessly sacrifices an important player in the 'game' of interpretation.

In this respect, it is perhaps worth noting that Nolan's critique concentrates on the contribution that my work has made to the interface between *film criticism* and biblical interpretation (much of the March 1998 issue of *Literature and Theology* is given over to this theme). However, in my opinion the place of literary texts underlying those film adaptations is not given its proper place within his assessment of my work.[18] To my mind this is to eliminate one of the partners within the overall discussion, namely the works of literature themselves, which, needless to say, are written by particular people, in a given set of cir-cumstances, usually to a specific purpose. Admittedly, I *am* interested in the authors of the literary works I investigate, and I *do* approach their literary contributions through what could be described as essentially a redaction-critical perspective. But is that any more methodologically suspect than assuming that we must remove the writer altogether from any consideration of his or her work? Somehow, I suspect not, particu-larly when my stated intention here is to explore how creators of 'classic' works of literature interact with the biblical materials which were very much a part of their conceptual world and which helped give shape to their literary efforts.

Thus, I would argue that there is a great deal to be gained in terms of our understanding of the Bible by an examination of the ways in which biblical ideas, themes and motifs are picked up, used, reworked and creatively adapted by later generations of writers and film-makers. To my mind, this is an essential means whereby the continuing relevance of the Bible can be demonstrated to contemporary people. Whatever we may feel about the 'rightness' or 'wrongness' of the current situation, we must admit that for many people today the Bible is largely viewed as an irrelevancy, a worthless trinket of a bygone era. Much more important to vast numbers of people today are great works of literature

18. Despite the fact that my two major publications in this area are deliberately designated as studies on fiction and film, the description of me as 'the guy who writes about films' is depressingly frequent. The review of my *The Old Testament in Fiction and Film* (1994) by Charles Mabee (1997: 88) is a case in point. Readers of the review are given precious little indication that the intention is to investigate the *three-way* hermeneutical process between biblical texts, a literary 'classic' and cinematic adaptations of that 'classic' work of literature.

and the efforts of creative film-makers. And yet, frequently underlying the work of both writers and film-makers are great stories and images from the Bible; at times the biblical bases seem to lie at an almost subliminal, even mythological, level. The four studies in this book are designed to explore some of the connections between the imaginative work of writers and film-makers on the one hand, and the biblical witness concerning the life and ministry of the apostle Paul on the other.

Finally, as I said within the Introductions to my two previous volumes in the Biblical Seminar series, I am all too aware that cross-disciplinary work of this nature is always going to be a risky affair. Somehow one is constantly made to feel under suspicion for 'letting the side down', or trivializing that which is sacred. After all, what do New Testament studies have to do with English literature, or (God forbid!) the cinema? As one person put it to me when he heard that I was working on another volume in the series on fiction and film, 'When are you going to do some *serious* New Testament work?'

For myself, I have found that inter-disciplinary studies such as those offered here have proved to be enormously rewarding professionally, as well as immensely enjoyable personally. I am more excited than I have ever been before about the relevance of the New Testament for the contemporary reader, and find again and again in teaching situations that biblical stories suddenly spring to life for students when they are approached through more familiar subjects, such as those contained in literature and film. I remain confident that inter-disciplinary hermeneutics is a sign of the future.

Chapter 1

ROBINSON CRUSOE: SHIPWRECK, SIN AND SALVATION

Daniel Defoe's *Robinsoe Crusoe*[1] remains one of the most beloved adventure stories of all times. Across the years it has thrilled readers, both young and old alike, titillating our imaginations as to how we might handle the prospect of being shipwrecked on a remote island with little to keep us from death but our wits. As Sir Walter Scott (1972: 78) once remarked:

> [T]here is hardly an elf so devoid of imagination as not to have supposed for himself a solitary island in which he could act Robinson Crusoe, were it but in the corner of the nursery.

The central figure of the story, the shipwrecked sailor Robinson Crusoe, might well be described as one of the few fictional characters who has become a modern Western mythological figure. Ian Watt (1951: 95) ranks Defoe's novel alongside *Faust, Don Juan* and *Don Quixote* in this regard, while James Joyce is said to have described the character Robinson as 'the English Ulysses'.[2] Defoe's classic tale has

---

1. The full title of the book is *The Life and Strange Surprising Adventures of Robinson Crusoe, of York. Mariner*. Defoe followed it with two quick sequels, *The Farther Adventures of Robinson Crusoe* (1719) and *Serious Reflections during the Life and Surprising Adventures of Robinson Crusoe, with his Vision of the Angelick World* (1720). In this study I am concerned only with the first of the three works and use the Penguin Classics edition of Daniel Defoe's *Robinson Crusoe* (London: Penguin Books, 1985); the edition is edited by Angus Ross who also provides an introduction. Citation from *Robinson Crusoe* always presents something of a difficulty in that the original novel did not contain substantial chapter divisions. I shall use page numbers from the Penguin edition unless otherwise stated, and designate them thus: *RC* 5 = *Robinson Crusoe*, p. 5.

2. According to Budgen (1960: 181). Budgen, a friend and critic of Joyce, was with him in Zürich during World War One when Joyce's own *Ulysses* was being written. Parallels between Homer's *Iliad* and *Odyssey* and Defoe's *Robinson Crusoe* are often identified. See Watt (1952), MacLaine (1955) and Spaas (1996) for further discussion along these lines.

been translated into most of the world's major languages, but the figure of Crusoe is also known by countless millions who have never read the book. A number of fictional spin-offs have appeared, which use the desert-island tale as their narrative backdrop.[3] Four of the more creative modern adaptations, one from each of the past four decades, are worth mentioning briefly. Together they illustrate not only the enduring popularity of the novel, but also the way in which it lends itself to artistic reworkings.

The first is Muriel Spark's story *Robinson* (1958), which creatively addresses Catholic–Protestant tensions by having its central character (whose full name is Miles Mary Robinson) live with his adopted servant-boy Miguel on an island off the Azores, appropriately known as *Robinson*. His island solace is disturbed by the appearance of three survivors of a plane crash, much as the appearance of cannibals on the island in Defoe's novel upset Robinson Crusoe. The second is Michel Tournier's *Vendredi ou les limbes du Pacifique* (1967), a postmodernist reading of *Robinson Crusoe* which playfully reverses the roles of Robinson and Friday within Defoe's novel and has Friday's easy-going lifestyle serve as the instrument of the English castaway's conversion from his economically corrupt world.[4] In the end Robinson elects to stay on his island rather than return to the world he once knew. The third is Adrian Mitchell's innovative *Man Friday: A Play* (1974), which similarly retells the story through the eyes of Friday and ends with Crusoe begging to be allowed to return to Friday's island. Friday, however, is afraid that Crusoe's presence will corrupt his people, and argues against it. The drama concludes with a clever little twist in which the audience watching the play is invited to judge whether Crusoe should be allowed to stay on the island or not (effectively the audience serve as members of Friday's tribe). The fourth is by the South African writer J.M. Coetzee, whose novel *Foe* (1986) recasts the story of *Robinson Crusoe* and blurs the boundaries between fictional character and historical personage. Coetzee achieves this by creatively inserting the historical person Daniel Defoe into the story-line. In Coetzee's plot the London-based Defoe becomes involved with a woman named Susan Barton, who had been Cruso's companion and lover on

3. Such books form their own literary sub-genre; in French these are even known as 'Robinsonnades', and in German as *Robisonaden*.

4. Recent studies of the novel include Green (1990: 185-95), Milne (1996), Purdy (1996) and Wilson (1996).

the island. Defoe learns through Susan of her life on the island with Cruso and Friday and how the three of them were eventually rescued, although Cruso died en route to England. Susan asks Defoe to tell Friday's story, since Friday has had his tongue cut out and cannot speak for himself. In effect this is to make Defoe the ghost-writer of the island reminiscences of *Friday* (as opposed to those of Robinson Crusoe). But is Defoe to be trusted to tell the story as Susan relates it? And what about the silent Friday? How is *his* story to be heard when he remains locked in silence? The result of all this is a subversion of the text as we have it, and the reader is invited to rethink what is meant by story-telling itself, particularly as it is exemplified by Defoe's classic tale of adventure, *Robinson Crusoe*.[5]

Our mental images of Robinson Crusoe are formed, in part, by the engravings, woodcuts, illustrations, photographs and drawings which have adorned the various editions of the text published over the past 280 years. These have done much to preserve Robinson Crusoe's place in the hearts and thoughts of the book's readership. At the same time, such visualization of the story provides generous scope for the artistic reinterpretation and creative adaptation of the Crusoe myth, for adaptability is an essential feature of any successful mythology. Little wonder, then, that the portrayal of Crusoe and his physical environs were made to fit the prevailing perceptions of the day. Conventions change in such matters as the presentation of Robinson's goat-skin clothing, his visage, his bodily appearance, the farming methods he adopts and the tools he uses, the construction of his island home in the style of an English manor-house, and the physical elements of nature (clouds, sky, waves, etc.).[6] He was at various times portrayed as a religiously minded Puritan, a hero in keeping with the spirit of the French Revolution, a Victorian explorer and empire-builder,[7] a romantic English Everyman,[8] an inventive North American frontiersman, and

5. Coetzee's novel has been the subject of considerable critical discussion. See, e.g., Post (1989); Roberts (1991); Spivak (1991); Macaskill and Colleran (1992); Hall (1993); Begam (1994); Burnett (1996); Corcoran (1996); Engelibert (1996); Gauthier (1996–97).

6. Blewett (1995) explores this thoroughly. The book contains many fine illustrations to highlight the extent to which *Robinson Crusoe* has been mythologically re-worked.

7. Joyce (1964: 24) describes him as 'the true prototype of the British colonist'.

8. Samuel Taylor Coleridge describes Crusoe as 'a representative of humanity in general' (Coleridge 1936: 194).

even a prefigurement of a Zionist Jew who is able to go to the idealized island-state of Israel and begin to build a new civilization there.[9]

Diversity as to the illustration of faithful man-servant Friday is also quite evident. At times he looks positively European, at times he is portrayed as if he were a Negro slave, and at times he is the perfect embodiment of the 'noble savage', a Native American Indian. All of this is but a brief demonstration of how vibrant a work *Robinson Crusoe* is and how readily the book lends itself to a variety of interpretations.[10]

I shall pursue my study by concentrating on a particular feature of *Robinson Crusoe*, one which has not always featured in the illustrations of the novel, and only infrequently within the critical discussion of it. My focus will be on the way in which theological elements of the story are conveyed, particularly as the shipwreck of Robinson Crusoe brings him to the point where he has a heightened sense of his sinfulness and undergoes a religious conversion. The brief New Testament descriptions of Paul's experience of shipwreck (2 Cor. 11.25-26; Acts 27–28) provide a convenient point of comparison, for they too provide a means of examining how the hand of providence is shown to be at work in the life of the apostle. The religious experience of Daniel Defoe, himself a prominent dissenter, is also an important factor to consider. I shall also have occasion to examine some recent film interpretations of *Robinson Crusoe* and the way in which they present the theological dimensions of Defoe's classic novel. Thus, the study shall be divided into four parts: (1) Paul: The Shipwrecked Apostle; (2) Daniel Defoe: The Dissenting Scribbler; (3) Shipwreck, Sin and Salvation in *Robinson Crusoe*; and (4) Shipwreck, Sin and Salvation in Film Interpretations of *Robinson Crusoe*.

1. *Paul: The Shipwrecked Apostle*

The story of Paul's missionary journeys in spreading the good news of the gospel message forms one of the central accounts of the New Testament witness. The Pauline letters and the Acts of the Apostles both testify to this concern, which is undertaken in the face of adversity. One of the demonstrations of this adversity is the threat of shipwreck. It is

---

9.   In Jean-Richard Bloch's article entitled 'Le Robinson juif' which originally appeared in a French newspaper in 1925. See Figuerola (1996) for more on this article.

10.   Wheeler (1995) is an up-to-date discussion of this topic.

this motif that I shall concentrate on in my study of Paul and his missionary calling.

a. *Shipwreck as a Basis for Paul's Boasting*
2 Corinthians 11.22-28 is a celebrated passage in which the apostle Paul lists some of the difficulties and trials that he has faced in his life of missionary service to the Gentiles. This is certainly not the only place where Paul catalogues his trials and tribulations (see Rom. 8.35; 1 Cor. 4.9-13; 2 Cor. 4.8-9; 6.4-5, 8-10; 12.10; Phil. 4.12 for similar passages), but the rhetoric reaches an unprecedented high in this section of the so-called 'Fool's Speech' of 2 Cor. 11.1–12.13.

It is generally recognized that Paul here is defending his apostolic ministry in the face of a hostile group of opponents in Corinth. In so doing he resorts to boasting in order to exalt his dedication to the cause of Jesus Christ and leave his opponents looking as if they were somehow second-rate. In 11.25, 26, as part of this heated harangue, Paul mentions his misfortunes on the open seas as one of the many hazards he faced on his missionary journeys for the sake of the Gentiles:

> Three times I have been shipwrecked; a night and a day I have been adrift at sea... [I have faced] danger at sea...

Paul presents in 2 Cor. 11.26 no less than *eight* different examples of 'dangers' (κινδύνοι) which he has faced in his apostolic ministry, including the threat of the open sea.[11] Most commentators agree that this is one of the clearest examples within the undisputed Pauline letters of the apostle's deliberate use of irony in order to get his particular point across.[12] This does not mean that the shipwrecks were without historical foundation; there is nothing to suggest that they did *not* take place. But pure history is not the use to which the events of his life are put here, and Paul is not interested in simply scoring historical points by relating to his readers who did what, when and where. Rather, these over-inflated boasts are injected into Paul's argument in order to serve as a point of contrast. Paul wishes to mark the difference between his own commitment to the Corinthian church and the commitment that his opponents within that church have for the members of their own

11. See Hodgson (1983); Furnish (1984: 512-18); Martin (1986: 370-79).
12. On this point, see Travis (1973); Spencer (1981); Forbes (1986); Marshall (1987: 339-95); Fitzgerald (1988: 107-14); Sampley (1988); Holland (1993); Witherington (1995: 442-64); Kreitzer (1996: 49-53).

congregation. In so far as his boastful comments arise from a purely human motive, they may even be described as a product of sin and pride. In 2 Cor. 11.17-18 Paul distances what he himself is here declaring from what he says elsewhere 'in the name of the Lord':

> What I am saying I say not with the Lord's authority but as a fool, in this boastful confidence; since many boast of worldly things, I too will boast.

In any event, the three shipwrecks that Paul survives are all the stuff of high drama and make his resumé an interesting read for us today. This is so even if, as appears the case, the apostle occasionally bragged about the things he had endured. Little wonder, then, that Paul was seen by his Corinthian opponents (as he is indeed still viewed today in many quarters)[13] as a vain, arrogant and conceited man who bullied his congregations into doing what he wanted.

b. *Shipwreck as a Demonstration of Paul's Apostolic Calling*
The story of Paul's shipwrecks becomes even more ironic if we take the story recorded in Acts 27.27-44 as relating an incident that took place *after* the writing of 2 Corinthians 10–13. This means that the fateful journey of Paul to put his case before the Emperor in Rome is punctuated by yet *another* shipwreck, this time on the island of Malta.[14] Thus, the Maltese experience becomes the *fourth* time that the New Testament speaks of Paul being shipwrecked and somehow managing to be rescued.[15] Needless to say, this hardly makes one thrill at the thought of

---

13. Shaw (1983: 101-25) is a case in point.

14. There remains some doubt about whether Malta (Μελίτη) was actually the site of the shipwreck. It has been suggested that an island off the Dalmatian coast (also known in antiquity by the name Μελίτη) was where Paul was actually stranded. On this point, see Acworth (1973); Meinardus (1976). The traditional view of the shipwreck as taking place on the island of Malta is put forward by Hemer (1975). Most commentaries also refer to the famous essay by James Smith, *The Voyage and Shipwreck of St Paul* (1848), for support of this thesis. Interestingly, the Jewish historian Josephus (a contemporary of Paul) also tells of a shipwreck he suffered while journeying to see the Emperor in Rome (*Life* 14–15). Apparently shipwreck was not an unfamiliar experience for the traveller of the first century CE, even though it was greatly feared. See Conzelmann (1987: 231-41) for some other examples of sea journeys within ancient sources.

15. Although Lüdemann (1989: 256-60) doubts whether the shipwreck on Malta actually happened. Johnson (1992: 444-60) offers an interpretation which attempts to do justice both to the historical and the fictional dimensions of the story. Part of the difficulty may be due to the fact that there appear to be two different

accompanying Paul on his danger-filled travels, particularly if he was as accident-prone as seems to be implied by the New Testament materials! Nevertheless, Paul's track record seems not to have deterred his sometime companion Luke, the beloved physician (traditionally said to be the author of Luke–Acts). Luke records the story of the sea journey and shipwreck in the first person, as if to signal that he was an eye-witness.[16] This is the last of a dozen or so sea journeys related within the Acts of the Apostles, but it is by far the most dramatic (see 9.30; 11.25-26; 13.4, 13; 14.25-25; 16.11; 17.14-15; 18.18-22, 27 for other examples of sea travels). Chapter 27 stands as one of the most highly polished stories in the New Testament and is filled with nautical terms and technical phrases which assist in making it a realistic, and therefore, credible narrative.

The journey to Rome is told in several stages. The initial part of the journey from Caesarea along the coastlines of Cilicia, Pamphylia and Lycia is made without too much difficulty. Paul and his Roman military escort from the Augustan Cohort, led by the centurion Julius, change ships in Myra in Lycia and board an Alexandrian grain-ship on its way to Rome (Acts 27.6). At this point in the narrative, portents of disaster are certainly to be found in the form of the unfavourable weather which drives them southward off their intended course. Still, the grain-ship with Paul and 275 other people on board eventually makes it to a small port town known as Fair Haven, on the south side of Crete (Acts 27.8). From here the plan was to travel to the western end of Crete and put in at the port of Phoenix; it was getting late in the year, travel was becoming increasingly dangerous and the harbour at Phoenix was more

versions of the story within the textual tradition (the differences between the Western and the Alexandrian texts of this section of Acts are substantial). See Murphy-O'Connor (1996: 351-54) for a helpful introduction to the matter.

16. We can assume that 'Luke', the companion of Paul, was the writer of Luke–Acts. 27.1–28.16 is one of the so-called 'we' sections of Acts (16.10-17, 20.5-15 and 21.1-18 are also written in the first-person plural). This unusual narrative feature of Acts has engendered a great deal of discussion, much of it revolving around the way in which travel narratives were written in the Hellenistic world and what implications such passages have for the historicity of Acts. For further discussion, see Dibelius (1956: 204-206); Cadbury (1956–57); Haenchen (1964: 235-54; 1965: 65-99); Pokorný (1973); Miles and Trompf (1976); Robbins (1978); Ladouceur (1980); Praeder (1984); Hemer (1985; 1989: 312-34); Barrett (1987); Kurz (1987); Fitzmyer (1989: 1-26); Porter (1994); Rapske (1994); Alexander (1996); Dunn (1996: x-xi); Witherington (1998: 754-93).

suitable for sitting out the winter months.[17] However, the weather was soon to take over as a howling, northeasterly wind (known as a Euraquilo)[18] descended upon the ship and drove it out to the open sea (Acts 27.14-17). For 14 days the ship was caught in the violent storm and drifted aimlessly. The narrative of Acts paints a vivid picture of the sense of hopelessness and despair which comes over the crew and its passengers before they finally come near to be able to land on the island of Malta (some 500 nautical miles to the west of Crete). In 27.26 Paul announces that the only hope for the beleaguered crew is that they shall have to run the ship aground on the island. This they attempt to do, but the ship is broken up by the violence of the storm and the people on board are forced either to jump overboard and swim for shore or be carried to land clinging to planks and other 'bits of wreckage' (or is it 'crew members'?—the Greek phrase ἐπίτινων τῶν ἀπὸ τοῦ πλοίου in 27.44 is ambiguous).

Most commentators on Acts 27.1–28.16 point out that the passage conveys important features of Lukan theology, including a pro-Roman political agenda which attempts to portray the Christian faith to the Romans in a positive light,[19] and the rather bizarrely interjected allusion to the Lord's Supper in 27.35-36 wherein Paul 'breaks bread' with the people on board before they attempt to beach the ship.[20] More importantly, throughout the story *God* is very much presented as in control of the situation in that he has a man (Paul) on the scene who is carrying out his heavenly commission as any good 'soldier' in the divine army should. In terms of dramatic narrative, Luke thus sets up a deliberate juxtaposition between Paul and the Roman centurion Julius,

17. Ogilvie (1958) discusses the precise location of the intended harbour of refuge.

18. Lake and Cadbury (1933: 338-44) offer a classic study of this.

19. See Walaskay (1983). Walaskay notes (101) how Luke–Acts consistently portrays Roman centurions in a highly favourable manner (as in Lk. 7.1-10; 23.47; Acts 10.1-48; 22.25-26; 23.23-24 and 27.1-44).

20. Willimon (1988: 184-85) sensibly comments on the breaking of bread image in 27.35: 'Of course, we are not told that this was what we call the sacrament of the Lord's Supper. Nor are we told whether or not the pagans on board joined with Paul in his blessed food. Yet surely Theophilus' church would make the connection between their Sunday meals together in whatever "storm" they were experiencing and this meal on a dark day at sea. The Eucharist is food of confidence shared in the middle of a storm.' See the discussion in the chapter on Dracula below (pp. 113-42) for more on the communion motif in Luke–Acts.

who also is doing his duty and is following the orders he has been given by his commander Festus (Acts 25.12; 27.1). True, Paul is a prisoner on board the ship, bound and with Julius's military escort to take him to Caesar. But Paul is nonetheless the one through whom *God* delivers the rest of the people on board to safety. Their salvation is revealed to Paul in a dream, and he is quick to capitalize on the situation by advising the centurion Julius how best to proceed. In Acts 27.21-26 Paul is made to say:

> Men, you should have listened to me, and should not have set sail from Crete and incurred this injury and loss. I now bid you take heart; for there will be no loss of life among you, but only of the ship. For this very night there stood by me an angel of the God to whom I belong and whom I worship, and he said, 'Do not be afraid, Paul; you must stand before Caesar; and lo, God has granted you all those who sail with you.' So take heart, men, for I have faith in God that it will be exactly as I have been told. But we shall have to run on some island.

The point of all of this is to suggest that God's purposes in having the good news spread to the ends of the earth will not be thwarted by *any* means, not even the awesome powers of a sea-storm which brings about a shipwreck. Gerd Lüdemann (1989: 258) sums up the essential point well when he says:

> The shipwreck is a narrative means by which Luke can show that the journey to Rome is in accord with God's plan. The buffeting of nature cannot hold up the divine plan.

In short, the shipwreck is to be seen as a demonstration of God's power and sovereignty. Even in the midst of something so disastrous as a shipwreck, there is to be seen the hand of God in effecting salvation.

Throughout the story we see another motif which is a distinctive theme in the second half of Acts—the centrality of Paul's role as God's ambassador within the narrative. More specifically, in 27.24 we detect the author presenting a hint to his intended readership about the ultimate success of Paul's aim of preaching the good news before the Emperor Nero.[21] Indeed, we are also given the impression in 27.24 that it is for Paul's sake that the rest of the people on board the ship are saved. The number of people concerned is given in 27.37 as 276, on the face of it a superfluous bit of information, but one which seems to have been included within the story by the narrator as a means of

---

21. So argues Haenchen (1971: 705).

establishing a relationship between himself and his readers (Sheeley 1992: 125, 157, 169-72). So Luke the narrator similarly concludes his dramatic story in 27.44: 'And so it was that all escaped to land.' This is in stark contrast to Defoe's story *Robinson Crusoe* where only the central character escapes to land and survives the shipwreck, which thus symbolizes not only the sin which is characteristic of his life but also the divine deliverance which comes to it (as we shall see below).

Before we turn to examine *Robinson Crusoe* in some detail, it is appropriate to acquaint ourselves with its author.

2. *Daniel Defoe: The Dissenting Scribbler*

Biographers of Daniel Defoe frequently comment on the paucity of hard evidence about the man himself.[22] Defoe's literary output was prodigious, with many Defoe scholars listing over 500 publications to his credit.[23] His writing covered an astonishing range of subjects, yet precious little is revealed within the various works about their author. In fact, much of his work was published anonymously, a nightmare scenario for anyone wishing to establish exactly what came from his pen. Nevertheless, some basic facts can be established which will help to introduce my study of the religious passages contained in *Robinson Crusoe*.

Defoe was born in 1660 (or 1661?) in Cripplegate, north London, the son of a City tradesman and candle-maker. His father, James Foe, was a Dissenter, possibly a Baptist,[24] but more likely a Presbyterian, who attended the church of Samuel Annesley, a Dissenting meeting-house in Bishopsgate. Defoe was originally intended to be a Dissenting preacher and at an early age was enrolled in the Reverend Charles Morton's Dissenting Academy in Newington Green[25] with that career

22. Defoe has been well served by biographers over the years. For recent examples, see Moore (1958); Earle (1976); Bastian (1981); Richetti (1987); Backscheider (1989); West (1997).

23. Furbank and Owens (1988) offer a fresh study on the complex question of attribution.

24. So Dottin (1928: 3) and Häusermann (1935: 299) argue, on the assumption that he did not approve of the christening of infants.

25. Morton studied at Wadham College, Oxford and was an excellent educator. He was forced to emigrate to America and eventually became Vice-President of Harvard University in Cambridge, Massachusetts. See Girdler (1953) for more on this matter.

in mind. His childhood experiences as a member of a Dissenting household were formative, particularly in the period immediately following Charles II's signing of the Act of Uniformity in May 1662. He participated in the Duke of Monmouth's unsuccessful rebellion of 1685, and probably fought at the battle of Sedgemoor (although he never says so unambiguously). In 1688 he joined the camp of William of Orange, following the 'Glorious Revolution' which drove the Catholic James II from the throne (and may have even plotted the 28-year long island exile of his fictional character Robinson Crusoe to coincide with the oppressive rule of the Stuart Kings from 1660–88).[26] True to his Dissenting roots, Defoe remained a staunch supporter of the Protestant William III throughout his reign.[27]

Until the publication of *Robinson Crusoe* in April 1719 (when Defoe was approaching the age of 60) his literary reputation rested predominantly upon his popular poem *The True-Born Englishman* (1701), which helped to calm public dissatisfaction with William III by its use of biting satire. He had also gained a certain degree of notoriety as a writer of political pamphlets, the writing of which embroiled him in the complex matter of Dissenting politics. In January 1703 a warrant was issued for his arrest for his political activism, notably the publication of the controversial pamphlet *The Shortest Way with the Dissenters* (1702). He was arrested in May at the house of a friend in Spitalfield, tried at the Old Bailey, and convicted. He was then heavily fined, made to stand three times in the public pillory,[28] and eventually imprisoned in Newgate prison. Imprisonment was a humiliating experience for Defoe, one from which he never fully recovered.[29] While in prison he founded a news-sheet entitled *The Review*, a bi-weekly, sometimes tri-weekly,

26. In the novel Crusoe lands on his island in September 1659 and returns to England in June 1687. In the words of Seidel (1991: 46): 'That Crusoe leaves just before the Stuarts return and returns just before they leave is a coincidence far too powerful to ignore.' Also see Seidel (1981).

27. For more on Defoe's religious sentiments, see Stamm (1936); Moore (1941; 1970–71); Shinagel (1968: 3-22); Earle (1976: 29-44); Backscheider (1989: 7-21).

28. Moore (1939: 3-22) discusses the vehemence with which Defoe was treated by the court.

29. However, it is often remarked that his prison experience helped make Defoe into a novelist. Thus, Forster (1990: 64) says, 'something occurred to him in prison and out of its vague, powerful emotion, *Moll Flanders* and *Roxana* are born'. Curtis (1984: 62-88) explores Defoe's creative use of prison/fortification imagery in *Robinson Crusoe*.

journal of political opinion and interpretation which was published until 1713. He was befriended by Robert Harley, the erstwhile Speaker of the House of Commons and at that time the Secretary of State, who secured his release from Newgate prison (although he was arrested again in 1713). Following his release Defoe became something of a political advisor to Harley (and others, including the Lord Treasurer Sidney Godolphin), working particularly hard for the union of England and Scotland. Much of this work was done under cover and the secretive nature of it meant that Defoe was frequently accused (not without some justification!) of acting in a duplicitous manner within the higher echelons of politics. His political career was chequered, to say the least.

So, too, was his business career. In 1692 Defoe suffered the humiliation of a bankruptcy (a second was to follow in 1703 with a further imprisonment in 1713); his financial affairs seemed to hang in the balance from the very beginning of his life as a merchant-trader. This was the case despite the fact that he had received a substantial dowry of £3700 when he married Mary Tuffley in 1864. Still, his union with Mary appears to have been a happy one, with little firm evidence of impropriety on Defoe's part;[30] the marriage produced eight children, six of whom survived to adulthood. For the last 23 years of his life Defoe lived in Stoke Newington, a well-known centre for Nonconformist activity, although there is some question about his involvement with the Dissenting meeting-house there (he appears to have fallen out with the local minister over the question of so-called 'occasional conformity').[31] It was while living in Stoke Newington that Defoe wrote *Robinson Crusoe*. Defoe died on 24 April 1731 in a lodging-house in Ropemaker's Alley in Moorfields, London, not far from where he had grown up. At the time he was on the run and hiding from his ever-pursuing creditors. He was buried two days later in Bunhill Fields, a graveyard for Dissenters which was located outside the city walls of London. His grave is only a few metres away from that of John Bunyan, author of *The Pilgrim's Progress*, with whom he is often compared.[32]

30. Novak (1970–71) and Moore (1972–73) debate this.

31. Secord (1951: 218) suggests that Defoe and his family attended the Presbyterian church in nearby Newington Green where he had grown up as a boy.

32. De la Mare (1930: 35) remarks: 'Roughly it may be said that in the one a poor castaway, named Christian, wins his way out of this world into a heavenly paradise; and that in the other a poor castaway, named Crusoe, wins his way out of an earthly paradise back into this wicked world; and both of them by their

With the publication of *Robinson Crusoe* Defoe entered into a new stage of his literary career, and it is generally as a writer of fictional novels, rather than as a journalist or pamphleteer, that he is now most remembered. The *Robinson Crusoe* cycle was followed by about eight other fictional works, among which *Journal of a Plague Year* (1722), *Moll Flanders* (1722) and *Roxana* (1724) are perhaps the most important. In any event, it was *Robinson Crusoe* that made him a literary figure of enduring importance, and it is to that masterpiece that I now turn my attention.

Robinson Crusoe was enormously popular when it first appeared and went through four editions (and six printings) in four months.[33] Like many works of literature which have stood the test of time and are deemed to be 'classics', *Robinson Crusoe* has enjoyed the praise of many famous men and women. In 1762 Jean-Jacques Rousseau (1994: 262) identified it as the first book which young people should read, since it 'affords a complete treatise on natural education'.

Robinson Crusoe has also been the subject of a host of political and ideological interpretations. One of the most celebrated is that of Karl Marx, who discussed it within the opening section of *Das Kapital* (1867). Marx criticized the novel as a tawdry fable of economic independence which failed to address the deeper social dimensions of labour and industry. There is certainly a strong economic sub-text running through the novel. Robinson Crusoe is driven by the pursuit of wealth in all of his various strange, surprising adventures, and there is more than a little preoccupation with book-keeping and ledger-making throughout Defoe's story-line (Marx asserts that account-making is a peculiarly British idiosyncrasy). But is this a sufficient picture of what Defoe presents to us in the form of his central character? One has to wonder if this is the case. Interestingly, Marx (1994: 274-75) also comments rather negatively about Robinson's religious experiences:

> Of his prayers and the like we take no account, since they are a pleasure
> to him, and he looks upon them as so much recreation.

Surely Marx goes too far when he dismisses out of hand the religious dimensions of the portrayal of Robinson Crusoe, for it is this feature which helps to give authenticity to the portrayal. Indeed, Defoe's clever

resolution, resource, and trust in Providence.' For more on the comparison between Bunyan and Defoe, see Damrosch (1994).

33. Hutchins (1925) and Shinagel (1994) provide details.

integration of the sacred and the secular dimensions of Robinson's life is one of the reasons why the story remains so intriguing. It has been argued that the character Robinson Crusoe is an embodiment of the Protestant work ethic, a rugged individualist who works hard and sees this as part of his duty to God. He is the supreme illustration of what Ian Watt (1957b: 82) describes as 'the secularization of the Calvinistic conception of stewardship'.[34] At the same time, Robinson evaluates all human relationships by what economic advantage they can bring him, and (in the tradition of the philosophical ideas of John Locke) comes to understand that the value of things on his island domain is inextricably bound up with their practical usefulness in his labours.

Other interpretative approaches to *Robinson Crusoe* are also on offer. In addition to specific investigations into theological matters which arise from *Robinson Crusoe*,[35] a bewildering number of psychological studies of the novel have been suggested (from both Freudian and Lacanian perspectives),[36] as have many philosophical,[37] politico-economic[38] and literary-critical analyses (most of which focus on the narrative complexities of Defoe's work).[39] In short, *Robinson Crusoe* has been examined from almost every conceivable angle. Robinson's attitudes to racism and slavery have been explored (Johnson 1973; Hayden 1981), as well as his seeming indifference, if not antipathy, to women. Even his sex life has been the subject of speculative (one almost needs to say *voyeuristic*) interest (Richardson 1971; Bell 1996).

On the face of it, *Robinson Crusoe* is an autobiographical work. The

34. Watt discusses the importance of the social and economic changes brought about by the rise of capitalism, as reflected in the characterization of Robinson Crusoe as *homo economicus*. Watt's study is extremely valuable, but he is not without his critics. See Novak (1963: 22-64; 1966: 32-66); Shinagel (1968: 122-41); Starr (1969); Richetti (1975: 21-62); Rogers (1979); Boardman (1983: 1-24); Bell (1985b: 42-114); McKeon (1987: 319-23); Armstrong (1996: 113-26).

35. Such as Blackburn (1984–85); Sim (1987) and Hudson (1988).

36. Berne (1956); Peck (1973); Perlman (1976–77); MacDonald (1976); Kavanaugh (1978); Maddox (1984); Jager (1987–88); Armstrong (1992); Foster (1992); Hentzi (1992); Sill (1994); and Hopes (1996), offer discussion along these lines.

37. Holmes (1972) is a case in point.

38. See Watson (1959); Novak (1962); Stein (1965); Ellis (1969); Cottom (1981); Sill (1983: 148-71); Birdsall (1985: 24-49); Braverman (1986); Schonhorn (1991); Vickers (1996: 99-131) on this.

39. Alkon (1979); Boardman (1983); and Merrett (1989) are cases in point.

title page of the book boldly declares that it was 'Written by Himself', and both parts of the work (the introductory narrative section as well as the journal proper) are written in the first person. Thus, one of the perennial questions faced by interpreters of *Robinson Crusoe* is to what extent the novel is intended to be read as a spiritual autobiography of Defoe himself, one which is written within the accepted literary conventions of the day (Starr 1965: 74-125; Hunter 1966).[40] Indeed, soon after the book was published it began to attract criticism precisely along these lines, with some reviewers accusing Defoe of fictionalizing his own life, particularly in those passages where the spiritual struggles of Robinson are detailed. It is not difficult to see Defoe's bankruptcy, or his imprisonment in Newgate prison, or his three stands in the public pillory as the 'shipwreck(s)' of his life, and to interpret the novel accordingly.[41]

An unauthorized abridgment of *Robinson Crusoe* appeared shortly after the book was published, which removed the religious and moral reflections of the central character and concentrated on the adventure story itself. Defoe condemned this in the preface to his sequel *The Further Adventures of Robinson Crusoe* (1719):

> Seeing, to shorten the book, that they may seem to reduce its value, they strip it of all those reflections, as well religious and moral, which are not only the greatest beauties of the work, but are calculated for the infinite advantage of the Reader.[42]

In short, the stage was set early on for a debate about the *historicity* of *Robinson Crusoe*, and Defoe certainly did much to muddy the waters on the matter, conveniently hiding as he did behind the mask of the anonymous 'Editor' within the prefaces of all parts of the *Robinson Crusoe* cycle. In the preface to the third volume in the series he describes *Robinson Crusoe* as 'a parable, or allegorick history', and says that the story, 'though allegorical, is also historical' (implying thereby that the work was an allegory for his own life).[43] Yet, as one of Defoe's biographers pointed out in 1879 (Minto 1879: 150, 169):

40. Starr (1973–74) contains some supplementary material.

41. Parker (1925) is a full-bodied attempt to identify personal events in Defoe's life with allegorical incidents in the novel. Bender (1994) is also worth consulting.

42. Defoe goes on to liken such abridgment to 'robbing on the highway, or breaking open a house'.

43. See Shinagel (ed.) (1994: 239-43) for the text of the prefaces of the two sequels.

> For all Defoe's profession that Robinson Crusoe is an allegory of his
> own life, it would be rash to take what he says too literally. The reader
> who goes to the tale in search of a close allegory, in minute chronologi-
> cal correspondence with the facts of the alleged original, will find, I
> expect, like myself, that he has been on a wild goose chase... He was a
> great, truly great liar, perhaps the greatest liar that ever lived.[44]

How much of *Robinson Crusoe* was based on historical fact, and how
much was simply invented by the author in order to promote the religious and moral reflections he describes within the story? Is Defoe
asserting the truth of historical occurrence, or merely the truth of narrative realism? The debate about the fictional nature of Defoe's story
inevitably gets tied up with discussions of the genre of the English
novel, and what place *Robinson Crusoe* has in the development of it.[45]
The deliberations over such matters are long-standing, with strong
opinions having been expressed from a variety of angles. Yet most
agree that there was, at the very least, a historical kernel underlying the
story of Robinson Crusoe, namely the experiences of a headstrong
Scottish sailor named Alexander Selkirk (1676–1721). Selkirk spent
over four years (from October 1704 to February 1709) in solitude on
the island of Juan Fernández off the coast of Chile, and news of his
deliverance made him the object of much public fascination.[46] He
became something of a celebrity and several accounts of his island
exile were published following his return to England in 1711.[47] It is

44. Minto goes on to suggest that Defoe came to the idea of calling *Robinson
Crusoe* an allegory as an afterthought, perhaps brought on by the appearance in
1719 of Charles Gildon's parody entitled *The Life and Strange Surprising Adventures of Mr. D—— De F——, Hosier*. Ellis (1969: 8) concurs. Sutherland (1938:
233) suggests that Defoe's Puritanism meant he was always apologizing for writing
'mere fictions' and that his stress on the moral lessons of the story for the benefit of
the reader lessened this sense of guilt. Backscheider (1989: 412-17) offers a useful
introduction to these matters.

45. Allen (1954: 37-41); Watt (1957b: 66-103); Novak (1964); Goldknopf
(1972: 42-58); McKeon (1987: 315-37); Seidel (1991: 13-35); Davis (1996: 154-
73); Doody (1997: 327-28, 334-43) all address this matter.

46. For more on Alexander Selkirk, see Mégroz (1939); Ross (1985); Gill
(1997: 301-302). Secord (1951: 225) offers another figure as the inspiration for
Robinson Crusoe, namely a sailor named Robert Drury who was shipwrecked on
the island of Madagascar for 14 years and returned to his home in Stoke Newington
in 1717.

47. Three of these contemporary accounts are contained in Shinagel (ed.) (1994:
230-38).

quite likely that Defoe even met Selkirk, and based some features of the Crusoe character on the man and his experiences.[48]

However, this in no way detracts from the creative work that Defoe produced in *Robinson Crusoe*, nor does it explain why he chose to include the introspective passages within the novel and why he regarded them as such an integral part of it. Robinson Crusoe's spiritual introspections are sometimes said to interrupt the action of the story, although they are one of the most persistent features of the narrative as a whole and carry on throughout the book, knitting it together and helping to create a sense of realism within the narration.[49] As one commentator remarks (Richetti 1987: 63):

> Crusoe's piety is often tedious but ultimately convincing because Defoe dramatizes it as a crucial means of survival that grows out of his hero's psychological stress at its most extreme.

The novel contains a surprising number of references and allusions to biblical texts, most of which occur within the controversial spiritual musings. The spiritual reflections of Robinson are often Puritan in form[50] and no doubt, in some sense, are an expression of the religious sensibilities of Defoe himself.[51] Even Ian Watt, who admits that he does not find Defoe's spiritual ruminations in the novel very convincing, concedes (1957a: 208) that

> Robinson Crusoe is not just a travel story; it is also, in intention at least, one of Defoe's 'honest cheats', a sincere attempt to convert a godless form of literature to the purposes of religion and morality.

48. William Cowper's poem entitled 'Alexander Selkirk' (first published in 1782) captures something of the despair that the melancholic Cowper imagined such isolation would bring. The first line of the poem reads: 'I am Monarch of all I survey'. See Cowper (1934: 311-12).

49. As Halewood (1964: 342) rightly notes. Halewood goes on to point out that Robinson's internal debate with his own conscience provides the only example of dialogue within the central section of the book; in effect, his religious soul has become his antagonist. Also see James (1972: 165-99) and Richetti (1975: 41-42) on this point.

50. Moffatt (1919) went so far as to describe Robinson's spiritualizing as expressive of the Presbyterian Shorter Catechism of the 1648 Westminster Assembly. Also see Smith (1925).

51. Although not, as Watt (1957b: 90) suggests, necessarily 'the result of an unresolved and probably unconscious conflict in Defoe himself'.

Are there any indications as to what these religious and moral purposes were for Defoe himself? Recently, Paula R. Backsheider (1989: 417-20) has put forward a suggestion which seems to fit the known facts and is gaining acceptance within the scholarly community. She argues persuasively that a specific religious controversy of the day is being addressed by Defoe via his *Robinson Crusoe*, namely the debate over the 'Salters' Hall meetings'. In essence this was a theological debate among the Dissenters about the nature of scriptural authority—whether the Bible and the Bible alone was a sufficient basis for decisions regarding faith and doctrine. Behind the debate, at least as Defoe perceived it, was the fear that ecclesiastical structures (including priests, eucharistic practices, and the use of *The Book of Common Prayer* in worship) might be imposed upon the Dissenting communities and that they would get in the way of a Christian's direct experience of God. In this sense, the fact that Robinson comes to his 'conversion experience' while living alone on an island with only his Bible to guide him, is a reflection of Defoe's position on this controversial matter.

This may be true, and it certainly tells us something about the religious aims of the Dissenter Defoe in composing *Robinson Crusoe*, but there is another factor to be considered. What about the function of the spiritual introspections within the story-line itself? There is much to be said for them as ingredients essential to the characterization of Robinson Crusoe; they help to define him as a realistic person, a flesh-and-blood human being that we can believe in and with whom we can identify. As one critic (Hearne 1967: 106) humorously describes the introspections:

> We may find them tedious and even disagreeable but they do help to establish Crusoe as a person. Without them, he would be only a pair of hands attached to a cash register.

3. *Shipwreck, Sin and Salvation in* Robinson Crusoe

The narrative perspective of *Robinson Crusoe* is predominantly that of a man recalling what had happened to him many years ago. The basic literary structure of the work is far from immediately clear. In short, the 'core' of the novel, as it were, consists of the diary-like journal of Robinson Crusoe's experiences on the island (these entries last ostensibly until his ink supplies run out). This journal is supplemented by an introductory narrative section, as well as the later explanatory comments of Robinson which are added to and interspersed with the various dated entries of the 'core' diary. To top it off there is also at operation here the hand of the presumed 'Editor', namely the redactional hand of Defoe himself in preparing the story for publication (at least if we are to take the prefaces of the second and third volumes in the *Robinson Crusoe* cycle at face value).[52] It is not always easy to determine the authorial level of any given passage, and at times there are inconsistencies, not to say contradictions, within them.[53] This means that within the story as it is related to us, there are great opportunities for personal reflection on, and interpretation of, the various experiences of Robinson's life (or is it the narrator's life, or the Editor's or Defoe's?—one can never be quite sure).[54] Albert Camus certainly caught sight of the force of this when he included a line from the preface to the third volume of Robinson Crusoe on the title page of his *The Plague* (1947):

> It is as reasonable to represent one kind of imprisonment by another, as
> it is to represent anything that really exists by that which exists not! –

Much can be made of these interpretative opportunities, particularly as the character Robinson Crusoe gives them to us as his spiritual introspections.

The central thesis of the book is the story of how the shipwrecked Robinson manages to survive on the deserted island and how he manages to transform it into his own little kingdom, a replica of the English world he has left behind.[55] The first 65 pages or so of the novel, in which the young Robinson tells how he leaves home and signs on as a crewman on a ship, how he survives the two 'preliminary' shipwrecks, how he is captured by the Moors and made a slave, how he manages to make his escape and how he finds financial success in Brazil, are really only a prelude to his escapades on the island. Similarly, the final 25 pages of the novel, in which Robinson relates how he returns to England via a hazardous overland journey through the Pyrenees, how he re-establishes himself as a businessman and how he again returns to

52. Blewett (1979: 15-24) discusses the development of Defoe's theory of fiction through the prefaces.

53. McKeon (1987: 315-17) is an excellent introduction to this critical question of interpretation.

54. Zimmerman (1971) and Bell (1985a) discuss this.

55. On this point, see Rogers (1974). Erickson (1982) also has some relevant discussion.

South America to assume oversight of his plantation, are all a postlude to his island experiences. Thus it is Robinson's shipwreck on the island, together with a description of how he copes with this situation, which has made *Robinson Crusoe* such an object of interest for generations of readers. The shipwreck is a powerful metaphor in the hands of a writer as capable as Defoe, and he makes much of it.[56] The theological dimensions of such a metaphor should not be overlooked. In the words of one commentator (Ellis 1969: 17):

> Robinson Crusoe's 'captivity' was primarily theological and only inci-
> dentally geographical. Or to put it another way: Robinson Crusoe's
> solitary confinement to the island is the vehicle of a metaphor of which
> the tenor is his captivity in sin.

Let us turn now to consider some of the ways in which that shipwreck is creatively presented by Defoe, particularly as this is conveyed through Robinson's spiritual introspections. We do not have space to cover every example of his anguish over his waywardness and sin, but we can provide enough instances to illustrate the essential point.

a. *Shipwreck as a Punishment for Sin: The Prodigal Son Disobeys his Father*

At several points the shipwreck is portrayed as a direct result of Robinson's sinfulness. Originally Robinson's sense of sin and guilt is brought on by his refusal to accept his father's advice about his career. Indeed, during one of the later spiritual introspections (set in his twenty-sixth year on the island), Robinson even describes this rebellion against his father as his 'ORIGINAL SIN', with the deliberate capitalization as a means of emphasis (*RC* 198). Precisely what constituted this 'original sin' has long been the subject of discussion among Defoe scholars, and the particularities of the debate need not detain us long here. However, one point is worth considering further since it does hint at a link between *Robinson Crusoe* and the letters of Paul, most notably the epistle to the Romans. This has to do with the origins of the sinful, human condition.

Given Defoe's theological mind-set and his familiarity with Puritan traditions, it is not difficult to see in his use of 'ORIGINAL SIN' an

---

56. Robins (1952) suggests that originally Defoe had intended an earlier rescue, or even a successful escape, by Robinson, but that in the process of writing the story he became fascinated with Crusoe's island life and so adjusted the story-line.

allegory of human rebellion against the heavenly Father. This is particularly the case if we take Robinson to be an Adamic figure and the island upon which he is a castaway as a symbol of a post-fall Eden wherein the man has to make his living by the 'sweat of his brow' (Gen. 3.19). If this is so, then Paul's teaching in Rom. 5.1-21 about Adam being responsible for 'original sin' also springs readily to mind, and one wonders if this is part of Defoe's intention all along.[57]

Within the story-line of *Robinson Crusoe* this 'original sin' is given concrete expression. Robinson's father wishes him to pursue a 'middle station' in life and become a lawyer, or perhaps a tradesman, but the young man finds such a prospect exceedingly boring. Instead, Robinson runs away from his home in York and signs on board a sailing ship in the port-city of Hull. On his first day at sea, when the ship is caught in a storm and Robinson begins to fear for his life, he becomes mortified, alarmed that he has disobeyed not only his earthly father, but his heavenly father. Robinson reminisces:

> The ship was no sooner gotten out of the Humber, but the wind began to blow, and the winds to rise in a most frightful manner; and as I had never been at sea before, I was most inexpressibly sick in body, and terrify'd in my mind: I began now seriously to reflect upon what I had done, and how justly I was overtaken by the judgment of Heaven for my wicked leaving my father's house, and abandoning my duty; all the good counsel of my parents, my father's tears and my mother's entreaties came now fresh into my mind, and my conscience, which was not yet come to the pitch of hardness to which it has been since, reproached me with the contempt of advice, and the breach of my duty to God and my father (*RC* 31).

As the young and headstrong Robinson defies his father's wishes and seeks a life of adventure on the high seas, he is brought to a point of near repentance by the terrifying storm. Robinson alludes to the parable

57. Defoe turns to Romans at several key points in the course of the story. For example, while contemplating the intricacies of divine providence, Robinson recalls the image of the potter and the clay-pot found in Jer. 18.2-6 and Rom. 9.21 (*RC* 213); in attempting to explain to Friday the Christian belief that God is stronger than evil, he alludes to Rom. 16.20 (*RC* 220); and following the celebration of his fourth year on the island he alludes to Rom. 7.7-8 and thanks God for his spiritual condition in which he conquered the sin of covetousness (*RC* 139). Most significantly, as Robinson agonizes over how he should respond to the cannibals in that they appear to follow their consciences and are a law to themselves, he alludes to Rom. 2.14-16 (*RC* 177, 212).

of Jesus recorded in Lk. 15.11-32 and describes himself in language reminiscent of it: 'I resolved that I would, like a true repenting prodigal, go home to my father' (*RC* 32).[58] The parable is also mentioned by Robinson after the ship upon which he was sailing from Hull was battered and sunk in a storm while anchored in the port of Yarmouth. Again he contemplates returning to his father:

> Had I now had the sense to have gone back to Hull, and have gone home, I had been happy, and my father, an emblem of our Blessed Saviour's parable, had even killed the fatted calf for me; for hearing the ship I went away in was cast away in Yarmouth road, it was a great while before he had any assurance that I was not drowned (*RC* 36-37).

The destruction of the ship is an ominous sign for Robinson's prospects at sea. Although he manages to escape to shore with the rest of the crew of the ship, all of the cargo on board is lost. Such a calamity prompts the master of the ship to exhort Robinson never to go to sea again. The master even goes so far as to compare the young would-be sailor to the Old Testament Jonah, whose presence on board a sailing vessel bound for Tarshish nearly spelled destruction for her (Jon. 1).[59] Robinson recounts a conversation he had with the master:

> My comrade, who had helped to harden me before, and who was the master's son, was now less forward than I; the first time he spoke to me after we were at Yarmouth, which was not till two or three days, for we were separated in the town to several quarters; I say, the first time he saw me, it appeared his tone was altered, and looking very melancholy and shaking his head, asked me how I did, and telling his father who I was, and how I had come this voyage only for a trial in order to go farther abroad; his father turning to me with a very grave and concerned tone, 'Young man,' says he, 'you ought never to go to sea any more, you ought to take this for a plain and visible token that you are not to be a

---

58. Ayers (1967); Hunter (1966: 133-38); and Backscheider (1982) discuss the importance of the Prodigal Son imagery. Flint (1988) argues that Robinson's rebellion against his father is best viewed against the backdrop of the social conventions of the eighteenth century. Both Novak (1974: 61) and Backscheider (1989: 423) suggest that Defoe's own struggles with his wayward son Benjamin may have informed the realism of the narrative on this point.

59. Luke appears to allude to Jon. 1.5 (LXX) in Acts 27.18, with his mention of the crew 'jettisoning the cargo' (ἐκβολὴν ἐποιοῦντο) in order to try to save the ship on which Paul is travelling. Williams (1953: 162) says, 'Paul plays exactly the opposite part to that played by Jonah'. Interestingly, Fisch (1986: 231) goes so far as to describe *Robinson Crusoe* as 'a midrash on Jonah'.

seafaring man.' 'Why, sir,' said I, 'will you go to sea no more?' 'That is
another case,' said he, 'it is my calling, and therefore my duty; but as
you made this voyage for a trial, you see what a taste Heaven has given
you of what you are to expect if you persist; perhaps this is all befallen
us on your account, like Jonah in the ship of Tarshish' (*RC* 37).

Much of the power of this part of *Robinson Crusoe* is concerned with
how young Robinson can discover and fulfil his 'calling' in life. Such
calling is defined as 'duty', and in this sense the 'duty' of the ship's
master is contrasted with the 'duty' of Robinson himself. The two characters are united in that they both perceive the call of duty upon them,
just as we noted both Paul and the Roman centurion Julius do in the
narrative of Acts 27.1-44 (see above, pp. 36-40).

Later in the novel, after the episodes with the Moors and his subsequent adventures in setting up his tobacco plantation in Brazil, Robinson is once again embarking on a hazardous sea journey to Africa in
order to cash in on the lucrative slave-trade. However, the consequences of this journey are much more severe, for it is this trip which
results in Robinson being shipwrecked on his isolated 'island of
despair', his 'island of solitariness', his 'island of meer desolation'.
And just to illustrate the narrative connection between that initial,
nearly fatal, storm at sea and this one, Defoe makes the two take place
on the same day of the year. Again the notion of rebellion against the
wishes of his father (and his mother!) figure in the recollection Robinson provides:

I went on board in an evil hour, the [first] of [September 1659], being the
same day eight year that I went from my father and mother at Hull, in
order to act the rebel to their authority, and the fool to my own interest
(*RC* 60).

The point here is that Robinson is looking back over his experience of
shipwreck and associating it with his rebellion against the rightful
authority of his parents, and beyond that, his rebellion against God. The
shipwreck is interpreted by him as a just punishment for this filial
rebellion.

b. *Shipwreck as the Instrument of Salvation: The Hand of Providence
Sustains*
When Robinson is swept overboard by the surging sea and finds him-
self, against all odds, alive on shore, he is understandably thankful to
God for his salvation. As he says:

> I was now landed, and safe on shore, and began to look up and thank
> God that my life was saved in a case wherein there was some minutes
> before scarce any room to hope (*RC* 65).

However, the wild and uncertain nature of his island refuge, as well as
the numbing fact that he alone of his 11 crewmates had survived,
means that such declarations of providential salvation are quickly
reassessed. Robinson soon describes it as 'dreaded deliverance' (*RC*
66). He questions whether the initial thankfulness to God he felt for his
salvation is warranted, and begins to wonder if he should commit
suicide:

> I had great reason to consider it as a determination of Heaven, that in
> this desolate place, and in this desolate manner I should end my life; the
> tears would run plentifully down my face when I made these reflections,
> and sometimes I would expostulate with my self, why Providence should
> thus compleatly ruine its creatures, and render them so absolutely miser-
> able, so without help abandoned, so entirely depressed, that it could
> hardly be rational to be thankful for such a life (*RC* 80).

This note of 'thankfulness to God' resounds again and again
throughout the novel, but it is frequently sounded against the counterpoint of despair and 'cries of affliction'. Perhaps the best illustration of
this occurs at the end of the narrative section of the novel where Robinson draws up a balance sheet upon which the credits and debts of his
position are set forth (*RC* 83-84):

Evil	*Good*
I am cast upon a horrible desolate island, void of all hope of recovery.	But I am alive, and not drowned as all my ship's company was.
I am singled out and separated, as it were, from all the world to be miserable.	But I am singled out too from all the ship's crew to be spared from death; and He that miraculously saved me from death, can deliver me from this condition.
I am divided from mankind, a soli-taire, one banished from humane society.	But I am not starved and perishing on a barren place, affording no sustenance.
I have not clothes to cover me.	But I am in a hot climate, where if I had clothes I could hardly wear them.

I am without any defence or means to resist any violence of man or beast.	But I am cast on an island, where I can see no wild beasts to hurt me, as I saw on the coast of Africa; and what if I had been shipwrecked there?
I have no soul to speak to, or relieve me.	But God wonderfully sent the ship in near enough to the shore that I have gotten out so many necessary things as will either supply my wants, or enable me to supply my self even as long as I live.

One of the most celebrated instances of God's provision for Robinson occurs when the shipwrecked sailor finds a bag which originally had been filled with corn for feeding the poultry on board the ship. Robinson detects nothing but some husks and dust in the bag and, wishing to use the bag for some other purpose, empties the husks of corn onto the ground outside his dwelling. Soon afterwards it rains and about a month or so later Robinson notices that some green shoots have sprouted from the husks. This meagre, if accidental, harvest challenges Robinson to reconsider God's care for him in the midst of his predicament. He interprets the corn as a miracle:

> After I saw barley grow there, in a climate which I know was not proper for corn, and especially that I knew not how it came there, it startled me strangely, and I began to suggest that God had miraculously caused this grain to grow without any help of seed sown, and that it was so directed purely for my sustenance, on that wild miserable place (*RC* 94).

Even when Robinson puts two and two together and realizes that he himself sowed the corn when he poured out the corn husks, he does not altogether remove providential care from his interpretation of the matter. He begins patiently to harvest his crop, replant it and harvest again until, after years of careful stewardship, he is self-sufficient in terms of grain. At one point he even likens God's provision in this matter to the Old Testament story in 1 Kgs 17.4-6 about Elijah being fed by the ravens.[60] Robinson determines:

> to give daily thanks for that daily bread, which nothing but a croud of wonders could have brought. That I ought to consider I had been fed

---

60. Brown (1971: 577) suggests that the saying of Jesus about a grain of wheat dying in the ground (Jn 12.24-25) lies behind the corn episode, and that Robinson is being encouraged to learn a spiritual lesson about death to self through the incident.

even by miracle, even as great as that of feeding Elijah by ravens; nay, by a long series of miracles... (*RC* 143).

Perhaps the most significant spiritual introspection within the novel concerns Robinson's so-called 'conversion experience', although the idea of conversion is a central motif within the novel as a whole, as Michael Seidel (1991: 57) states:

> *Robinson Crusoe* works and reworks the motif of conversion. Conversion is at the heart of the narrative. To set a man on an empty island means that everything has to be converted to Crusoe's use to have significance; hence the novel is in a direct and metaphoric sense about the varieties of conversion: fear to salvation; stuff to structure; nature to culture; accident to providence; paranoia to toleration. Crusoe makes over his island, turns his religious sensibility, shifts his politics, transforms his life.[61]

Robinson becomes seriously ill with a fever and begins to pray to God 'for the first time since the storm off of Hull' (*RC* 102). In a state of spiritual agitation he falls asleep and dreams of God coming from heaven to kill him for his lack of repentance. The vision is an integral part of his 'spiritual conversion' and moves him inexorably on to a new identity, in much the same way that Paul the apostle's Damascus road experience is the event which gives him a new identity and results in him being given a new name ('Saul' becomes 'Paul').[62] Robinson awakens and, still in the grip of his fever and in great turmoil, goes to a chest which he had salvaged from the shipwreck and in which are stashed his tobacco stores, together with some bibles. 'I went', he says, 'directed by Heaven no doubt; for in this chest I found a cure, both for soul and body' (*RC* 108); whether the tobacco or the Bible constitutes the cure is something which Defoe leaves delightfully ambiguous.[63] He chews some of the tobacco, mixing it with rum, and then inhales smoke from some of the tobacco which he has thrown on the fire. He begins to read from the Bible and stumbles across the words of the Psalmist in 50.15. We read:

61. Similarly, Boreham (1955: 13) says: 'The biggest thing that ever happened to Robinson Crusoe was his conversion ...Crusoe's conversion dominates the entire book and adds a lustre to every page'.

62. The importance of the Damascus road episode for the writer of Luke–Acts is evident by the fact that he records three different versions of it. See Hedrick (1981) for an introduction to the matter.

63. As Sill (1994–95: 47) notes.

> [O]nly having opened the book casually, the first words that occurred to
> me were these: *Call on me in the day of trouble, and I will deliver, and
> thou shalt glorify me* (*RC* 108).

This is closely followed by a reference in the journal to Ps. 78.19b (*RC*
109); here the rebellion of the people of Israel in the desert following
their miraculous deliverance from Egypt is cited. God's people mock
the salvation which has come to them; as the Psalmist records:

> Yea, they spake against God; they said, Can God furnish a table in the
> wilderness?

It is a particularly apt quotation, given that Robinson has been delivered
from the storm which killed his fellow seamen, yet seems to entertain
doubts about the level of God's provision for him. Robinson returns to
the promise of God which is recorded in Ps. 50.15,[64] questioning
whether he himself has upheld his part in the covenant and coming to a
critical moment within his spiritual struggle:

> Had I done my part? God had delivered me, but I had not glorify'd Him;
> that is to say, I had not owned and been thankful for that as a deliver-
> ance, and how could I expect greater deliverance?
>   This touched my heart very much, and immediately I kneeled down
> and gave God thanks aloud, for my recovery from my sickness... (*RC*
> 110).

The next entry within the journal is dated 4 July. It is this entry
which marks Robinson's so-called 'conversion experience', perhaps *the*
defining event within the novel as far as the spiritual introspections are
concerned.[65] The section is rather long, but it is worth citing in its
entirety:

> In the morning I took the Bible, and beginning at the New Testament, I
> began seriously to read it, and imposed upon my self to read a while
> every morning and every night, not tying my self to the number of
> chapters, but as long as my thoughts shou'd engage me: It was not long
> after I set seriously to this work, but I found my heart more deeply and

---

64. Together the two verses from Psalms become something like proof-texts for
Robinson within his spiritual diary. He continues throughout much of his island
experience to contemplate not only his divine deliverance in the form of the shipwreck, but also the surety of God's provision for him on the island (allusions to the
two verses from Psalms recur in *RC* 111, 114, 157, 165, 270).

65. For more on the importance of the conversion episode, see Benjamin
(1951); Grief (1966); and Zimmerman (1975: 20-47).

sincerely affected with the wickedness of my past life: The impression
of my dream revived, and the words, *All these things have not brought
thee to repentance*, ran seriously in my thought: I was earnestly begging
of God to give me repentance, when it happened providentially the very
day that reading the scripture, I came to these words, *He is exalted a
Prince and a Saviour, to give repentance, and to give remission*. I threw
down the book, and with my heart as well as my hands lifted up to
heaven, in a kind of extasy of joy, I cry'd out aloud, 'Jesus, thou son of
David, Jesus, thou exalted Prince and Saviour, give me repentance!'

This was the first time that I could say, in the true sense of the words,
that I prayed in all my life; for now I prayed with a sense of my condition, and with a true scripture view of hope founded on the encourage-
ment of the word of God; and from this time, I may say, I began to have
hope that God would hear me.

Now I began to construe the words mentioned above, *Call on me, and
I will deliver you*, in a different sense from what I had ever done before;
for then I had no notion of any thing being called deliverance, but my
being delivered from the captivity I was in; for tho' I was indeed at large
in the place, yet the island was certainly a prison to me, and that in the
worst sense in the world; but now I learned to take it in another sense.
Now I looked back upon my past life with such horrour, and my sins
appeared so dreadful, that my soul sought nothing of God, but deliverance from the load of guilt that bore down all my comfort: as for my
solitary life it was nothing; I did not so much as pray to be delivered
from it, or think of it; it was all of no consideration in comparison to
this. And I add this part here, to hint to whoever shall read it, that whenever they come to a true sense of things, they will find deliverance from
sin a much greater blessing, than deliverance from affliction (*RC* 110-
11).

This is the moment within the novel where Robinson begins to spiritu-
alize the meaning of his island prison, where he 'finds' himself even
though for all outward appearances he is 'lost'. In the insightful words
of Michael McKeon (1987: 318),

It is the beginning of the movement of narrative 'atonement,' when
Character and Narrator come together, and this can be seen in the ease
with which Robinson will shortly distinguish between not aimless past
and repentant future but anguished past and contented present: between
'Before,' when he felt he 'was a Prisoner lock'd up with the Eternal Bars
and Bolts of the Ocean, and 'now,' when 'I began to exercise my self
with new Thoughts'.

The religious conversion of Robinson is marked in several ways
throughout the rest of the story, a fact which serves to illustrate the

importance of it within the overall story-line. Perhaps the best illustration of this concerns the way in which Robinson marks time spent on the island. Not only does he set up a 'counting post' onto which he carves notches to mark the days, but he begins to mark the anniversary of his arrival on the island (30 September 1659).[66] The language used to describe these anniversaries reflects the change that has come over Robinson as a result of his 4th of July experience; in effect the special marking of 30 September makes that day an annual celebration of God's salvation and of Robinson's deliverance to the island. And to ensure that we do not fail to pick up on the connection between the two dates, Defoe provides us with an intriguing paragraph designed to set out the significance of 30 September for Robinson. Within the extended spiritual reflection which arises out of Robinson's marking of his fourth anniversary on the island, we read:

> The same day of the year I was born on (viz.) the 30th of September, that same day, I had my life so miraculously saved 26 year after, when I was cast on shore in this island, so that my wicked life, and my solitary life begun both on a day (*RC* 144).

In other words, 30 September was not only the day on which Robinson began his earthly life, it was also the day on which he was delivered by the hand of providence to begin a new, solitary life lived under the watchful eye of Heaven. The novel is littered with chronological coincidences such as these which stretch credulity to the limit,[67] but the fact remains that they are present and do serve a purpose. Thus, 30 September witnesses to Robinson's physical birth to life, but also to his spiritual re-birth from death. It is not without significance that Robinson's conversion on 4 July 1660 comes *nine months* (and *two* days!)[68] after

---

66. The significance of this date within the chronology of *Robinson Crusoe* has been the subject of some discussion, particularly as it relates to the possibility that Defoe inserted the episodes involving Friday at a later stage in the composition of the novel. For more on the issue of chronology, see Hastings (1912); Ganzel (1961); James (1972: 192-93).

67. Even one of Defoe's contemporary critics complained about what he described as Robinson's 'Coining of Providences'. This charge is found in Gildon (1719: 9).

68. Remembering that the narrator of the novel relates that the calculations for Crusoe's length of stay on the island, based on the number of notches on the 'counting post', was only off by one *or two* days: 'I found at the end of my account I had lost a day or two in my reckoning' (*RC* 117).

his salvation from shipwreck, as if to suggest his 'gestational period' as a newly born Christian.[69]

There is space to cite four of the 'anniversary' passages that illustrate the importance of the annual celebrations as essential parts of Robinson's spiritual reflections. Careful reading will also show them to be deliberate echoes of the conversion experience of Robinson. We detect within the first of these passages not only a glimpse of Robinson's keeping of the Sabbath, but also the nearest that he is able to come to a celebration of the Lord's Supper:

> September the thirtieth, I was now come to the unhappy anniversary of my landing. I cast up the notches on my post, and found I had been on shore three hundred and sixty five days. I kept this day as a solemn fast, setting it apart to religious exercise, prostrating my self on the ground with the most serious humiliation, confessing my sins to God, acknowledging His righteous judgments upon me, and praying to Him to have mercy on me, through Jesus Christ; and having not tasted the least refreshment for twelve hours, even till the going down of the sun, I then eat a bisket cake, and a bunch of grapes, and went to bed, finishing the day as I began it (*RC* 117).

Interestingly, the eating of bread and wine (or the nearest equivalent available to Robinson in his primitive island setting) is preceded by a defined period of fasting, a feature that was also given prominence in the account of the breaking of bread recorded in Acts 27.33-38. Both the author of Luke–Acts and Defoe appear to allude to the celebration of the Lord's Supper within their accounts of shipwreck and salvation. The first *anticipates* deliverance from shipwreck which has been foretold but has not yet happened, the second *commemorates* deliverance from the shipwreck which has already taken place.

Defoe returns to this 'bisket and grapes' image of the Lord's Supper later in the novel immediately following Robinson's rescue of Friday from the cannibals (although in this instance it is now *dried* grapes that are used). Robinson has killed two of the cannibals who were chasing the fleeing Friday, and Friday buries them in the sand so as to avoid detection by the other cannibals who are still on the island. Then Robinson takes Friday to the safety of his small cave hideaway on the

69. The importance of 30 September 1660 within the story-line of *Robinson Crusoe* has led to speculation that this was also Defoe's own birthdate. The exact date of Defoe's birth remains something of a mystery, although 1660 appears to be the most likely year.

other side of the island. 'Here I gave him bread, and a bunch of raisins to eat' (*RC* 208), declares Robinson within his journal. The eucharistic gesture not only marks Friday's deliverance, but also anticipates his eventual conversion. Thus, the image functions for Friday in exactly the same way that the eating of 'bisket and raisins' did for Robinson when he was washed ashore following the shipwreck.

The second anniversary of the shipwreck is spent in the same solemn manner as was the first, with Robinson beginning to demonstrate peace and contentment about his situation. Slowly he develops an ability to see the physical poverty he suffers on the island as more than compensated for by the spiritual wealth he discovers there. Not only has he begun to master his island home and assert his dominion over it, he is at the same time mastered by it, or to be more accurate, he finds his spiritual Master while shipwrecked on it. The description of the second anniversary is as follows:

> I spent the whole day in humble and thankful acknowledgments of the many wonderful mercies which my solitary condition was attended with, and without which it might have been infinitely more miserable. I gave humble and hearty thanks that God had been pleased to discover to me, even that it was possible I might be more happy in this solitary condition, than I should have been in a liberty of society, and in all the pleasures of the world. That He could fully make up to me, the deficiencies of my solitary state, and the want of humane society by His presence, and the communications of His grace to my soul, supporting, comforting, and encouraging me to depend upon His providence here, and hope for His eternal presence hereafter (*RC* 125).

Thus, despite the fact that he suffers from occasional bouts of doubt and spiritual depression, Robinson's devotional patterns begun at his conversion are continued. One day he reads in his Bible the promise of God in Josh. 1.5, 'I will never, never leave thee, nor forsake thee', and takes heart. He is even able 'to give thanks to God for bringing me to this place' (*RC* 126).

The celebration of his fourth year on the island illustrates the continuing spiritual growth and development of Robinson. He is becoming more and more distanced from the outside world, viewing it as something foreign and remote to him. The parable of Dives and Lazarus (Lk. 16.19-31) is invoked as a parallel to his situation:

> I finished my fourth year in this place, and kept my anniversary with the same devotion, and with as much comfort as ever before; for by a constant study, and serious application of the word of God, and by the

> assistance of His grace, I gained a different knowledge from what I had
> before. I entertained different notions of things. I looked now upon the
> world as a thing remote, which I had nothing to do with, no expectation
> from, and indeed no desires about: in a word, I had nothing indeed to do
> with it, nor was ever like to have; so I thought it looked as we may per-
> haps look upon it hereafter, viz. as a place I had lived in, but was come
> out of it; and well might I say, as Father Abraham to Dives, *Between me
> and thee is a great gulph fix'd* (*RC* 139).

The twenty-seventh anniversary of Robinson's arrival on the island is spoken of in similar terms, even though much has happened in the interim. Most importantly, by this stage in the story-line Robinson has rescued his man-servant Friday from the cannibals who had been intent on eating him. Friday has now been with Robinson for three years, and has even come to Christian faith. Friday's conversion is a nice dramatic counterpoint to Robinson's, for it gives us as readers external evidence of Robinson's own conversion.[70] The sincerity of Robinson's repentance is confirmed by his evangelistic zeal in bringing Friday to faith. A hint of this is contained in the description of the celebrations marking the twenty-seventh anniversary on the island:

> I was now entred on the seven and twentieth year of my captivity in this
> place; though the three last years that I had this creature with me, ought
> rather to be left out of the account, my habitation being quite of another
> kind than in all the rest of the time. I kept the anniversary of my landing
> here with the same thankfulness to God for His mercies, as at first; and if
> I had such cause of acknowledgment at first, I had much more so now,
> having such additional testimonies of the care of providence over me,
> and the great hopes I had of being effectually, and speedily delivered; for
> I had an invincible impression upon my thoughts, that my deliverance
> was at hand, and that I should not be another year in this place (*RC* 230).

c. *Shipwreck and the Crisis of Faith: The Single Footprint in the Sand*
Several years ago Sir William Golding gave a public lecture in Oxford in which he discussed his experiences as a novelist. As one of his illustrations of how a writer can sometimes stumble upon an image or an idea, the significance of which he perhaps only *begins* to suspect, Golding spoke of Defoe's *Robinson Crusoe* and how the hero of the story finds a lone footprint in the sand. Golding, who used the desert-island

---

70. Hunter (1963) discusses how Defoe strives to present a realistic picture of Friday's conversion. Also see Egan (1973) for a discussion of Robinson's decision to share his faith with Friday.

1. Robinson Crusoe: Shipwreck, Sin and Salvation

setting to great effect in his own *Lord of the Flies* (1954) and *Pincher Martin* (1956), said that he wondered if Defoe had any idea what a true stroke of genius the 'flying footprint' really was. Certainly the discovery of the lonely footprint on the beach has captured the imagination of illustrators of the novel, for it is one of the most commonly portrayed scenes from the book.[71]

The scene is introduced simply and abruptly, so that the unexpected nature of the narrative of the discovery is made to match its content. As readers, we are as unprepared as Robinson was for what follows. The discovery of the footprint takes place during Robinson's fifteenth year on the island, exactly at the mid-way point in the narrative of the novel.[72] Robinson himself can only describe it as 'a new scene of my life':

> It happened one day about noon going towards my boat, I was exceedingly surprized with the print of a man's naked foot on the shore, which was very plain to be seen in the sand: I stood like one thunder-struck, or as if I had seen an apparition... (*RC* 162).

Robinson recoils in horror at the sight of the footprint and what it might mean for his life on the island. He imagines cannibals behind every tree and bush; every distant stump is transformed by his imagination into the shape of a man. He runs quickly to the safety of his home compound and does not dare to venture forth for three days and three nights. There, within the relative safety of his fortress, he ponders the meaning of the footprint. He wonders if it is a sign of the presence of the devil on the island,[73] or possibly a sign of cannibals from a neighbouring island or the mainland who have come to devour him (*RC* 163).[74] At one point he convinces himself that it was one of his own footprints, left in the sand during one of his excursions around the island (this is later disproved by careful measurement of the size and shape of the print).

The significance of the naked footprint within the story has been endlessly discussed, and a variety of interpretations have been put forward. At one level the scene is certainly a humorous one; the mental picture

71. As Blewett (1995) clearly demonstrates.

72. So Hammond (1993: 73) suggests.

73. For an intriguing study of Defoe's preoccupation with the supernatural, see Baine (1968).

74. Ellis (1969) suggests that the novel is organized around images of devouring.

of Robinson reacting in the manner that he does is certainly enough to cause readers to giggle. Thus John Sutherland (1997: 5) has recently remarked:

> Was the single footprint made by some monstrous hopping cannibal? Perhaps Long John Silver passed by, from Treasure Island, with just the one foot and a peg leg? Has someone played a prank on Robinson Crusoe by raking over the sand as one does in a long-jump pit, leaving just the one ominous footprint?

Defoe makes much of the fact that it is a *single* footprint which causes such upheaval in Robinson's life. It is really only by rescuing Friday from the cannibals, and befriending him, that Robinson is able to overcome the terror occasioned by the discovery of the footprint. In effect, this suggests that fear cannot be overcome alone and that human beings are only whole when integrated within society (Novak 1961).

However, what is perhaps more significant for our purposes is to note the way in which the discovery of the footprint challenges Robinson's sense of his deliverance by the hand of providence. The footprint shatters his confidence in God, and raises doubts about his interpretation of the shipwreck as proof of his miraculous deliverance from sin and self. Fear gives rise to doubt within the frightened soul of Robinson, as the realization of how fragile his cosy little world is comes crashing in on him. He says:

> Thus my fear banished all my religious hope; all that former confidence in God, which was founded upon such wonderful experience as I had had of his goodness, now vanished, as if He that had fed me by miracle hitherto, could not preserve by His power the provision which He had made for me by His goodness (*RC* 164).

Robinson likens himself to King Saul, who, according to 1 Sam. 28.15, was so afraid of the army of the Philistines that threatened him that he also believed God had abandoned him (*RC* 167). The experience of finding the footprint causes Robinson to recall his sinfulness before God and to resign himself to whatever might be the intentions of Providence. He considers dismantling all of the evidences of his presence on the island, destroying his carefully cultivated fields and releasing his penned animals. In the end he opts for an even greater fortification of his living quarters, building a second wall and constructing strategic firing sites for his seven muskets. He also divides his crop-stores and herd of goats, stashing them at various secured places on the island. All of this is due to the discovery of a single footprint in the sand, a discovery which heralds a spiritual crisis. One of the best descriptions of Robinson's agony of spirit comes within a passage given over to the discussion of his attempts at making his island home more secure. In an extended reflection Robinson says:

> I must observe with grief too, that the discomposure of my mind had too great impressions also upon the religious part of my thoughts, for the dread and terror of falling into the hands of savages and canibals, lay so upon my spirits, that I seldom found my self in a due temper for application to my Maker, at least not with the sedate calmness and resignation of soul which I was wont to do; I rather prayed to God as under great affliction and pressure of mind, surrounded with danger, and in expectation every night of being murthered and devoured before morning; and I must testify from my experience, that a temper of peace, thankfulness, love and affection, is much more the proper frame for prayer than that of terror and discomposure; and that under the dread of mischief impending, a man is no more fit for a comforting performance of the duty of praying to God, than he is for repentance on a sick bed (*RC* 170-71).

While there is by no means agreement among critics as to the meaning of the naked footprint within the fictional world of *Robinson Crusoe*, all agree that Defoe has here produced an imaginative scene which is as terrifying as it is timeless. Robert Louis Stevenson, whose own *Treasure Island* (1883) owes much to Defoe's work, described it as one of the four unforgettable images of imaginative literature.[75] James Joyce compared Robinson's sight of the naked footprint with the vision of John at Patmos. Effectively this identifies the two events as cataclysmic portents of a new age to come, an age which irretrievably alters the one in which we now live. Joyce (1994: 323) says:

> Saint John the Evangelist saw on the island of Patmos the apocalyptic ruin of the universe and the building of the walls of the eternal city sparkling with beryl and emerald, with onyx and jasper, with sapphire and ruby. Crusoe saw only one marvel in all the fertile creation around him, the print of a naked foot in the virgin sand. And who knows if the latter is not more significant than the former?

In sum, the evocative image of the 'single footprint' is used to illustrate Crusoe's fears and apprehensions, reactions which are understandable for someone in his position, a solitary figure stranded on a deserted

---

75. See Stevenson (1882) on this point. The other three images were Achilles shouting over against the Trojans, Ulysses bending his great bow, and Bunyan's story from *The Pilgrim's Progress* of Christian running with his fingers in his ears.

island. More importantly, in a powerful fashion Defoe uses Crusoe's reactions to highlight a deeper, spiritual crisis that takes place within the soul of the man. Thus, the 'single footprint' remains one of the most memorable and thought-provoking images of the work.

I turn now to consider how Defoe's novel has been interpreted by modern film-makers. I shall consider two very different adaptations of the novel: the first by a French film-maker from the 1960s, the second, a full-bodied adaptation from the 1980s with an up-and-coming Hollywood star in the title role. In both instances I shall concentrate on how the idea of Robinson's shipwreck is portrayed within the films.

4. *Shipwreck, Sin and Salvation in Film Interpretations of* Robinson Crusoe

Defoe's *Robinson Crusoe* has yielded a rich harvest as far as film adaptations are concerned. Some of film-making's most celebrated directors have turned their hand to it; perhaps the best example is Luis Buñuel's *The Adventures of Robinson Crusoe* (1952), generally acknowledged to be one of the most imaginative and entertaining versions of the novel ever made. The film starred Dan O'Herlihy in the role of Robinson and Jaime Fernández in the role of Friday (with O'Herlihy winning an Oscar nomination in the 1954 Academy Awards for his performance). A version made for BBC television, simply entitled *Robinson Crusoe*, appeared in 1974. It was directed by James MacTaggert and starred Stanley Baker in the title role and Ram John Holder as Friday. A somewhat unusual space-age adaptation by Byron Haskin was released in 1964 entitled *Robinson Crusoe on Mars*. This starred Paul Mantee as a stranded astronaut, and captured the sense of isolation integral to Defoe's novel by successfully transferring it to a modern equivalent setting. Friday in this instance is a refugee from a nearby interplanetary war.

Several cinematic versions of adaptations of Defoe's novel have also been produced, perhaps the most notable of which is based on Adrian Mitchell's *Man Friday: A Play* (1974). This 1976 film[76] was directed by Jack Gold and starred Peter O'Toole as Robinson and Richard Roundtree as Friday. As mentioned above (p. 32) the adaptation inverts

---

76. An earlier version of Mitchell's play was produced for the BBC programme *Play for Today* in 1972. This was directed by James MacTaggert and produced by Graeme McDonald.

the relationship of Robinson and Friday and thereby attempts to address questions of racism and exploitation. In this version, however, the audience does not decide whether or not to allow Robinson to stay on Friday's island, for, in one version of the film at least, the rejected Crusoe commits suicide by blowing his brains out. However, it is to two other film versions of *Robinson Crusoe* that I now turn our attention.

a. *Jean Sacha's* The Adventures of Robinson Crusoe (1964)
The first film adaptation which I shall consider is the black-and-white television serialization made by the French director Jean Sacha for Franco-London Films in 1964.[77] Originally made in French, it was dubbed into English and shown on the BBC in weekly installments during October–December 1965.[78] The series was produced by Henry Deutschmeister and the screenplay was written by Jean-Paul Carrière, Pierre Reynal and Jacques Somet. The title character Robinson was played by an Austrian actor named Robert Hoffman, with English dubbing for his voice being supplied by Lee Payant. Much of the story is told via a voice-over narration done in the first person, although there are flashback scenes to help fill out sequences explaining Robinson's earlier life. The island scenes within the series were shot on location in the Canary Islands, which greatly enhances their realism. The series has a haunting musical score and each of the 13 episodes lasts approximately 27 minutes (within the following discussion I shall identify the episodes by their sequential number).

Episode 1 begins with the shipwreck on the island and Robinson being washed up on the island as the only member of the fated *Esmeralda* to survive a violent storm; Episode 13 concludes with Robinson

77. The series has recently been released on video by Sound and Media Ltd (1997). The publicity blurb on the four-part video set explains that the last remaining prints of the English version were discovered after being exiled to a French film archive in 1982.

78. There are one or two scenes that play on the differences between the French and the English and attempt to interject an element of humour. This is understandable, given that what we have here is a French interpretation of an English classic. The best example occurs when Robinson is attempting to cook a bird over his open fire. The voice-over narrator explains Robinson's thoughts: 'I am going to make my first attempt at cooking. I am doubtful about the results. We English are not very gifted for cooking; we leave that to the French. We have, thank God, enough qualities to get along without that one, if it is one.'

and Friday being rescued from the island by an English ship and travelling to England where they write their memoirs about the experiences
on the island. Thus, the series as a whole is a fairly faithful adaptation
of the *core* of Defoe's book, the experiences on the island. Most of the
major scenes of the island experience are represented at some point
within the 13 episodes. At the same time, there are chronological
adjustments that are made to Defoe's basic story-line. For example, the
day of his shipwreck is given as 16 September 1697, and the length of
Robinson's stay on the island from that date is drastically shortened. In
Sacha's version Robinson spends only six years in exile on the island,
with Friday arriving during his fourth year, that is in Episode 10 (in
Defoe's novel Friday arrives in the twenty-fourth year of Robinson's
28-year long stay). No doubt one of the reasons for this chronological
alteration is the difficulty in sustaining an audience's interest and ability to believe in a character's experiences over such a long period
(Defoe had difficulty in handling this aspect of his story-line as well, as
his feeble attempt to explain the uneven length of the journal by having
Robinson run out of ink illustrates). Yet even beyond this understandable curtailment of time, there are some other difficulties in the
chronology of the series. As an illustration, it can be seen that in the
beginning of Episode 9 Robinson describes the Spanish pirate ship
which he plunders as having been shipwrecked during his *first* year (in
the novel this takes place in the twenty-fourth year). Less than two
minutes later Robinson mentions that he has been on the island *three*
years, and a few moments later, in a state of drunkenness, he goes on
board the ship in search of rum. The implication is that the pirate ship
has been near his island's shoreline for two years and, astonishingly,
that it has never been fully explored. Shortly after that Robinson tells us
that he has taken everything of value off the ship; but if that is so, why
has he boarded it in search of rum? The on-ship sequence here is an
awkwardness within the story-line, although (as we shall see below) it
does serve an important end. However, these are trivialities of plot
continuity within the series which need not concern us too much.

What about the central themes of shipwreck, sin and salvation within
Defoe's novel? How are these presented in Sacha's series? Robinson's
thankfulness to God for his deliverance certainly comes through at several points, and it is often mixed with his bewilderment about the work-
ings of providence in saving him (just as occurs in Defoe's novel).
Thus, in Episode 1, after Robinson has been washed overboard by a

wave and manages to drag himself into the sandy beach of the island, he exclaims: 'I was lucky. *My God* I was lucky.' Early in Episode 2 Robinson mistakes a set of footprints on the beach as evidence of other survivors and painfully comes to realize that they are indeed his own prints. The voice-over narration reveals his thoughts as he contemplates his imprisonment on the island: 'I had set out to conquer the ocean, and it is the ocean which has made me a prisoner.' These are words reminiscent of Defoe's Robinson as he similarly describes the prison-like nature of the island: 'I was a prisoner locked up with the eternal bars and bolts of the ocean' (*RC* 125). Sacha's Robinson then drops to his knees in the sand, holds out his hands in a gesture of petition and prays:

> O God, why did you rescue me if only to abandon me on a desert island? Why did you save my life? Why just me and not the others? Have mercy on me, dear Lord! Don't abandon me!

Episode 7 opens with an echo of this mixture of despair and gratitude. Robinson's narrative voice tells us: 'I can't bear being imprisoned on this island any longer, even on this hospitable island where I live comfortably.' This prompts him to decide to leave the island and reach the nearest inhabited land. Nevertheless the prospect of leaving the island prompts recollection: 'I recall my arrival, half-dead; my first steps on this land which saved my life.' The idea that the shipwreck on the island was providential is also brought out in Episode 13 when Robinson is in England and is reflecting with hindsight about his experiences. He describes the cave in which he had lived during his time on the island as 'the home which the Almighty had provided for me'.

The accidental miracle of corn-planting, which is made so much of in Defoe's novel, is found within Episode 4 of Sacha's series, although Robinson's dropping of corn seeds on the ground is only briefly portrayed and comes as some of the seed he is feeding his pet parrot Polly falls to the earth. However, this is followed by two or three scenes in which images of corn fields in various stages of growth are presented. In Episode 8 the sprouting of the corn is called 'a miracle', and Robinson recognizes his need to cultivate and harvest 'this God-given grain'. In Episode 11 Robinson and Friday harvest the corn in order to make bread.

Robinson's reading of the Bible as an expression of his religious life is also brought out within the series. In Episode 3 he discovers a large Bible on board the wrecked *Esmeralda* and takes it with him to the island, describing it through the voice-over narration as 'my friend for life'. In Episode 9, following his plundering of the Spanish ship, Robinson decides to celebrate his third anniversary of arrival on the island by holding a celebration meal with his faithful companions, the dog and the parrot. He reads words (ostensibly from the Bible) which exhort him to give thanks to God for his salvation:

> Remember the long difficult road along which Almighty God has made you walk, to test your obedience and also your strength, to know the innermost secrets of your heart, and to see if you shall remain faithful... Observe the commandments of the Almighty by walking along his paths and by fearing them. Never let yourself say in your heart, that the strength and work of my hands were the only source of these blessings.

However, the most innovative feature of the series is the way in which Robinson's conversion and the discovery of the famous 'footprint in the sand' are handled. This occurs in Episode 9 and involves a rather freehanded re-working of the story-line of the original novel. Following his three-year anniversary banquet, Robinson goes to the pirate ship in search of rum. In a drunken stupor he falls asleep on the ship and awakens to find the ship moving; he has been swept out to sea by the currents and is once more adrift and lost. Eventually the ship runs aground and Robinson jumps into the water and swims ashore, thinking that he has hit the mainland. Of course, he has only come ashore on another part of his own island, as he realizes when his dog comes out of the bush to greet him. Robinson is thrilled that once again he has been delivered. As he walks along the beach with his dog the voice-over narration gives us his thoughts:

> I just can't believe that I am saved! Here is my dog. It is really *my* island. From out at sea I didn't recognize it. Here are my footprints! My footprints ... *my* footprints? It wasn't I who made those footprints!

As Robinson looks down he realizes with horror that the set of prints he sees are from feet larger than his (the scene virtually reproduces the same images that we noted above in Episode 2 when Robinson followed his own prints along the beach). Fear and paranoia overtake him and Robinson retreats into his cave-enclosure where he is overcome with a fever and hallucinations. The so-called 'conversion experience' is then portrayed, with Robinson making himself a tobacco inhalation in an attempt to break the fever (there is no mixing of rum and tobacco as in the novel!).

Effectively this unites three incidents which are all firmly separated within Defoe's *Robinson Crusoe*. In the novel Robinson's conversion takes place in his *first* year on the island, while the foolhardy attempt to go around the island in his canoe (the equivalent of the escapade on board the Spanish pirate ship) takes place in the *sixth* year on the island, and the discovery of the footprint takes place in the *fifteenth* year. Sacha's film brings all three of these incidents together and so gives an altogether different dramatic force to the conversion episode. It makes the discovery of the footprints (and in the film there is a trail of footprints along the beach) the event which precipitates Robinson's conversion. Robinson's conversion experience is very much down-played, at least as far as his religious introspection is concerned. There is not the agonizing over his sinful condition which is so important within the novel, although the shipwreck on the island is presented as something which is caught up with the mysteries of divine providence.

In Episode 11 Robinson does introduce Friday to his Christian beliefs, while explaining that Friday's worship of Benamuckee is primitive and unacceptable. Friday raises questions about good and evil and asks why if God is stronger than the devil he does not kill him now and be done with it. At this point Robinson's over-voice narration has him pray that he be given power to explain love and goodness to Friday. In the end Friday says he understands that God will forgive us all and is (presumably) converted. In Episode 12 this state of rightness with God is alluded to when Robinson says at one point that their industry on the island has been rewarded. Speaking of himself and Friday he notes 'our peaceful souls turn toward God with ease'. The experience of salvation certainly unites Robinson and Friday, and just as Robinson saves Friday from the cannibals in Episode 10, so too does Friday reciprocate and save Robinson from the pirates in Episode 13. As Robinson and Friday prepare to leave the island on the English ship, there is a final opportunity to give thanks to God for the salvation which has come to them through the experience of being shipwrecked on the island. Robinson's narrative voice says:

> Finally my prayers have been answered. Yes, I am leaving my island, but with great regret. I arrived there a rash young man full of arrogance; I am leaving with a sense of peace and fulfilment. This island has brought out the best in me. I owe it everything.

b. *Caleb Deschanel's* Crusoe (1988)

I next consider an adaptation of Defoe's novel which is perhaps the most visually striking of all cinematic versions of *Robinson Crusoe*. Much of Caleb Deschanel's *Crusoe* was filmed on location in the Seychelles, and the director of photography, Tom Pinter, certainly takes advantage of the spectacular ocean scenery, as well as the diverse tropical forest on the island. The film stars Aidan Quinn as Crusoe, Ade Sapara as The Warrior, and Hepburn Graham as Lucky. The screenplay for the film was written by Walon Green and there are several distinctive twists to the standard plot which make this a highly original effort on his part. Three of these creative adaptations are worth noting at the outset.

First, the chronological setting of the film is not the end of the seventeenth century, as Defoe would have it, but the beginning of the nineteenth—in 1808, to be exact. Beyond that, Crusoe is not immediately identified as an Englishman who longs for travel and adventure, but as a slave-trader who lives in Tidewater, Virginia. The shift of time and place is important, for it sets up a psychological tension within Crusoe as he has to reconsider his views about race and the selling of human beings, about the nature of bondage and imprisonment, and what it is that makes a person truly human. By placing Crusoe within an eighteenth-century context where slave-trading was a commonplace, the stage is set for us to watch the development of the character Crusoe. He is seen initially as a ruthless and greedy slave-owner, who seems unmoved by the suffering that goes on around him. Indeed, if the opening sequence depicting Crusoe chasing down a runaway slave is anything to go by, he is responsible for a great deal of misery in other people's lives. He buys and sells human beings with apparent indifference.

Secondly, the characterization of Defoe's Friday is very much reworked in the film. In fact, there are really *two* characters whom Crusoe meets on his island, and together they assume the role that Friday has in the novel. Given the slave-trading scenario mentioned above, it will come as no surprise that both of these men are black. The first of these is a man whom Crusoe helps to escape from a ritual blood sacrifice; Crusoe names him Lucky. The second is one of the native warriors who was participating in the ritual sacrifice; he is simply identified in the film credits as The Warrior.[79] It is significant that

79. The publicity blurb on the video box for the film completely misunderstands the relationship between these two characters. It erroneously summarizes the plot of the film thus: 'This stunning beautiful film stars Aidan Quinn as the tortured hero

Crusoe never assigns him a name, for he exists in his own right and his identity comes from the place that he has in his own world, not one that is provided for him by Crusoe. If anything, the two men are equals, each seeking to live within the bounds of his respective world. At one point The Warrior even saves Crusoe's life as the two are fighting and become trapped in a pit of quicksand (perhaps a deliberate allusion to the Slough of Despond in Bunyan's *The Pilgrim's Progress*). The Warrior manages to extract himself and only decides to save Crusoe at the last minute by bending a tree branch down to allow Crusoe to haul himself from the life-threatening mud.

Thirdly, the narrative perspective of the film is quite different from that used by Defoe in telling his story of *Robinson Crusoe*. As I had occasion to note earlier in this study, Defoe makes much of Crusoe's narrative comments on his island journal as a means of relating his tale many years after they were supposed to have happened. This, together with the fiction of an editor who helps bring the story of *Robinson Crusoe* to print, produces a complex narrative web, involving levels of authorship, and is characteristic of Defoe's fiction. However, there is nothing quite like this in Deschanel's film, for there is no journal to be found, and no narrative voice-over which offers an insight into Crusoe's mind. The film contains no internal dialogue; a deliberate absence of retrospective thought on what was happening to Crusoe on the island pervades.[80] In fact, there is precious little dialogue at all within the film (Crusoe talks more to his dog than he does to anyone else). This is a *visual* film, to a degree that is quite remarkable. The viewer is forced to rely on the camera to reveal what is happening, or on his or her imagination to offer a perspective for interpreting the scenes which are portrayed. There are no flashback scenes; everything is happening in the present, as we watch it. This is a film which explores the development of a human being, but the development traced is always subtle and internal, never overt or external. The result

alongside Ade Sapara, the noble savage he rescues from a ritual blood sacrifice.' Not only is the grammar incorrect, but the relationship between the 'civilized hero' and the 'pagan savage' which lies at the heart of the film is missed. It is not Ade Sapara who is rescued in this film.

80. Meagher (1996) offers an extremely stimulating study along these lines. Unfortunately she has misspelled the name of the film director throughout the article, and I am not altogether sure whether or not she has made the mistake of confusing the characters of Lucky and The Warrior within it.

is that we watch and interpret the scenes which are presented to us from Crusoe's visual point of view and find ourselves drawn into his mental world (this is achieved via a sophisticated inter-cutting of camera shots). In short, Crusoe's introspections become *our* introspections.

So how does Deschanel's film handle the ideas of shipwreck, sin and salvation with which we are concerned? The visual imagery of a ship-wreck is powerfully and realistically portrayed, even to the point of seeing close-ups of rats trying to escape the sinking ship. But there are also subtle hints about how Crusoe responds to this disaster of ship-wreck, a metaphor of his life. The island certainly is a prison and a means of punishment for Crusoe, and there are several scenes which intimate that he perceives this to be so. At one point after the ship-wreck, when he has climbed to the highest point he can find and confirmed that he is indeed on an island, he shouts defiantly, 'No! I am cursed on this island'. In another scene, after Crusoe has salvaged what he can from the shipwreck and is sitting with it on the beach, he opens a trunk and comes across the ship's log (no Bible in *this* film!—that would be too blatant). He opens to the last entry and reads the ironic declaration, 'We shall reach the slave coast tomorrow'. And now, in a sense the log-entry was prophetic, even providential, for Crusoe is sitting on the coast of his island, a man enslaved, a soul imprisoned. Several other passages also speak ironically of Crusoe's predicament on the island as his slavery. For example, he finds a bag of gold coins on board the ship when salvaging her, but recognizes that it has no real value now. The half-naked Crusoe begins to re-enact a slave auction for the money, mocking the auctioneer's time-honoured words which con-clude a transaction: 'Going, going, gone! ...to the man with no shirt.' Or again, after he has rescued Lucky from the ritual killing and hidden him from the pagan warriors, he turns to the frightened man and declares:

> You are a lucky man. First, because you are alive. Second, because you have a man like me as your master. And third, because I have no one to sell you to.

He then breaks out into maniacal laughter, the laughter of a man who has come to realize the absurdity of his former way of life. Ultimately things are not so fortunate for the mis-named Lucky, for he is soon re-captured and killed by The Warrior in fulfilment of the ritual blood sacrifice which Crusoe had interrupted.

What about the idea of divine deliverance, the hand of providence?

How is this portrayed as working within Crusoe's life? How is the idea of salvation expressed? Many of the standard images we associate with Defoe's novel are simply not found in Deschanel's film. There is no 'miracle of the corn', no mention of the annual celebrations of deliverance at the counting posts, no eucharistic meals or bread and raisins, no prayers on the beach after the folly of the attempt to go around his island in his canoe. In point of fact, there are only a couple of scenes in which theological themes or images are explicitly presented. The first overt mention of God, or providence, comes early on within the film as Crusoe is on board the ship en route to Guinea in West Africa to make another lucrative slaving-run. It is late in the season for such a journey to be undertaken (shades of Acts 27.9!), but Crusoe has managed to persuade his business associates that the risk is worth it. As the ship is rolled about in heavy seas, Crusoe, Captain Harding (the captain of the ship) and Reverend Milne meet for dinner at a dining table below deck. Reverend Milne is obviously quite sea-sick and more than a little worried about the state of the sea. After Reverend Milne says a blessing over the food, he begins a conversation with his fellows:

Reverend Milne: Usual weather, Captain?
Captain Harding: Ask the Lord, Reverend Milne. This is our first autumn crossing.
Reverend Milne: Ah, Providence willed it.
Captain Harding: Don't thank Providence, Reverend. *(Nodding across the table to Crusoe.)* Mr Crusoe is our benefactor.
Crusoe: *(Smiles but remains silent.)*
Reverend Milne: Oh no! No, no! Providence it is, sir, though it wears Mr Crusoe's face. The ship carries Christ's spirit into Africa.

A second subtle theological point is made in the scenes concerned with Crusoe's building of a boat. This is the equivalent to the account in Defoe's novel where Robinson constructs a raft in which he attempts to go around his island. In the film Crusoe spends considerable time and effort in constructing a boat and a ramp with which to launch her into the water. However, when the boat, which bears the highly symbolic name *Deliverance*, is released to rumble down the ramp into the sea, it all goes awry and the ramp collapses, leaving the boat a broken hulk on the water's edge. Deliverance will not come through his own efforts, for they will fall short and fail.

The third overt reference to God occurs after Crusoe has been shipwrecked on the island for some time. A dog named Scamp has also survived the shipwreck and has been Crusoe's faithful and true companion throughout his ordeals on the island. At one point, Scamp refuses to eat his dinner and Crusoe, examining the dog, suddenly realizes that Scamp is seriously ill with a fever. He gives him a spoonful of rum, lifts him from the place where he usually sleeps on the floor, and places him in his own bed. Crusoe then sits at his table and prays in turmoil of spirit to God:

> Lord, I beg you for my dog's life. He is such a good dog. I have come to need him. Without him ... I shudder to think of life on this island all alone. Thank you, Lord. Amen.

A fourth religious image occurs after Crusoe has rescued Lucky from the natives who were just about ready to slit his throat and add his blood to the ritual sacrifice. Crusoe takes Lucky to his cave and prepares a bird for them to eat. They sit at the table across from each other, and Crusoe folds his hands in prayer before eating. Lucky does not understand what the meaning of the gesture is, but Crusoe motions that he too should adopt the pose. Lucky does so and then proceeds to eat his portion of the bird hungrily. Again, it is characteristic of how Crusoe is portrayed within the film that he does not *say* any prayer as he folds his hands before eating; we are to assume that he voices it in the quietness of his heart and that this piety hints at a change of heart within him. Has the sinful slave-trader now 'got religion'? We can only guess that this is indeed the case, but if so, when? Are there any indications about when this 'conversion' might be said to have taken place?

There is only one episode which addresses this, namely the scene in which Crusoe prays for Scamp's (his dog's) life and finds his prayers are not answered—the beloved dog dies. What is quite remarkable about this scene is that it has many features in common with Robinson Crusoe's conversion experience within Defoe's novel. The mention of Scamp having a fever, as well as the giving of medicinal rum, seem to point in this direction. Something of the spiritual anguish Crusoe undergoes when Scamp dies is evident in the brief scenes depicting the dog's burial. Crusoe takes a shovel and buries the dog in the sand on the beach. He then walks slowly and despairingly into the ocean, dropping the shovel in the water as he goes. A large wave comes towards him and Crusoe strikes out viciously at it with his fist. No words are spoken, but the anguish is vividly portrayed. The loss of his beloved canine companion results in a spiritual crisis for him, and there are vivid scenes of Crusoe sitting on the beach, isolated and lonely, illustrating his melancholy and despair. The experience breaks him, and, paradoxically, eventually frees him; he becomes a transformed man, as demonstrated by his behaviour from then on. Now he is able to accept the arrival of the pagan warriors on his island (the very next scene!) without the same fear or hostility. Now he can laugh at the folly of his former existence as a slave-trader. Because he himself has been set free from his former life, he can, in the end, *not* sit back and watch The Warrior be taken back to England to become a side-show attraction to a scientific lecture tour. So he slips on board the English ship and secretly releases The Warrior, helping him to escape in a canoe. By this action the debt Crusoe owes to The Warrior for saving his life in the quicksand pit is repaid. Crusoe shows how his own shipwreck has led him to overcome his sinful, slave-trading nature and to discover the salvation of wholeness, of authentic personhood. So he sails off into the sunset, silent, but saved from the sin that has cast such a dark shadow over his life. In this sense his shipwreck has proven to be salvific.

In summary, Deschanel's film addresses the issues of shipwreck, sin and salvation in a highly innovative fashion. It offers a reinterpretation of *Robinson Crusoe* which is quite at odds with much that is in Defoe's novel. But the intensely personal way in which the spiritual experiences of Crusoe's life are portrayed make it a film which speaks powerfully to the contemporary audience.

5. *Summary*

I began my study by noting how the New Testament documents present the story of Paul the apostle's shipwrecks, noting differences of emphasis within the two places where it is mentioned (2 Cor. 11.25-26; Acts 27.1–28.16). I then turned to another famous story of shipwreck, Daniel Defoe's classic novel *Robinson Crusoe*, and explored how the ideas of shipwreck, sin and salvation are portrayed within the novel, noting along the way how Defoe's life as a Dissenter helped shape his fictional story. The exploration was then expanded to include two very different film versions of Defoe's novel. At every step along the way, I have sought to listen to the dialogue taking place between the New Testament documents, Defoe's work, and more recent adaptations of Defoe's work. The exploration has been a rich and rewarding one, particularly as it relates to how narration of a story of shipwreck (along with its theological underpinnings) is achieved. There is a sense in which the narrative perspectives of Defoe's *Robinson Crusoe* and the account of Paul's journey to Rome in Luke–Acts begin from a common point, but nevertheless proceed in opposite directions. What is meant by this?

Most readers agree that it is the accounts of Robinson Crusoe's experiences *on the island* which are the most realistic and entertaining within the book. They hold our attention and titillate our imaginations, precisely because they transport us to that island and give us an insider's point of view on things. We view matters from Robinson's perspective, and are invited to make his experience our own. This is the magic that Defoe has worked upon us. It is also one of the reasons why the final pages of the book seem to be such a let-down for most readers. Speaking of the concluding land-journey across the Pyrenees, wherein Robinson and Friday and the rest of their party make their way to England, Michael M. Boardman (1983: 41) remarks:

> So now the solitary speaker who forms the heart of Defoe's greatest stories recedes into the anonymity of the travelling party, the pronouns shift from 'I' and 'me' to 'we' and 'us', and events wrestle the story away from the narrator.

In short, it is the personalized account of the island experiences which makes *Robinson Crusoe* such a memorable work of fiction, and of course this can only really be achieved because the book was written in the first-person singular. Indeed, this first-person singular perspective of relating the story also figures in both of the film adaptations of *Robinson Crusoe* I have examined (although each film handles this narrative technique in its own distinctive way). The maintenance of this perspective is one of the key ways in which the films demonstrate continuity with the original novel, and, in a roundabout way, it also serves to illustrate how central the first-person singular perspective is in Defoe's story.

The account in Acts 27.1–28.16, on the other hand, relies on the first-person plural perspective of its narrator in order to convey a similar sense of realism. Through this narrative technique he attempts to get his audience to identify with the central character Paul as the apostle helps to spread the Christian faith to Rome. This is as it must be, given that in this instance it is Luke, and not Paul, who is narrating the story. But the contrast is nonetheless significant, if subtle. For solitary Robinson sitting alone on his island for most of his 28-year exile, his events *are* the story; for the anonymous writer of Luke–Acts, appearing to join

Paul's party on the fateful trip to an unknown future in the capital city of Rome, *his story* is the event. The only question that remains to be answered is to whom the *his* refers. What is the relationship between the author and the narrator of this narrative (is God the author and Luke the narrator?).

As I noted above, very similar questions abound within critical studies of Defoe's *Robinson Crusoe*. In the end, whatever we may decide about the vexing question of the precise relationship between Daniel Defoe and his creation Robinson Crusoe—whether or not it is right in some sense to view the novel as a spiritual autobiography and thus anchor it in the historical events of Defoe's own life—the truth remains that Defoe has been almost completely effaced by the character he created. As Edgar Allan Poe (1994: 270) remarked, whenever readers read the novel,

> Defoe has none of their thoughts—Robinson all. The powers which have wrought the wonder have been thrown into obscurity by the very stupendousness of the wonder they have wrought!

Maybe it is no wonder that discussions about the 'we' sections of Acts and their implications for the question of the authorship of Luke–Acts have never been settled matters. Perhaps here too within this unique document, a stupendous wonder has been wrought and the message, rather than its mediator, should, in Poe's words, have all our thoughts.

Chapter 2

THE PICTURE OF DORIAN GRAY:
LOOKING IN THE MIRROR DARKLY

In his recent commentary on Leviticus, the renowned Old Testament scholar Jacob Milgrom makes an intriguing reference to Oscar Wilde's novel entitled *The Picture of Dorian Gray* (1891).[1] Milgrom (1991: 260) likens the role played by the painting of Dorian Gray in Wilde's novel to the role played by the temple of Yahweh within the life of the nation Israel. He says:

> On the analogy of Oscar Wilde's novel, the Priestly writers would claim that sin may not leave its mark on the face of the sinner, but is certain to mark the face of the sanctuary; and unless it is quickly expunged, God's presence will depart.

The meaning of the sacrificial system of Israelite religion is thus viewed in a new light. A shortcoming within the life of the people of Israel is immediately registered upon the sanctuary, which inevitably stands as the focal point of their religious life, inasmuch as it is the place of their meeting with God. It is this impurity that the sacrifices offered by the people are intended to cleanse. This is analogous to the situation within Wilde's novel in which changes to the portrait of Dorian Gray are a reflection of the changes that take place within the life of its subject. The mysterious painting of Dorian Gray becomes the lens through which we are invited to watch the fate of a man who is hurtling headlong on a pathway of self-destruction. One asks in alarm, as the novel progresses, what will serve as the sacrificial means of purification for Dorian Gray and his ever more hideous portrait?

Within this study I shall concentrate on the theme of how mirror

---

1. I shall cite passages from the novel by noting their chapter and page number (thus *PDG* 1.5 denotes p. 5 of chapter 1). The edition used here is that within the Penguin Classics series (London: Penguin Books, 1985). The edition contains an introduction by Peter Ackroyd.

imagery is used within the story and how a contrast between the portrait of Dorian and the man himself is presented by means of that imagery.[2] Wilde uses the mirror metaphor frequently within *The Picture of Dorian Gray*; it has even been described as a key to the structure of the novel as a whole (Dickson 1983: 13). Crucial interpretative questions arise. What is being reflected within the portrait, and how does its transformation signal a contrast between what is and what ought to be? Are the changes which take place in the portrait meant to be understood as an indication of reality, and how do they relate to Dorian Gray's unchanged physical appearance? Most importantly, how is the tension between Dorian Gray and his portrait to be resolved? What does the future hold for him and how is the man to be reconciled to his own fate? In short, the importance of the mirror imagery in the novel is indisputable, particularly as the portrait of Dorian Gray functions as a *reflection* of the state of the man's soul. When Dorian looks at the portrait it is as if he is looking into an ever-darkening mirror, one which offers a reflection of his inner corruption and moral decay. Thus, the novel is concerned with the nature of human existence, and how we are to understand what it means to live as true human beings within this fallen world.

The connection between what we experience *now* within our day-to-day existence and what we are to expect in the *future* is also a central concern within the New Testament. Indeed, these are matters with which Paul is pre-eminently concerned within his various letters to the church at Corinth, as he seeks to provide some perspective for the members of the congregation there. Undoubtedly Paul felt some personal responsibility for the Corinthian church (according to Acts 18.1-18 he was instrumental in founding the church in the city). The heightened sense of eschatological balance, wherein the present is compared to what is to be in the future, is readily illustrated in the Corinthian correspondence through Paul's use of mirror imagery. This imagery serves as an excellent point of comparison between the apostle's eschatological thought and similar imagery as it appears in the highly creative novel by Wilde.

---

2.   Gillespie (1992) warns against the dangers of adopting thematic approaches to the novel on the grounds that they are too narrow for a work as rich and multi-layered as this. Nevertheless, there is much to be gained by looking at the mirror imagery as *one facet* of Wilde's novel, just as it is but *one facet* of Paul's letters to the church at Corinth.

I shall pursue this study in four parts: (1) mirror imagery in 1 Cor. 13.12 and 2 Cor. 3.18; (2) the writing of *The Picture of Dorian Gray*; (3) mirror imagery in Wilde's novel; (4) some film interpretations of Wilde's masterpiece.

First, let us consider how such mirror imagery is used within Paul's letters to the church at Corinth, especially as the apostle uses the imagery as a way of expressing his understanding of eschatological existence. Christians, he asserts, live out a tension between the 'now' and the 'not yet', insofar as their present earthly lives are but a pale reflection of what they shall be in the future.

1. *Mirror Imagery in 1 Corinthians 13.12 and 2 Corinthians 3.18*

The idea of a mirror as a symbol for self-knowledge is widespread within ancient Greek literature, particularly within later Gnostic writings of the second and third centuries CE.[3] The unusual properties of mirrors as objects that provided reflections of the physical world meant that they were not only highly prized possessions, but also that they became the subject of frequent philosophical discussion. Mirrors were seen as instruments of revelation, with the focus of philosophical interest being either the revelation itself or the *indirect nature* of that reflection, namely the fact that what was visible was a secondary reflection of reality.

It is commonly asserted by students of antiquity that ancient Corinth was one of the centres for the production of high-quality bronze mirrors. This may help explain the fact that at two points within his correspondence to the church at Corinth, Paul invokes the image of 'looking in a mirror'[4] as part of his argument about the nature of the eschatological existence of Christians (Bassett 1928; Danker 1960).[5] Thus, in 1 Cor. 13.12 he says: 'For now we see in a mirror dimly, but then face to face. Now I know in part; then I shall understand fully, even as I have been fully understood.' The juxtaposition between what is true *now*, and what will be true *then*, underlies the use of the mirror image in this verse.

---

3.   Conzelmann (1975: 226-29) provides details.

4.   Fee (1987: 647) notes that Greek generally speaks of 'looking *through* a mirror' as opposed to our English idiom.

5.   Hays (1997: 230) remarks: 'Paul is using a metaphor well suited to his audience'. Seaford (1984) suggests that the Hellenistic mystery religions, particularly the Dionysiac initiation rite, may provide the background for the image.

Similarly, in 2 Cor. 3.18 Paul builds upon the Old Testament story of Moses having to veil his face following his encounter with the living God on Mt Sinai, and contrasts this with the unveiled faces of the Christian believers, who even now reflect the eschatological glory of God. In Moffatt's translation of this verse the rendering of the unusual participle κατοπτριζόμενοι as 'mirror' brings out the looking-glass imagery well: 'But we all *mirror* the glory of the Lord with face unveiled, and so we are being transformed into the same likeness as himself, passing from one glory to another—for this comes of the Lord the Spirit.'[6]

Both passages show Paul's creative adaptation of Old Testament texts and demonstrate the way in which he picks up unusual features of the particular verses and uses them to make his theological point. Most commentators agree that 1 Cor. 13.12 is a deliberate allusion to Num. 12.8 (LXX) in which God rebukes Aaron and Miriam for their speaking against Moses for taking an Ethiopian wife. In this regard, Paul's use of the text is similar to that of contemporary Jewish writers, notably Philo of Alexandria, as well as other later rabbinical writers, who also offer imaginative interpretations of stories about Moses' face-to-face encounter with God on Mt Sinai.[7] In this context, Philo (*Quaest. in Gen.* 2-3.101-103) cites Num. 12.6 and describes Moses as the supreme example of someone who, when wishing to see God, does not want to see mere reflections (μηδὲ κατοπτρισαίμην) which are channelled through the mirrors of the physical order (heaven, earth, water, air, or other created things). Rather, Moses desires to see the form of God directly, face to face and without intermediaries.

In Num. 12.8, God declares that he has a special relationship with Moses, one in which he reveals himself in a special and direct way, and not through the medium of dreams and visions as he does with Aaron and Miriam. The verse reads:

στόμα κατὰ στόμα λαλήσω αὐτῷ ἐν εἴδει καὶ οὐ δι᾽ αἰνιγμάτων καὶ τὴν δόξαν κυρίου εἶδεν.

With him I speak mouth to mouth, clearly, and not in dark speech; and he beholds the form of the LORD.

Here the *directness* of God's revelation of himself to Moses is emphasized (στόμα κατὰ στόμα λαλήσω αὐτῷ), as well as the *clarity*

---

6. See Kreitzer (1996: 66-68) for more on this verse.
7. Kittel (1964) provides reference for some of the rabbinic materials.

of that communication (ἐν εἴδει). This is contrasted to the dream-like, visionary communication that God has with other prophetic figures such as Aaron and Miriam, a level of communication which is described as coming through 'dark speech' (δι' αἰνιγμάτων). The word translated as 'dark speech' in the RSV is the most important link with 1 Cor. 13.12 and gives us a clear indication that Paul is alluding to the Old Testament verse within his letter. 1 Corinthians 13.12 reads:

> βλέπομεν γὰρ ἄρτι δι' ἐσόπτρου ἐν αἰνίγματι, τότε δὲ πρόσωπον πρὸς πρόσωπον· ἄρτι γινώσκω ἐκ μέρους. τότε δὲ ἐπιγνώσομαι καθὼς καὶ ἐπεγνώσθην.

> For now we see in a mirror dimly, but then face to face. Now I know in part; then I shall understand fully, even as I have been fully understood.

The Greek term αἴνιγμα which is used only here in the New Testament and is rendered within the RSV as 'dimly', carries with it the idea of 'riddle' or 'puzzle'. In this context it means that a prophetic utterance is so enigmatic that it requires further explanation.

The term αἴνιγμα occurs in a number of ancient Greek texts, including Aeschylus, *Agamemnon* 1112, where the Chorus complains that the prophetess Cassandra does not make her proclamations about the fate of the royal family of Argos in a manner which is at all clear. They complain that she uses 'riddles' (αἰνίγματα) and 'dark oracles' (ἐπάργματα θέσφατα) which are open to misunderstanding. Perhaps the most famous illustration of an enigma within the ancient world is the one associated with the legendary figure of the sphinx. The substance of the story is well known in the ancient world and involves the unfortunate character Oedipus, who is on his way to the city of Thebes and is confronted by the dreaded sphinx.[8] The legendary monster, who had a body like a winged lion and the breasts and face of a woman, had laid siege to the city and would not let anyone pass into it unless he could answer a 'riddle' (αἴνιγμα). The riddle was, 'What creature walks on four feet in the morning, on two feet at midday, and on three

---

8. It is perhaps not without coincidence that Oedipus was the adopted son of King Polybius, the ruler of *Corinth*! Could it be that Paul is cleverly alluding to the story of Oedipus and the enigmatic sphinx within his letter to the church at Corinth? One wonders if this is sheer coincidence or if it is another example of the apostle demonstrating that he is a widely read man who appeals to the background and legends of his readership in an attempt to win them over to his theological position.

feet in the evening?' Oedipus correctly answered that the creature was man, who crawls on all fours in infancy, walks erect on two legs when in the prime of his life, and walks with the aid of a staff in old age.[9] Oedipus saved the day, and the city of Thebes was released from the tyranny of the sphinx (who killed herself in humiliation). What endures about the story is the association of the riddle—the enigma—with the legendary sphinx. Indeed, several ancient sources, including Apol- lodorus's *The Library* 3.5.8, Sophocles's *Oedipus the Tyrant* 391 and Diodorus Siculus's *Library of History* 4.64.3, specifically describe the 'riddle' that the sphinx puts to Oedipus as an αἴνιγμα.

The significance of the classical legends surrounding the enigmatic sphinx was certainly not lost on Oscar Wilde, who had distinguished himself while at Oxford University by gaining a rare double-first in Greats in 1878.[10] In fact, Wilde was to return at several points to the legend of the sphinx within his writing, most notably in his poem *The Sphinx* (1894), a work which occupied his attention for nearly 20 years.[11] Nor was the significance of the sphinx imagery overlooked within the best-known film adaptation of *The Picture of Dorian Gray* which appeared in 1944. As we shall see below, imagery associated with the legend of the sphinx figures prominently in the way in which the story of Dorian Gray is presented in the film. Indeed, it is difficult to imagine a more suitable image than that of the sphinx to apply to the person of Oscar Wilde himself. He remains an enigmatic figure, one whose life seems to embody riddles and paradoxes at virtually every turn. Little wonder that he has been described recently as 'an Irish Sphinx' (Edwards 1998).[12] In this sense, it is entirely fitting that Wilde's grave in the Père Lachaise Cemetery in Paris is marked by a

9. It may well be that Paul's contrast of children and adults (1 Cor. 13.11) is a further allusion to the riddle of the sphinx in the Oedipus myth.

10. A course in *Literae Humaniores* ('Greats') included a study of Greek and Latin literature and history up to the first public exams at the end of the second year of the course, followed by two further years of study. The degree was then awarded on the basis of the results in the final examinations which were conducted at the end of the fourth year. Wilde achieved first-class marks in both the Honour Moder- ations of Trinity term 1876 and the final examinations of Trinity term 1888.

11. The poem, although not published until 1894, was substantially finished in the late 1880s. Holland (1966: 93) contains an illustration of the title page of the work with a decorative design by Charles Ricketts.

12. Kiberd (1996: 33-50) addresses Wilde's Irish background and his attempts to adapt to the English scene. Marez (1997) also has some relevant discussion.

large monument designed by Jacob Epstein which contains a winged figure resembling an Egyptian sphinx as its central motif.[13]

For now, however, I move to consider briefly how Oscar Wilde came to write the one novel of his short but glittering literary career.

2. *The Writing of* The Picture of Dorian Gray

Wilde's *The Picture of Dorian Gray* was published in two distinct stages. The story was first published in Philadelphia where it appeared in the July 1890 issue of *Lippincott's Monthly Magazine* and occupied pp. 3-100. It was then reissued in April 1891 by the London publishers Ward, Lock & Company. There were six extra chapters added, along with a preface,[14] and a number of corrections and alterations.[15] Perhaps the most significant of these alterations occurs in 12.180, where the date of Dorian Gray's murder of Basil Hallward is shifted from 7 November, the eve of Dorian's thirty-second birthday, to 9 November, the eve of his (Dorian's) thirty-eighth birthday.[16] Generally this is taken to intimate that the murder is a turning point in Dorian Gray's life, and that it is a mirror of Wilde's own personal life, given that he first engaged in homosexual activity in 1886 when he was 32 years old. In effect, the earlier date is something of a autobiographical clue which Wilde, for reasons which are perfectly understandable, obscured by changing the time reference within the novel.[17] Critical scholarship is generally agreed about the sub-theme of homosexuality within *The*

13. Hyde (1976: 381-83) discusses the difficulties in erecting the monument over Wilde's gravesite.

14. The preface was originally published on 1 March 1891 as an independent essay in the *Fortnightly Review*. The preface is an important feature of the work as a whole, particularly as it contains some 25 epigrams expressing Wilde's thoughts about the relationship between art and interpretation and encourages pluralistic readings of the story. For more on this subject, see Gillespie (1995: 92-106).

15. Lawler has made a specialized study of the various versions of the work. See Lawler (1972, 1974, 1988a). Also important are Murray (1972) and Espey (1977: 23-48).

16. Albert Lewin's film *The Picture of Dorian Gray* (1944), discussed below, is true to the novel and keeps the latter date.

17. Ellmann (1970: xviii) discusses this point. Also see Ellmann (1988: 260-62). Lawler (1988b: 445) argues that Wilde continued to purge the homoerotic allusions and overtones within the various versions of the story, beginning with the first surviving manuscript and continuing right through to the final revision.

Picture of Dorian Gray, as is the case for another of Wilde's short stories, namely 'The Portrait of Mr W.H.' (1889).[18] The choice of the name 'Dorian' for the central character in the novel also seems to point in this direction (Cartledge 1989).

Wilde was a master at incorporating ideas from the work of other writers within his own compositions; nowhere is this more evident than within *The Picture of Dorian Gray*. Consequently, critical scholarship has had a field-day attempting to identify the various sources which are echoed within the novel.[19] As one recent critic (McCormack 1997: 110) puts it:

> As if in two facing mirrors, the novel and its analogues seem to multiply towards a possible infinity, in a kind of self-perpetuating critical machine... One thing is clear: careers can still be made in the hunt for originals of *The Picture of Dorian Gray*.

Several works are commonly cited as being particularly influential upon Wilde's novel, including Philip Massinger's *The Picture* (1629) (see Powell 1978–79), Goethe's *Faust* (1832) (see Rossi 1969), Joris Karl Huysmans' *A Rebours* (1884),[20] Charles Robert Maturin's *Melmoth the Wanderer* (1820),[21] Alfred Tennyson's *The Lady of Shallot* (1832) (see Portnoy 1974; Joseph 1987), Edgar Allen Poe's *William Wilson* (1839) (see Julian 1988: 407), Robert Louis Stevenson's *The Strange Case of Dr Jekyll and Mr Hyde* (1886), Arthur Conan Doyle's *A Study in Scarlet* (1887) (see Hodgson 1996–97), Benjamin Disraeli's *Vivian Gray* (1826–27), Théophile Gautier's *Mademoiselle de Maupin* (1835), Walter Pater's *Studies in the History of the Renaissance* (1873) (see Martin 1983), and Edward Heron-Allen's *Ashes of the Future* (1888) (see Murray 1974: xxi-xxiv), with the list recently being expanded to include some of the works of Louisa May Alcott (see Murray 1994). Important Gothic dimensions of the novel have also been identified, particularly with regard to the mysterious power of the

---

18. The literature on this subject is vast. More recent studies include Sedgwick (1985: 94, 176); Cohen (1987); Cohen (1989–90); Danson (1991); Nunokawa (1992); Lane (1994); and Bristow (1997).

19. Kohl (1989: 160-66) offers a helpful introduction to this matter.

20. This book is most commonly identified as the 'yellow book' which Dorian Gray received from Sir Henry Wotton, the book which led to Dorian's eventual absorption into wickedness (see *PDG* 10.154-57).

21. Roditi (1969) discusses this point, noting the family connection between Wilde and Maturin (the uncle of Wilde's mother). Also see Zeender (1994).

portrait itself (Poteet 1971; Lawler 1994). In this regard, three literary works almost certainly read by Wilde are of special note in that they all use portraits or pictures within their story-line as a means of conveying the magical properties of such objects. By this means an exploration of the relationship between reality and art is pursued, one which is now increasingly recognized as widespread within Victorian literature. These three works are Edgar Allen Poe's *Oval Portrait* (1842), Nicholai Gogol's *Portrait* (1867) and two stories from Nathaniel Hawthorne's *Twice-Told Tales* (1842), namely 'The Prophetic Pictures' (1837) and 'Edward Randolph's Portrait' (1838). Together they form part of what Kerry Powell (1983) has described as a preoccupation with the 'magic-picture'.[22] Finally, it also seems clear that Wilde was not above using ideas and images previously published in his own short stories and developing them within *The Picture of Dorian Gray*. There are marked similarities between the novel and two of Wilde's short stories, namely 'The Portrait of Mr W.H.' and 'The Fisherman and his Soul' (1891) (see Lawler and Knott 1975–76).

So much for the literary influences that helped to make the novel the composite work that it is. What about its central message? Within *The Picture of Dorian Gray*, according to Joyce Carol Oates (1988: 429), 'Wilde's great theme is the Fall—the Fall of innocence and its consequences'. Thus, at one level, Wilde's story is a tale about a man who is a divided self. A body–soul dualism is at the centre of the story, with the soul of Dorian resident within the portrait and separated from the man himself (Korg 1967–68).[23] The struggle against the human tendency to bifurcate existence can readily be viewed as an illustration of Christianity's engagement with the Hellenistic thought-world.[24] In the words of the controversial Camille Paglia (1991: 514), 'The novel's major premise is Dorian's repudiation of the Christian inner world for the pagan outer world'.[25] Yet the precise nature of this bifurcated

22. For more on Hawthorne's influence upon Wilde, see Powell (1980).

23. Hasseler (1993) discusses Wilde's use of the ideas of T.H. Huxley on this point.

24. Gordon (1967) discusses the bifurcation of conscience in the novel and plots it against the struggle between a Hebraic concern for moral commitment and the Hellenistic pursuit of the artistic ideal which is detached and self-sufficient. Sedgwick (1990: 136-41) similarly discusses Wilde and Nietzsche as two figures whose thought is concerned with the clash between Christianity and the wider Graeco-Roman world.

25. Dale (1995) discusses the Hegelian ideas underlying Wilde's thought. Also

existence of Dorian Gray (and by extension, the writer who gave birth to him!) quickly became the subject of intense scrutiny by those opposed to Oscar Wilde and all that he represented.

The intimate relationship between the three male characters in *The Picture of Dorian Gray* has long been a focus of critical debate about the novel's underlying preoccupation with homosexuality.[26] As Lawrence Danson (1997: 9) writes:

> In *The Picture of Dorian Gray*, a book that never describes an act of physical intimacy between men, many readers think they recognize a particular notion of homosexual identity.

Even the major male–female relationship of the novel, that between Dorian and the actress Sibyl Vane, can be read as a veiled homosexual fantasy, given that when Dorian is most attracted to Sibyl she is playing the role of the cross-dressing Rosalind from Shakespeare's play *As You Like It*.[27] Indeed, *The Picture of Dorian Gray* was used against Wilde in his high-profile trials in 1895, wherein Wilde foolishly followed the advice of his lover Lord Alfred Douglas to file a libel lawsuit against the Marquis of Queensberry (Douglas's father). Sections were even read out in the subsequent trial proceedings against Wilde as evidence of his homosexuality.[28] Thus, Peter Ackroyd (1985: 8) remarks: 'The publication of *The Picture of Dorian Gray* marked the first stage in Wilde's long descent into open scandal and eventual infamy'.[29] Or, again, as Ackroyd (1983: 122) has Wilde speak about the novel within his imaginative reconstruction of Wilde's diary for the last four months of his life: 'I date my downfall from that period—it was the moment

see Gagnier (1997) on this point.

26. Ellmann (1977); Beckson (1986); and Dellamora (1988) offer helpful introductions to this much-discussed topic.

27. Gold (1997) pursues this point. The reference to Rosalind has an even deeper meaning when it is remembered that in Shakespeare's day *all* of the parts in plays would have been played by male actors. Wilde is here hinting at a disguised sexuality.

28. Hyde (1973: 109-15) provides details. James Joyce remarked in 1906 on *The Picture of Dorian Gray*: 'I can imagine the capital which Wilde's prosecuting counsel made out of certain parts of it. It is not difficult to read between the lines' (cited in Bergson 1970: 269).

29. Knox (1994) traces how Wilde's syphilis (contracted through a prostitute during his undergraduate years in Oxford) helped to shape his career and contribute to his downfall. The controversy over Wilde's alleged syphilis continues, as Holland (1997: 12-14) illustrates.

when the prison gates swung open for me, and awaited my arrival'. Certainly Wilde himself was aware of the way in which the three male characters of *The Picture of Dorian Gray* reflected aspects of his own personality, and stated as much in a celebrated letter written to Ralph Payne on 12 February 1894. Within the letter Wilde declares (Hart-Davis 1962: 116):

> I am so glad you like that strange coloured book of mine: it contains much of me in it. Basil Hallward is what I think I am: Lord Henry what the world thinks me: Dorian what I would like to be—in other ages, perhaps.[30]

In short, there is a sense in which *The Picture of Dorian Gray* is a mirror of Wilde's own life,[31] although the extent to which this is true is not something that is easily quantifiable. It is often overlooked, as it was also overlooked by the prosecution lawyers who questioned Wilde about the book, that within the novel Dorian Gray pursues women as much as he does men. Indeed, the destruction that he brings upon the lives of both Sybil Vane and Hetty Merton is arguably much greater than that which he inflicts upon any male character within the story (with the singular exception of the painter Basil Hallward!). Quite simply, the novel lends itself to a variety of interpretations, and this is nowhere better illustrated than in the multiple readings which are on offer concerning its message about sexuality (Gillespie 1995). Here, too, the parallels with Wilde's own life are striking.

The Picture of Dorian Gray is a highly structured novel,[32] although the plot is somewhat mechanical and at times moves rather ineptly from one chapter to the next. Wilde was clearly at ease within the upper echelons of British society, and the sections of the novel which reflect this are the most realistic in the book. The descriptions of high-class

30. For more on the importance of the triumvirate (Basil Hallward, Lord Henry Wotton and Dorian Gray) as a basis for understanding Wilde's own personality, see Shewan (1977: 112-30). Charlesworth (1988) describes each of the three central characters as 'masks' of Wilde.

31. Nethercot (1944: 835) plays with the idea of the portrait of Dorian Gray as a reflection of the man's character and applies this to Wilde's own writing when he says, 'Oscar Wilde himself unfortunately had no magic portrait; he had only a mirror: his writings, in which already, for over a decade, he had been faithfully reflecting himself to all who had eyes to see'.

32. Brînzeu (1994) discusses how the novel is arranged in concentric circles around the placement of the portrait of Dorian Gray within its owner's house.

dinner parties, for example, sparkle with insight and wit. Much less effective are the accounts of the back streets, the opium dens and the seedy houses in which sexual liaisons were arranged. The description of the less seemly side of life is much less convincing. In contrast, one of the most satisfying aspects of the novel is the relationship between Dorian and Lord Henry Wotton. The mesmerizing influence of Lord Henry Wotton upon Dorian Gray is frequently noted (Powell 1984), as is his role in stimulating Dorian to make his deal with fate. The fatal Faustian contract that Dorian proposes, in a moment of frivolous fancy, ultimately comes to wreak havoc upon him. Dorian stands before the painting and whispers the ominous words:

> If it were I who was to be always young, and the picture that was to grow old! For that—for that—I would give everything! Yes, there is nothing in the whole world I would not give! I would give my soul for that! (*PDG* 2.49)

With this incautiously uttered prayer, the stage is thus set for an intriguing story of the relationship between the man and his portrait. Indeed, one of the dominant sub-themes of the novel concerns the relationship between art and life. Within the story, living itself is transformed into something of an art-form. At the same time, the normal connection between a real person and an artistic work which is based upon that person becomes distorted and confused.[33] The attempt to create life by means of art is an error which the painter Basil Hallward makes, and it ultimately means that he will have to pay for his mistake with his own life. He declares that he has poured too much of himself into the painting and there is a price to be paid for such *hubris*. Not surprisingly, some critics have stressed the importance of the painter Basil Hallward within the novel's plot, effectively making him responsible for the moral downfall of his subject Dorian Gray.[34]

Ironically, Basil Hallward also represents the voice of reason, of conventional morality within the novel.[35] As such he functions as the embodiment of the conscience of Dorian Gray, as does, by extension, Hallward's painting of his young friend. In the end, however, the

33. Gagnier (1986: 7) suggests that the vision of aestheticism which Wilde presented in the novel was unacceptable to Victorian society because it seemed unaccountable to public values.

34. So Keefe (1973) argues. Powell (1986–87) discusses the identity of the artist who may have inspired Wilde to create the character of the painter.

35. As Spivey (1960) notes.

'conscience', Basil Hallward, is cruelly slain before his masterpiece, brutally stabbed by the subject—Dorian himself. In the attic school-room Dorian takes a knife and kills Basil in a frenzied attack. This is an action which serves as the fulfillment of a comparable scene early on in the novel (chapter 2). In this often overlooked passage from the begin-ning of the novel, Basil, whose conscience is stricken by the knowledge of what he has done by creating the portrait and putting too much of himself into it, picks up a palette knife and moves to stab the portrait and destroy it. He is prevented from doing so by Dorian, who declares, 'Don't, Basil, don't! It would be murder!' (2.51). However, this 'murder' of the painting is later committed by its subject, when the troubled Dorian Gray stabs the portrait with the same knife that had been used to kill Basil Hallward, a knife that Dorian is said to have cleaned many times (20.263); inexplicably, the knife is later found to be in Dorian's own chest (20.264).[36]

The intimate relationship between portrait and subject is mysteri-ously conveyed in this scene and the attempt to live life as if the soul is separate from the body is thereby adjudged a failure. Belief in a body–soul dualism is undercut as the novel comes to its predictable, but nonetheless spectacular, conclusion. It is difficult to know precisely what Dorian was intending when he takes the knife and stabs his por-trait. Is Dorian here committing suicide or homicide (the ending can been read in both ways)?[37] Is he attempting merely to destroy another representation of his conscience, as he had done when he murdered Basil Hallward? If so, then perhaps he is unaware that the act of attack-ing the portrait will have the fatal consequences that it does. Or is the stabbing a deliberate act of suicide in which the distraught Dorian repents of his sin and attempts to reunite his soul with his body in the only way he knows how? The final act of Dorian stabbing the painting, which inadvertently means that he is also ending his own life, has fre-quently been read as the desperate act of a repentant sinner who realizes the error of his ways. The penitent Dorian attempts to eradicate the evil of his life, and accepts divine punishment for his depravity in the pro-cess. Thus, the ultimate destruction of the portrait represents the victory

36. Ellmann (1988: 473) recalls Wilde's poem 'Humanitad' (1881) in which men kill themselves when they kill Christ: 'And we were vain and ignorant nor knew/That when we stabbed thy heart it was our own real hearts we slew'. For more on the importance of Christ in the thought of Oscar Wilde, see Albert (1988).

37. Paglia (1991: 527) discusses this.

of Dorian's conscience against the prevailing philosophical opinions of his day.[38]

There is some indication that Wilde felt that the ending he offered was something of an artistic error, at least in terms of the composition of the novel as a whole. The moralizing ending could be regarded as false and misleading, since it contradicted the core message of the novel as the declaration that the importance of beauty and art supercede all other ethical considerations. It is not without significance that Wilde chose an oil painting as the vehicle for tracking the disintegration of his character Dorian Gray; it fits well within Wilde's artistic thought-world. Much has been made of the importance of nature, art and aesthetics within *The Picture of Dorian Gray*, particularly for what the novel reveals about Wilde's own ideas on these matters.[39] These subjects remain among the most discussed aspects of the work, and rightly so, for they are exceedingly attractive and are creatively treated by Wilde for whom they obviously meant so much. Indeed, the contribution that Wilde has to make to the rich philosophical discussion of the late Victorian era is becoming increasingly recognized (Haley 1985; Brown 1997),[40] as is the importance of *The Picture of Dorian Gray* for the understanding of Wilde's thought as a whole.

Let us turn now to consider more specifically how *The Picture of Dorian Gray* makes use of mirror imagery.

3. *Mirror Imagery in Wilde's Novel*

What are we to make of the mirror imagery such as that which occurs in Paul's letters to the Corinthian church? In what ways is this used within *The Picture of Dorian Gray*? The use of mirror imagery within the novel is similar to that contained within Paul's letters to the church at Corinth, although within the apostle's thought the juxtaposition of the present and the future is in the opposite direction. In 1 Cor. 13.12

---

38. See Gagnier (1986: 216-17).

39. Baker (1969–70); Pappas (1972); Gillespie (1994); and Waldrep (1996) all offer important discussions. Gall (1992: 55-58) interestingly suggests that the blurring of the artistic boundaries within the novel is strongly reminiscent of Mikhail Bakhtin's theory of the grotesque as the place in which opposites merge.

40. The discovery of some of Wilde's notebooks from his days in Oxford has helped to highlight his philosophical thinking. See Smith and Helfand (1989) on this.

and 2 Cor. 3.18 Paul wishes to contrast the imperfections of existence, as it is now, with the perfection of the future existence, as it will be in Christ. This is in stark contrast to the situation with the mirror-like portrait of Dorian Gray. The enigmatic portrait is transformed from an artistic work displaying beauty and perfection into one which can only be described as hideous and grotesque; it is supremely an image of ever-progressing decay and corruption, rather than an image of the 'transformation from one degree of glory into another'. As readers of the story, we instinctively know that the day of reckoning will somehow come, that the relationship between picture and subject will be reversed and that Dorian will eventually have to face the music. In this sense we could say that the picture is a reflection of Dorian's inevitable *future*. In the meantime, as the portrait is transformed from that which is perfect into that which is not, Dorian himself retains his youthfulness and beauty as if frozen in the past, effectively halting the physical decay associated with the progression of time. Present and future are both to be viewed in the enigmatic mirror, whether that be a theological construct (as in Paul's letters) or an image within a creative work of fiction (as in Wilde's novel).

But let us turn to some more specific examples of how imagery drawn from the Corinthian letters is used by Wilde. One of the intriguing ways in which the imagery of 1 Cor. 13.12 is employed in the novel concerns the phrase 'face to face'. This appears five times within the novel: three times to describe encounters that Basil has with Dorian Gray himself, and twice to describe encounters with the portrait of the man. Thus, it is twice used when Basil Hallward is describing to Lord Henry Wotton his initial meeting with Dorian at a dinner party. He mentions that he 'had come face to face with a personality who was … fascinating' (*PDG* 1.28), and later, during the course of the evening, describes his encounter with Dorian thus: 'Suddenly I found myself face to face with the young man whose personality had so strangely stirred me' (*PDG* 1.29). Similarly, it is used in 9.144 when Basil describes to Dorian that when he met him he had discovered a new level of artistic beauty: 'I only knew that I had seen perfection face to face'. More significant are the two uses of the phrase in connection with the portrait of Dorian itself. The first of these occurs in 8.124 following Dorian's cruel rejection of Sibyl following her performance as Juliet. Dorian has already noted, when he returned from the theatre the night before, that the portrait appears altered. Half in disbelief, he has placed a screen in front of the picture to prevent anyone seeing it. The next morning he examines the portrait again:

> He got up and locked both doors. At least he would be alone when he looked upon the mask of his shame. Then he drew the screen aside and saw himself face to face. It was perfectly true. The portrait had altered (*PDG* 8.124).

The final occurrence of the phrase is in 12.186 where Dorian discusses the state of his soul with Basil Hallward and invites him to see the portrait which has been safely secreted in his schoolroom in the attic. He says: 'You have chattered enough about corruption. Now you shall look on it face to face.' What is interesting about these final two uses of the phrase 'face to face' is the way in which both language of perfection ('It was *perfectly* true'), and imperfection ('You have chattered enough about *corruption*') is incorporated within them. This is the kind of language which is quite central to Paul's eschatological thought and, as we have noted, it is twice used within the Corinthian correspondence to express the 'now/not yet' tension of Christian existence in both 1 Cor. 13.12 and 2 Cor. 3.18.

Descriptions of 'mirrors' and 'reflections' also occur at key points in the story, and often these illustrate Wilde's familiarity with the ancient world where such imagery was greatly discussed. *The Picture of Dorian Gray* is peppered with allusions to Graeco-Roman myths, notably the story of Narcissus who looks into a pond of water and falls in love with his own reflection.[41] Moreover, there are several passages in the novel where the portrait of Dorian Gray is described as a mirror or a looking-glass. Similarly, the portrait is sometimes said to function as a looking-glass, 'mirroring' the condition of Dorian's soul. For example, after Dorian has treated Sibyl Vane so shamefully, rejecting her love for him because of her uninspiring performance as the female lead in Shakespeare's play *Romeo and Juliet*, he returns to his home, and as he walks through the library toward his bedroom he notices that the portrait has altered.

> In the dim arrested light that struggled through the cream-coloured silk blinds, the face appeared to him to be a little changed. The expression looked different. One would have said that there was a touch of cruelty in the mouth. It was certainly strange.

---

41. Keefe (1973); Beckson (1984); and González (1994) explore this.

> He turned round and, walking to the window, drew up the blind. The
> bright dawn flooded the room and swept the fantastic shadows into
> dusky corners, where they lay shuddering. But the strange expression
> that he had noticed in the face of the portrait seemed to linger there, to
> be more intensified even. The quivering ardent sunlight showed him the
> lines of cruelty round the mouth as clearly *as if he had been looking into
> a mirror* after he had done some dreadful thing.
>
> He winced and, taking up from the table an oval glass framed in ivory
> Cupids, one of Lord Henry's many presents to him, glanced hurriedly
> into its polished depths. No line like that warped his red lips. What did it
> mean?
>
> He rubbed his eyes, and came close to the picture, and examined it
> again. There were no signs of any change when he looked into the actual
> painting, and yet there was no doubt that the whole expression had
> altered. It was not a mere fancy of his own. The thing was horribly
> apparent (*PDG* 7.119).

In this particular instance, the 'mirror' of the portrait is contrasted with
another hand-mirror on the table, one which is adorned with Cupids,
figures associated with the sensuality of Venus within classical mythology. Dorian compares his own visage in the hand-mirror with that
being reflected from the portrait; apparently the hand-mirror and the
portrait-mirror are kept together and the image of an infinite regression
of reflections is suggestively placed before the reader. Dorian's inspec-
tion of himself in a mirror, as he stands before the portrait, is repeated
at several points. Note the following passage, which speaks of the portrait being safely hidden in his boyhood study in the attic:

> For there would be a real pleasure in watching it. He would be able to
> follow his mind into its secret places. This portrait would be to him the
> most magical of mirrors. As it had revealed to him his own body, so it
> would reveal to him his own soul (*PDG* 8.136).

Two other passages also mention Dorian's examination of himself in
a mirror as he stands before the portrait in the locked upper room. The
first of these is used to convey the moral decay that takes place within
Dorian's life after the suicide of Sibyl Vane. Dorian begins to model
his life on the fictional Parisian whose immorality was chronicled in the
infamous 'yellow book' given to him by Lord Henry Wotton. One
notable exception is interjected, however. The young Parisian has a
grotesque fear of mirrors and polished metal surfaces, a phobia even
extending to still water. In contrast, Dorian positively delights in the

changes that have taken place within his portrait as a result of his corrupt lifestyle:

> Often, on returning home from one of those mysterious and prolonged absences that gave rise to such strange conjecture among those who were his friends, or thought that they were so, he himself would creep upstairs to the locked room, open the door with the key that never left him now, and stand, with a mirror, in front of the portrait that Basil Hallward had painted of him, looking now at the evil and aging face on the canvas, and now at the fair young face that laughed back at him from the polished glass. The very sharpness of the contrast used to quicken his sense of pleasure (*PDG* 11.159).

The second passage is one that Wilde added to the original *Lippincott's Monthly Magazine* version of the story. This in itself testifies to the importance of the mirror motif for the overall story-line:

> The curiously carved mirror that Lord Henry had given to him, so many years ago now, was standing on the table, and the white-limbed Cupids laughed round it as of old. He took it up, as he had done on that night of horror when be had first noted the change in the fatal picture, and with wild, tear-dimmed eyes looked into its polished shield. Once, someone who had terribly loved him had written to him a mad letter, ending with these idolatrous words: 'The world is changed because you are made of ivory and gold. The curves of your lips rewrite history.' The phrases came back to his memory, and he repeated them over and over to himself. Then he loathed his own beauty, and flinging the mirror on the floor, crushed it into silver splinters beneath his heel (*PDG* 20.260).

Dorian's destruction of the mirror hints at the destruction of his portrait which is imminently to take place. Insofar as the portrait serves as a mirror of his life, the destruction of the hand-mirror is closely linked to the annihilation of Dorian Gray himself. The attack on the portrait will bring about his own death.

Finally, it is worth noting that the character Sybil Vane also uses mirror imagery at one point in the story. She alludes to the idea of a mirror producing a reflection of reality when she expresses her movement from the make-believe world of stage-acting to the reality of her love of the real-life Dorian Gray.[42]

---

42. For a stimulating study on how Wilde followed the Victorian attitudes of his day in his negative portrayal of actresses, see Powell (1997). Also see the unpublished prose poem entitled 'The Actress' in Holland (1954: 225-27) which contains some remarkable reminiscences of the character Sibyl Vane.

The painted scenes were my world. I knew nothing but shadows, and I
thought them real. You came—oh, my beautiful love!—and you freed
my soul from prison. You taught me what reality really is. Tonight, for
the first time in my life, I saw through the hollowness, the sham, the
silliness of the empty pageant in which I had always played. Tonight, for
the first time, I became conscious that the Romeo was hideous, and old,
and painted, that the moonlight in the orchard was false, that the scenery
was vulgar, and that the words I had to speak were unreal, were not my
words, were not what I wanted to say. You had brought me something
higher, *something of which all art is but a reflection*. You had made me
understand what love really is. My love! My love! Prince Charming!
Prince of life! I have grown sick of shadows. You are more to me than
all art can ever be (*PDG* 7.114-15).

Having noted some of the particular ways in which mirror imagery is
used within *The Picture of Dorian Gray*, let us now turn to consider
how this motif figures within some of the many film interpretations of
Wilde's novel that have been produced over the years.

4. *Some Film Interpretations of Wilde's Masterpiece*

The Picture of Dorian Gray captured the imagination of playwrights
and film-makers soon after Wilde's death in November 1900. A stage
adaptation of the novel was written by G. Constant Lounsbery in 1913
and another by M. Nozière in 1922. Marion Mills Miller published a
dramatization of the story in 1931 which considerably expanded the
place that the murder of Basil Hallward has in the story line. The
award-winning playwright John Osborne also adapted Wilde's novel
for his play entitled *The Picture of Dorian Gray: A Moral Entertain-
ment* (1973).

About a dozen or so film versions of the story from around the world
have been made over the years, beginning with the Danish director
Axel Strøm's *Dorian Grays Portraet* in 1910. Several other silent versions also appeared in the early days of cinema, including Phillips
Smalley's *The Picture of Dorian Gray* (USA, 1913), Vsevolod Mejer-
chold's *Portret Doriana Greja* (Russian, 1915), Fred W. Durrant's *The
Picture of Dorian Gray* (Great Britain, 1916), Richard Oswald's *Das
Bildnis des Dorian Gray* (Germany, 1917), and Alfréd Deésy's *Az élet
tzirálya* (Hungary, 1917). There is space to consider two of the more
recent film interpretations of the work, one from a British director made
in 1944, and one from an American director made in 1973. In both

instances I shall concentrate on how mirror imagery is used within the films.

a. *Albert Lewin's* The Picture of Dorian Gray *(1944)*

Albert Lewin's film adaptation of Wilde's novel offers a star-studded cast. It includes George Sanders as Lord Henry Wotton, Hurd Hatfield as Dorian Gray, Donna Reed as Gladys Hallward, Angela Lansbury as Sibyl Vane, Peter Lawford as David Stone, and Lowell Gilmore as Basil Hallward. Sir Cedric Hardwicke provides the voice of the narrator throughout the film, while the screenplay is by the director Albert Lewin himself. Special paintings of Dorian Gray, which feature prominently within the film, were created by Ivan Le Lorraine Albright and Henrique Medina.[43] The actress Angela Lansbury won a Golden Globe Award for Best Supporting Actress for her role as Sybil Vane; the film also won an Academy Award for Best Cinematography in 1946.

In the main, the film is a fairly faithful adaptation of Wilde's novel, with most of the central events of the work being presented in fine fashion by a collection of highly skilled actors and actresses. At the same time, several additional scenes and characters are added within the screenplay, all of which serve to illustrate that the film is not slavishly following the novel, but that it has its own creative contribution to make to the story of Dorian Gray as well. Not least of these is the way in which reference to Oscar Wilde himself is injected at one point within the story-line. The opening scenes of the film are set in London during the year 1886, slightly earlier than the actual publication of the novel itself in 1891. Precisely *why* the film opens with this year, prominently declared by means of a title-board, is never made clear. Could it be that this is a deliberate allusion to the year in which Wilde befriended Robert Ross, a man who was to remain his life-long friend and, following Wilde's death in 1900, became the executor of his literary estate? In this regard, it is perhaps also not without significance that Ross was, apparently, the first man with whom Wilde had a homosexual relationship, although (as we shall see below) this dimension of Wilde's life is downplayed within the film as a whole. One cannot help but wonder about such matters, although it must be stressed that such suggestions remain mere speculation. Nevertheless, several other additional features of Lewin's film from 1944 are worth noting.

43. Albright's painting is on display at the Kennedy Galleries in New York City.

First, there is the way that the religious struggle for Dorian Gray's soul is portrayed. Following the suicide of his friend Alan Campbell, whom Dorian Gray had coerced into assisting dispose of the body of Basil Hallward, Dorian decides to go to Blue Gate Fields, a seedy part of London filled with opium dens and houses of prostitution. As his hansom cab draws up in the area, there is a scene in which a street-preacher is exhorting an assembly of down-and-outs, one of whom is Jack Vane (the brother of Sibyl, who was driven to suicide 18 years ago by Dorian's cruelty towards her). The preacher delivers a sermon which summarizes well the theological tension that lies at the heart of *The Picture of Dorian Gray*. A citation of Jesus' words, as recorded in Mk 8.36, is contained within the sermon and illustrates the point:

> Eternal words are as true today as when He uttered them. '*What shall it profit a man, if he gain the whole world and lose his soul?*' The soul is not an illusion. It is a terrible reality. It can be bought and sold and bartered away. It can be poisoned or made perfect. That man, rich or poor, who has the light of charity and faith within himself, even though he were plunged into the very pit of darkness, would still enjoy the clear light of day. But the wretched creature whose soul is filled with dark thoughts and foul deeds, must dwell in darkness, even though he walk under the noon-day sun. He must carry his own vile dungeon around with him.

The spiritual struggle which is being fought for Dorian Gray's soul is set forth in other ways as well. To illustrate, the film opens with a quotation from *The Rubaiyát of Omar Kháyyám* which helps to set the stage for much of the psychological drama which follows. Within the opening sequences we see a story-board which proclaims:

> I sent my soul through the invisible,
> Some letter of that after-life to spell:
> And by and by my soul returned to me,
> And answered, 'I myself am Heaven and Hell.'

These lines are alluded to later within the film when Dorian Gray ask Alan Campbell to help him dispose of the body of the murdered Basil Hallward. Campbell, his now estranged friend, comes to the house and Dorian reads a selection of the words to him as a cryptic declaration of the state of his (Dorian's) own soul. The same four lines from *The Rubaiyát of Omar Kháyyám* are also presented as the final shot of the film, where they are visually linked with the all-important image of the cat-sphinx (this connection is more fully explored below). Effectively, this means that the presentation of the section from *The Rubaiyát of Omar Kháyyám* forms a literary *inclusio*, with the film beginning and ending on the exact same note. In short, the film could be legitimately described as an exploration of how it is that 'heaven and hell' co-exist within each human breast.

The opening scenes of chapter 1 of the book are fairly faithfully preserved within the film. Thus, we see the witty dialogue between Basil Hallward and Lord Henry Wotton as the artist goes about the task of finishing the portrait of Dorian Gray, as well as the delayed arrival of Dorian himself in the studio. The interaction between the three main characters is quickly established and the seductive influence of Lord Henry upon Dorian is convincingly conveyed. There is one significant variation from the novel within these early scenes, namely the introduction of a new character, a little girl named Gladys who is Hallward's niece. In effect, she becomes a replacement for the character of Hetty Merton within the novel, serving as a love-interest for Dorian in the second half of the film when she has blossomed into a young woman and finds herself attracted to the ever-youthful Dorian. Eventually, Dorian makes plans for Gladys to marry him, once he has disposed of the meddlesome Uncle Basil.

The significance of the portrait of Dorian itself is brought out in several ways within these opening scenes, which are set in Basil Hallward's studio. Not only is it the centre of the conversation between the three men at the heart of the story, but its importance is also emphasized by the use of colour footage within what is otherwise an exclusively black-and-white film. In other words, at several points, when the camera closes in on the portrait itself, the film suddenly bursts into a rich explosion of technicolour. This serves to heighten the mysterious nature of the portrait, as does the continual association of it with an enigmatic Egyptian sphinx-like cat throughout the story-line of the film.

The novel's central suggestion that the portrait is a reflection of the soul of Dorian Gray comes through clearly within the film, and in this sense the mirror imagery of 1 Cor. 13.12 and 2 Cor. 3.18 is an underlying theme of the film. The incidents in chapters 11 and 20 of the novel wherein Dorian is described as examining his visage in a mirror and comparing it against the portrait are conflated into one crucial scene within the film. The narrator describes the scene for us as we watch

Dorian scrutinizing his visage in the mirror and comparing it to the portrait:

> He would stand in front of the picture, sometimes loathing it and him-
> self, but filled at other times with that pride of individualism which is
> half the fascination of evil. He would examine with minute care the
> hideous lines that scarred the wrinkling forehead, or crawled around the
> heavy, sensual mouth, wondering which were more horrible: the signs of
> sin, or the signs of age.

However, it is with the frequent use of the image of a sphinx-like cat, a figure not contained within the novel, that perhaps the most interesting allusion to the 'enigmatic mirror' of 1 Cor. 13.12 is made. Clearly, the writers of the screenplay for the film are consciously building into the story-line an image long known to have been a formative one in Wilde's thought, as the quotation of some lines from his poem *The Sphinx* within one scene mid-way through the film demonstrates.

The very first indication of the importance of the cat-sphinx occurs as Basil Hallward and Lord Henry are sitting in the garden of the painter's studio. Basil holds a sketchpad upon which he has produced a line-drawing of the cat-sphinx within his studio. Moreover, the cat-sphinx is intimately connected with the portrait of Dorian itself. Note, for instance, the way in which the cat-sphinx figures within the scene in which Dorian's fateful Faustian pact is made:

Dorian:	*(Looking at the portrait.)* As I grow old this picture will remain always young. If it were only the other way; if it were I who was to be young and the picture that was to grow old.
Lord Henry:	*(To Basil.)* You would hardly care for such an arrangement, Basil. It would be rather hard lines on your work.
Basil:	I should object strongly, Harry.
Lord Henry:	*(Speaking to Dorian.)* You oughtn't to express such a wish in the presence of that cat, Dorian. *(The camera cuts to a close-up of a marble cat-sphinx standing on a table.)* It is one of the seventy-three great gods of Egypt and it is quite capable of granting your wish.
Dorian:	Lord Henry is right. I know now that when one loses his youth, one loses everything.
Basil:	Perhaps a cup of tea will bring you round, Dorian. You'll have some too, won't you Harry? Or do you object to such simple pleasures?

Lord Henry:	I adore simple pleasures. They are the last refuge of the complex.
Dorian:	*(Standing before the painting and speaking half to himself, half to the other two men.)* It's more than a painting. It is part of myself.
Basil:	As soon as you are varnished and framed, Dorian, you will be sent home. Then you can do whatever you like with yourself.
Lord Henry:	You had better send along the Egyptian cat. I don't think the god and the picture should be separated.
Basil:	I will, if Dorian wants it.
Dorian:	*(Again speaking to the painting.)* If only the picture could change, and I could be always what I am now. For that I would give everything. Yes, there is nothing in the whole world I would not give. I would give my soul for that!

If one looks very closely it is possible to see that the enigmatic cat-sphinx itself appears in the portrait of Dorian, on a stand just next to the subject's right arm. The cat-sphinx of antiquity is thus closely associated with the mysterious portrait of Dorian Gray, and serves to highlight its enigmatic nature.

The next appearance of the cat-sphinx within the film occurs in connection with the love affair between Dorian Gray and Sibyl Vane (who within the film is transformed from an actress into a singer in a vaudeville act at *The Two Turtles* tavern). Sibyl goes to Dorian's house, ostensibly to see the wonderful portrait of Dorian painted by Basil Hallward. Dorian plans to test the extent of her love for him by inviting her to stay the night with him (a suggestion which has been made by the wicked Lord Henry). As the clock strikes two in the morning Sibyl begins to prepare to go home, putting on her hat and adjusting it by looking in a large mirror which stands in the library. Behind her, standing on a small table, is the Egyptian cat-sphinx, which Sibyl sees via the mirror. The shot is carefully framed, placing Sibyl in a middle position between the cat-sphinx and the mirror. Sibyl is startled by what she sees in the mirror and turns around and addresses Dorian who is seated at the piano:

Sibyl:	It's that cat! I thought I saw its eyes move.
Dorian:	*(Rising from the piano and coming to the table where the cat-sphinx is located.)* Perhaps you did. Lord Henry says it is one of the seventy-three great gods of Egypt.
Sibyl:	Doesn't it frighten you?

Dorian: It does a little. *(He picks up a book of poetry from the table
               and begins to read.)* Listen to this: 'Dawn follows dawn and
               nights grow old and all the while this curious cat/ Lies
               crouching on the Chinese mat with eyes of satin rimmed
               with gold./ Get hence, you loathsome mystery! Hideous
               animal, get you hence!/ You wake in me each bestial sense,
               you make me what I would not be./ You make my creed a
               barren sham, you wake foul dreams of sensual life.'

Sibyl: What a strange poem. Who wrote it?

Dorian: A brilliant, young Irishman out of Oxford. His name is
               Oscar Wilde.

The interjection of the person of Oscar Wilde into the film via the
lines from his poem *The Sphinx* is another clever means of underlining
the classical heritage of the enigmatic cat-sphinx and associating it with
the portrait. Sibyl unwisely succumbs to the temptation put to her by
Dorian, who is growing in wickedness day by day and seduces her. She
is then rejected by Dorian for spending the night with him (this is a
significant change from the novel, where it is her failure as an actress
that causes his rejection of her). Interestingly, this is one of the clearest
instances in the film where the sexual appetites of Dorian Gray are presented as decidedly heterosexual in nature.[44] Another example occurs
when Dorian's presence at some of London's clubs is depicted as a
cause of scandal among other club members and is deliberately interspersed with shots of blushing women, who drop their eyes when
Dorian enters. The narrator explains:

> Some of those who had been most intimate with him appeared, after a
> time, to shun him. Women who for his sake had set convention at
> defiance seemed to grow pale when Dorian Gray entered the room.

A similar reworking of the novel's homosexual sub-theme occurs in
connection with Dorian Gray's blackmailing of Alan Campbell in an
attempt to get the scientist to dispose of Basil Hallward's body. In the
novel the impression is that Dorian threatens to reveal a secret homosexual relationship in which Campbell was involved; in the film this is
altered to a heterosexual relationship which would shame his wife. In
fact, there is virtually *nothing* within the film that would suggest the
homosexual sub-theme of the novel which was made so much of within

---

44. Tyler (1947: 60) remarks: 'Implicitly Dorian becomes in the movie a typical
young man about town who consistently goes whoring and gains an evil reputation
as a seducer of wives'.

Wilde's public trials in 1895. All of the quasi-homosexual relationships within the novel are made into male–female relationships within the film. No doubt homosexuality would have been viewed as a taboo subject within Hollywood at the time the film was made, and this is reflected in the presentation of Dorian's relationships with others.

Following Dorian's rejection of Sibyl for her failure to meet his cruel test of her character, he returns to his house in Mayfair and notices the subtle change in his portrait. As he examines the portrait and then moves across the room to look at his own visage in the mirror, the Egyptian cat-sphinx is again centrally framed within the shot. A narrative voice-over repeats the Faustian prayer which Dorian uttered earlier as he moves to stand beside the cat on the table:

> If only the picture could change, and I could be always as I am now. For that I would give everything. Yes, there is nothing in the whole world I would not give. I would give my soul for that!

Dorian moves a screen to hide the portrait and leaves the room, attempting to convince himself that the changes in the portrait are only his imagination. He leaves the library with the camera closing in on the Egyptian cat-sphinx which sits on the table at the centre of the room. The cat-sphinx is also made a focal point in a subsequent scene when Basil Hallward comes to offer his condolences to Dorian following the suicide of Sibyl Vane. He moves to the library and attempts to remove the screen in front of the portrait before being halted by a panicking Dorian. The two men do a carefully choreographed dance around the watchful cat-sphinx on the table at the centre of the room. Similarly, when Basil Hallward comes to Dorian's house and confronts him about the decadence of his life, he is invited by Dorian to go up to the attic and see for himself the state of his 'soul'. As the two men leave the room and begin to climb the stairs the camera again lingers on the Egyptian cat-sphinx on the table at the centre of the library. The object also figures as the introductory shot when Alan Campbell comes to Dorian's house, at Dorian's request, and is asked to dispose of the body of the dead painter hidden in the attic.

At one point toward the end of the film Gladys' suitor David steals into the room in the attic, driven by jealousy over the impending marriage between Gladys and Dorian. He is attempting to gain some evidence to prevent the marriage. Lord Henry asks him to describe in more detail the portrait which he saw within it. David replies:

> There is a curious cat in it, like the one in Dorian's drawing room. Only
> in the portrait the eyes shine in an evil way that is indescribable.

A final shot of the cat-sphinx occurs in the very last scene of the film,
following Dorian's stabbing of the portrait and the discovery of his
hideous body by Lord Henry, Gladys and David. The cat-sphinx is
shown standing in its normal place on a table within Dorian's library,
with a copy of *The Rubaiyát of Omar Kháyyám* opened to display the
words with which the film began:

> I sent my soul through the invisible,
> Some letter of that after-life to spell:
> And by and by my soul returned to me,
> And answered, 'I myself am Heaven and Hell.'

One expression of this agony in his soul concerns Dorian's relationship
with Gladys. Towards the end of the film Dorian spares Gladys by
rejecting her and breaking off their engagement. Dorian goes to examine the portrait to see if the condition of his soul, as evidenced by the
portrait, has improved as a result of this sacrifice. The narrator's voice
explains:

> Was it true that one could never change? He longed for the unstained
> purity of his youth before he had prayed in a monstrous moment of pride
> and passion that the painting should bear the burden of the years of his
> corruption. Sibyl Vane was dead, and now her brother would be hidden
> in a nameless grave. Alan Campbell had shot himself, and Basil...
> nothing would alter that. It was of the future that he must think. He had
> spared Gladys. Would there be any sign of his one good deed in the
> portrait? *(Dorian removes the covering from the portrait and gazes
> expectantly at it.)* It was there. Almost imperceptible, but surely, it was
> there in the eyes. Struggling through the eyes' horror and the loathsome-
> ness. There was hope for him, then.
>   He would go away, leave England forever, live obscurely in a distant
> country, find peace in a life of humility and self-denial. He would expel
> every sign of evil from the painted face. He would watch the hideous-
> ness fade and change. But the painting would always be there to tempt
> his weakness. Better to destroy it! To grow old inevitably, as all men
> grow old. If he fell into evil ways, to be punished as all men are pun-
> ished. Better if each sin of his life were to bring sure, swift penalty. *(The
> camera closes in on a knife on the table.)* The knife that had killed Basil
> Hallward would kill his portrait also and free him at a stroke from the
> evil enchantment of the past.

Dorian picks up the knife and lunges towards the portrait, stabbing it in
the heart. He then staggers backward, mortally wounded, and leans

heavily on a table before collapsing on the floor. The camera shifts to the portrait of Dorian which is shocking in its hideousness. The portrait slowly begins to alter in its appearance, dissolving into the form that it had on the fateful day that Dorian uttered the prayer which determined the fate of his soul.[45] As the portrait is in mid-transformation, we hear a voice-over in which Dorian frantically offers up another prayer:

> Pray Father forgive me! Pray Father forgive me, for I have sinned! Pray Father forgive me, for I have sinned! Through my fault, through my most grievous fault!

The film thus ends with Dorian offering a prayer of contrition, as earnest and as heart-felt as the one at the beginning of the film in which he mortgaged his soul for the folly of eternal youthfulness.

b. *Glenn Jordan's* The Picture of Dorian Gray *(1973)*
Glenn Jordan's adaptation of Wilde's novel, first broadcast in the USA in 1973 as a made-for-TV film, introduced the actor Shane Briant in the title role. It also starred the accomplished British actors Nigel Davenport in the role of Sir Harry Wotton and Charles Aidman in the role of Basil Hallward. The role of Sibyl Vane was played by Vanessa Howard, with Beatrice Hallward being played by Linda Kelsey, and the role of Felicia by Fionnuala Flanagan. The screenplay for the film was written by John Tomerlin, and the various paintings of Dorian Gray were produced by Solie. An opening screen graphic tells us that the beginning of story is set in London in 1891.

Although the production levels are quite high throughout the film, there are several points at which the story-line departs radically from that of Wilde's novel. One of the most significant is that Dorian is here a double murderer. He not only kills Basil Hallward for making the portrait, but murders James Vane in an attempt to keep the man from revealing his part in the unfortunate death of Vane's sister Sibyl. In fact, the murder of James Vane functions in this film version in much the same way that the murder of Basil Hallward does in both the novel and in the 1944 film version (for example, Alan Campbell is called

---

45. Dickson (1983: 13) remarks: 'the restoration of the portrait to its original splendor—mimetic though it may be—seems to represent the only triumph of art over life in this novel'. Thus, Dickson argues, Wilde's intention in writing *The Picture of Dorian Gray* is to demonstrate the failure of the aesthetic ideal in which art was said to express nature, and not nature art.

upon to dispose of the body of Vane, not Hallward). The influence of Albert Lewin's film from 1944 is clearly in evidence, particularly with the interjection of the character of Basil Hallward's niece into the story—here she is named Beatrice (rather than Gladys as in Lewin's film). However, the hatred that Dorian feels against Basil Hallward over the influence that the painter has upon his niece is not taken up within this adaptation. Indeed, the love affair between Dorian and a woman (in this case, Beatrice) is carried further in this version than it was in the novel (in the person of Hetty Morgan) or in the earlier film (in the person of Gladys Hallward). In fact, Dorian even marries the niece of the man he murders and attempts to build a new life with her as an atonement for all his past acts of wickedness. In order to accommodate this dramatic change in the circumstances of Dorian's life, the time-scale of the novel is considerably altered. Within Jordan's film Basil is murdered two years after the suicide of Sibyl Vane (in the novel it is many years later, on the ninth of November, the eve of Dorian's thirty-eighth birthday). Beatrice, on the other hand, comes back on the scene and into Dorian's life some 18 years later in 1911 (having moved away from London following the death of her uncle).

The characterization that is given to Sibyl Vane is quite distinctive within this film. Here, she is not an actress, which means that the exploration of the relationship between art and reality in the life of an artist, so central to the novel, is left unexplored. In this film Sibyl Vane is a barmaid with whom Dorian becomes infatuated one night when he, Sir Henry and Basil go carousing. Soon Dorian is engaged to the beautiful Sibyl, much to the surprise of his friends. Moreover, the way in which the 'fall' of Sibyl is portrayed is similar to that which I noted in my discussion of the 1944 film. Here too it is Dorian's seduction of Sibyl (at the instigation of Sir Henry) that is stressed. Dorian places her in a moral dilemma and when she submits to his sexual advances he rejects her cruelly. Following this affair Dorian does not see Sibyl for weeks, although she attempts many times to visit him at his home, always wondering why he now spurns her. Eventually she suspects him to be involved with another woman, a dark-haired temptress named Felicia, and this betrayal of her love and commitment drives Sibyl to commit suicide by jumping off a bridge into the river (in contrast to suicide by the taking of poison as in the novel). Interestingly, it is the affair with Felicia which first causes a change in the portrait of Dorian Gray. A slight cruelty around the mouth becomes visible. This is very cleverly portrayed within the film, with three quick frames of the portrait being shown to the audience, like subliminal cuts. What we thought we detected is confirmed as Dorian goes to examine the portrait more closely and sees that a change has indeed taken place within his face. The progressive disfigurement of the portrait is well handled in the various portraits which are shown. In all we see eight different stages of corruption within the picture of Dorian Gray, most of which are tied to the way in which he treats, or mistreats, other people. As we noted in connection with Albert Lewin's film from 1944, there is here a decided portrayal of Dorian's sexuality as predominantly heterosexual in nature. Thus we are given several scenes in which Dorian pursues women prostitutes, and in one case even the underage daughter of a prostitute.[46]

The film does not dwell much on the mirror imagery so important within Wilde's novel. In fact there are only three or four scenes within the film where mirrors are used at all, notably one in which Dorian examines his face in a mirror following the suicide of Sibyl. There are no scenes in which Dorian is shown to be comparing his image in a mirror with that of the portrait, the 'mirror of his soul'. In this sense, the mirror imagery so important within Paul's letters to the church at Corinth is not developed within the film. However, the film does use another expression contained within those letters to good effect, namely the idea of seeing 'face to face'. The examination of the 'face' of a person is all-important here, for the face serves as an index into the character of a person; it is a means whereby the soul can be examined. As Basil says to Dorian just before he ascends to the attic nursery to examine the portrait of his friend which is now so disfigured, 'Sin is a thing that writes itself across a man's face; it cannot be concealed'. As he pulls back the sheet covering the portrait, Dorian replies: 'Here is the face of my soul!' The importance of the face as a place where reality can be viewed is stressed, particularly as a means by which the future can be grasped (at one point Dorian explains to Basil that the portrait even registers wicked deeds planned but not yet done!). We note, for instance, the opening scenes which help set the exploration of this theme.

The film opens with the camera panning around the upstairs nursery

46. This is to be contrasted with the way in which sexual appetites are handled in Massimo Dallamano's film entitled *The Secret of Dorian Gray* (1970). Within this film, which is given a contemporary setting in London, Dorian pursues *both* men and women in fulfilment of his sexual appetites.

of Dorian's house, and moving in turn to introduce us to the main characters in the drama. A narrator's voice (we discover later it is Dorian's) intones:

> A man's destiny, some say, is written in the stars. All he'll ever do, all he'll ever love, all he'll ever be. The whole of his life is inscribed in the heavens, some say. Others claim to see the truth in other places—in a deck of cards, the palm of a hand, a crystal ball, or the bottom of a cup. Perhaps it is in all of those. Perhaps in none of them. For my part, the only glimpses of the future Fate ever provided were in men's faces. There I've read passion, greed, hate, envy. And, knowing what had been, knew also what had to be.
>
> So many faces—too many—and most of them not very pleasant. The face of Sir Harry Wotton: rich idle, bored with life. A man who, to use his own words, 'Knew the price of everything, the value of nothing.' The face of Basil Hallward: a kind and generous man, a superb painter, as good a friend as I ever knew. So many faces to read the future in— their futures and my own.

The camera comes to focus on a large ruby ring which rests on a pedestal in Basil's studio (ultimately it will be the ring by which the withered body of Dorian Gray will be identified). The ring then fades into the representation of the ring on the hand of Dorian within the portrait of him which has been painted by Hallward. The voice of Dorian continues in narration, setting the stage for what follows:

> The stars, the cards, the human face. What good does it do to read the future in any of them if the words cannot be changed? And if they cannot, then only one question remains: Who does the writing? If I knew the answer to that, if I could be sure, then I would know whether to curse God for what my life has been, or praise the devil.

As this is said we see some words come on to the screen, words which help us to interpret the meaning of the film as a whole. The words are taken from the preface that Wilde wrote to *The Picture of Dorian Gray* and are attributed to him within the on-screen citation. They are a curtailment of one of Wilde's better known epigrams about the nature of art:

> Those who go beneath the surface do so at their peril...

A shortened form of these words of narration is used at the conclusion of the film, as is the citation from the preface to the novel. Together they form an inclusio for Jordan's effort as a whole. They conclude the final scenes in which Dorian has made plans to leave

England with Beatrice, and has arranged to have the attic sealed up so that no one can ever see the hideous portrait that is contained within the nursery. However, Dorian is curious to know if the picture reflects the change of character brought about by his new life with Beatrice and he cannot resist one final look at the work. Of course he finds it more hideous than ever, and he attacks it with a knife, driving the blade through the heart of the portrait.[47] This causes the exchange between picture and person which we have come to expect, and the film concludes as we watch Beatrice, having heard Dorian's cry of anguish through the self-inflicted stabbing of the painting, rise from her bed. She ascends the stairs to the nursery and finds a withered, ring-fingered corpse at the foot of the now beautiful portrait.

5. *Summary*

Oscar Wilde's *The Picture of Dorian Gray* is a haunting story; once read it is difficult to forget. At its heart is the image of an idealized portrait which reveals the inner corruption of its subject, the beautiful and tragic figure who is the novel's central character, Dorian Gray. The picture tracks each sin and underlines each evil act committed by Dorian through its slow but relentless transformation into an object of unspeakable hideousness. In this sense the portrait of Dorian is an enigmatic mirror reflecting his true spiritual condition.

We have noted some of the ways in which *The Picture of Dorian Gray* uses phrases and images which are found within Paul's letters to the church at Corinth. Two of these have been singled out as of special worth, namely the central image of a mirror (or looking-glass) as a means of reflecting the nature of human existence, and the mysterious, enigmatic character of that reflection.

In short, the mirror motif has provided an opportunity to compare and contrast how the present and the future are presented by Paul the apostle and Oscar Wilde. I have also examined some of the film interpretations of Wilde's novel and have noted how the mirror imagery has been portrayed within them. Perhaps the most intriguing of these

47. Interestingly, Massimo Dallamano's film *The Secret of Dorian Gray* has Dorian stab *himself* with the knife rather than attack the portrait. The age-old debate about whether or not Wilde intended Dorian to commit suicide is settled in this film version, although it is worth pointing out that the portrait of Dorian Gray undergoes metamorphosis nonetheless.

cinematic adaptations is Albert Lewin's film from 1944 which interjects a cat-like sphinx at key points so as to highlight the enigmatic dimension of the portrait of Dorian Gray. The classical allusion is something which no doubt would have delighted Wilde, especially as it also conveys something of the ultimate indeterminacy of artistic endeavour, let alone human existence. As Wilde stated in one of the epigrams contained within the preface to the 1891 version of *The Picture of Dorian Gray*.[48]

> All art is at once surface and symbol.
> Those who go beneath the surface do so at their peril.
> Those who read the symbol do so at their peril.

It is not difficult to apply this double-sided epigram anachronistically to the situation that Paul was facing in the church at Corinth. Insofar as human existence is lived out in the midst of the tension between the 'now' and the 'not yet', it is both surface and symbol. To Paul's mind Christians who never bother to go 'beneath the surface', those who see human existence as wholly absorbed with the present realities of earthly life and do not recognize that there is an eternal dimension beyond, are in danger. Those in Corinth who are caught up in the self-deceit of an 'over-realized eschatology' which denies a future consummation live their lives at their own peril. At the same time, Christians who 'read the symbol', those who see life as exclusively concerned with the future realities of heavenly existence and do not recognize that there is a sense in which eternity has *already* invaded time, also do so at their peril.

48. The connection between the preface and the story proper remains an important consideration of Wilde's overall purposes within *The Picture of Dorian Gray*. Stokes (1978: 30) suggests that 'the maxims that Wilde put forward in his Preface act as a kind of smokescreen to the honourable confusions within the novel'.

Chapter 3

DRACULA: 'THE BLOOD IS THE LIFE!'

'There Is a Fountain', one of the best known hymns of William Cowper (1731–1800), is based on a rather bizarre image contained in Zech. 13.1. The verse contains a reference to a fountain being opened for the house of David and the inhabitants of Jerusalem, a fountain to deal with the sin and impurity of the people of God. The precise religious significance of this fountain within the life of the nation Israel remains a matter of some dispute. However, the image is a provocative one, and it has yielded at least one bountiful harvest in the form of Cowper's hymn. The hymn was written in about 1772 and later published in the influential collection of *Olney Hymns* (1779). The first verse of the hymn emphasizes the centrality of a sacrificial imagery, concentrating on the shedding of divine blood, which lies close to the heart of one particular evangelical way of understanding the meaning of Christ's death:

> There is a fountain filled with blood
> Drawn from Immanuel's veins;
> And sinners, plunged beneath that flood,
> Lose all their guilty stains:
> *Lose all their guilty stains, Lose all their guilty stains;*
> *And sinners plunged beneath that flood, Lose all their guilty stains.* [1]

1.   It is perhaps worth noting that Cowper's hymn is used within Aldous Huxley's novel *Island* (1962). Huxley's novel explores the idea of a utopian existence, and has the central figure, a journalist named Will Farnaby who has recently come to the island community, cite the first stanza of Cowper's hymn. The barbarity of the sacrificial image is noted by Susila, one of Farnaby's listeners, who goes on to contrast the blood-thirsty image of Christianity with that of the less violent Buddhism. The essential point is that Christ's death on the cross at Golgotha is portrayed as a place where the sacrificial shedding of blood takes place, however 'obscene' such an idea may be.

Clearly within the thought-world of this hymn, sacrificial blood is invested with tremendous power. It cleanses and transforms, bringing life and a new order of existence. In this sense, there is little doubt that 'the blood is the life' (Deut. 12.23).

My task within this study is threefold. First, I shall note briefly how such blood–sacrifice imagery helps to frame Paul's theological understanding of the death of Christ. Next, I will consider how the importance of blood, or more precisely, *the drinking of blood*, is creatively employed within Bram Stoker's classic novel *Dracula* (1897). Third, I shall examine in detail some of the cinematic adaptations of Stoker's novel and the ways in which the sacrificial shedding of blood, and related communion imagery, are used within them. I shall begin by examining one of the places where the sacrificial imagery surrounding Christ's death is most clearly exhibited in Paul's thought, that is, in his understanding of the Lord's Supper.

1. *The Lord's Supper in Paul's Thought*

The controversy in the church of Corinth surrounding the celebration of the Lord's Supper has been the subject of special interest in recent years. Nowhere is this more true than among New Testament scholars seeking to explore the sociological implications of the controversy. Gerd Theissen's work in this area has been seminal,[2] with a number of others building upon his basic reconstruction of the Corinthian situation and making refinements to it.[3] It now seems clear that the theological debate over the celebration of the Lord's Supper in the church at Corinth was inextricably bound up with tensions between richer and poorer members of the congregation. In short, it appears that traditional social distinctions and classifications were spilling over into the corporate celebrations of the ritual meal. This resulted in unacceptable practices being adopted wherein one wealthier group (the 'strong') was taking advantage of another poorer one (the 'weak'), probably with regard to seating arrangements as well as the timing and quality of food distributed. Paul reacts strongly against such divisive practices and exhorts the congregation to live more in keeping with the unity that they have in Christ. However, I shall concentrate not on the

2.   Especially Theissen (1982: 121-74).
3.   Barton (1986) is an important advance along these lines. Also see Winter (1978) and Witherington (1995: 241-52).

sociological question of the Lord's Supper as it was celebrated in the church at Corinth, but rather on the theological idea of the 'body and *blood* of Christ' which was an integral part of how Paul conceived of those celebrations.

The precise relationship between the Jewish Passover celebration and the Christian celebration of the Lord's Supper (as it came to be known) has long been a matter of discussion. A variety of terms were used to describe these early Christian ritual meals, including 'the Lord's Supper' (1 Cor. 11.20), 'the breaking of bread' (Lk. 24.30; Acts 2.42, 46; 20.7, 11; cf. 27.35?), the 'agape feast' (Jude 12), and 'the eucharist' (*Didache* 9.1; Ignatius, *Letter to the Smyrnaeans* 8.1; Justin Martyr, *Apology to the Jews* 66.1).[4] Exactly how such overtly religious celebrations were integrated into Graeco-Roman banquets and guild meals is also a subject which has engendered considerable scholarly debate (Smith 1981). It is commonly, though not universally, agreed that the Lord's Supper was based upon the celebration of the Passover which Jesus shared with his disciples in the upper room (Mt. 26.26-29/Mk 14.22-25/Lk. 22.15-20).[5] Paul alludes to this Passover celebration when he writes in 1 Cor. 11.23-26:

> For I received from the Lord what I also delivered to you, that the Lord Jesus on the night when he was betrayed took bread, and when he had given thanks, he broke it, and said, 'This is my body which is for you. Do this in remembrance of me.' In the same way also the cup, after supper, saying, 'This cup is the new covenant in my blood. Do this, as often as you drink it, in remembrance of me.' For as often as you eat this bread and drink the cup, you proclaim the Lord's death until he comes.

Most scholars agree that in this passage Paul creatively adapts the traditions concerning the Lord's Supper which have been handed down to him. Both elements of the Lord's Supper—bread and wine—are spoken of in the passage, as are their spiritual equivalents, the body and blood of the Lord. From the way that the two eucharistic elements are described in this passage, it seems that the idea of the 'body of Christ' was a much more important theological concept for Paul than was the 'blood of Christ'. He certainly has much more to say about the 'body of

4. Klauck (1992); Stein (1992); and Marshall (1993) offer helpful surveys of the matter.

5. On this, see Higgins (1952); Hunter (1961); Schweizer (1967); Marxsen (1970); Martin (1974: 110-29); Jeremias (1977); Marshall (1980b); and Barrett (1985: 60-78).

Christ' than he does about the 'blood of Christ', although the latter expression does function elsewhere in Paul's letters as an expression for the death of the Lord Jesus (as we shall see in a moment). Paul does not explicitly say that the cup of wine *is* Jesus' blood, nor does he suggest that Jesus himself ever made such a declaration at the Last Supper. Indeed, it is difficult to imagine that Jesus would have made such a crass equation between the ritual cup of wine and his own blood (although Mk 14.24[6] does suggest it). An outright identification like this would presumably have made the Lord's injunction to his disciples extremely objectionable, given that they were religiously minded Jews for whom there was a prohibition in the Torah against the ingesting of blood (Lev. 17.10-12). Rather, here Paul reworks the sacrificial imagery contained within the eucharistic traditions of the synoptic gospels and stresses the shedding of Christ's blood as the basis of a 'new covenant', invoking the imagery of Jer. 31.31.[7] Such participation in the new covenant also seems to lie at the heart of another passage from 1 Corinthians wherein Paul alludes to the eucharistic imagery of the Lord's Supper. In 1 Cor. 10.16, within a passage given over to discussing Christian participation in pagan sacrificial meals, we read:

> The cup of blessing which we bless, is it not a participation in the blood of Christ? The bread which we break, is it not a participation in the body of Christ?[8]

The phrase 'in the blood of Jesus' (or 'through the blood of Jesus') occurs in several other places within the Pauline letters and is generally taken to be a reference to his death on the cross (Rom. 3.25; 5.9; Eph. 1.7; 2.13; Col. 1.20). The point is that Christ's crucifixion is invested with sacrificial significance and the shedding of his blood is interpreted

---

6. For more on this controversial verse, see Bultmann (1952: 146); Higgins (1952: 29-34); Emerton (1955); and Jeremias (1977: 193-95).

7. Käsemann (1964: 131-32). Maccoby (1991) argues that the idea of the Lord's Supper came to Paul in a vision in which the risen Lord laid out for him the significance of the bread and wine. The suggestion distances Paul from the Last Supper/Passover traditions recorded in the Gospels and effectively makes Paul the creator of the Lord's Supper, as it came to be known and celebrated in the church. The thesis is not without its difficulties.

8. Too much can be read into the reversal of the normal order of the elements here ('cup' usually follows 'bread' in eucharistic passages). Paul probably makes the alteration in order to set up his statement in 10.17 that the church is the united body of Christ.

against the backdrop of the cultic sacrificial system of Judaism (Dunn 1974: 133). In the words of Herman N. Ridderbos (1974: 80): [9]

> When therefore the blood of Christ is regularly referred to, it is not so much because of the manner of his death but because of its significance as a sacrifice, especially as an atoning sacrifice, in which the blood was shed to cover and eradicate sin.

Thus, in 1 Cor. 5.7 Paul can go so far as to describe Christ as 'our Passover lamb who has been sacrificed' (τὸ πάσχα ἡμῶν ἐτύθη Χριστός).[10] The unspoken implication of this unusual statement, which helps to give the metaphor its force, is that the Christian life is likened to a spiritual Passover festival and that the Corinthian Christians should live their lives accordingly. This is quite an astonishing declaration and demonstrates one way in which eucharistic imagery served to communicate the reality of new life brought about 'by the blood of Christ'. Little wonder that Christians down through the ages have seen the eucharist as a ritual celebration of the salvation which is made possible by Christ's death.

I move now from the New Testament materials to begin my consideration of Bram Stoker's *Dracula*, one of the most influential and enduring of modern vampire myths.[11]

2. *Communion Imagery in Bram Stoker's* Dracula *(1897)*

Before I turn to examine the place that communion imagery has within *Dracula* itself, it is worth reviewing how it was that Stoker came to write the novel and what sorts of critical discussion it has engendered, not least in the realm of theological matters. A brief consideration of some of these issues will also serve to set the proper context for the religious imagery I am concentrating on in this study.

---

9. For more recent discussions, consult Travis (1994); Carroll and Green (1995: 113-32).

10. The immediate context of this passage (5.1-13) is that of the disciplining of an errant member of the congregation. The description of Christ as the sacrificial Passover lamb is made as a passing remark by the apostle, possibly in preparation for the church's celebration of Easter. See Howard (1969) on this.

11. Hollinger (1997: 201) describes the vampire as 'a metaphor for certain aspects of postmodernism', which perhaps helps to account for its abiding popularity.

a. *Bram Stoker and the Writing of* Dracula

The year 1997 marked the centenary of the publication of *Dracula*. The novel has been phenomenally successful; it has been translated into approximately 20 languages worldwide and it has never been out of print in English since it first appeared in June 1897, sporting a mustard-yellow cover with blood-red lettering.[12] Paradoxically, the author of the celebrated novel, which is often described as the quintessential Gothic horror story, remains something of an obscure figure. Many people today know of his creation largely because of the numerous film adaptations of the novel, but remain totally unaware of the author's identity. Indeed, the recent biography of Bram Stoker by Barbara Belford (1996: x) goes so far as to describe him as 'the soulless invisible man' and suggests that the paper trail left by him is very faint indeed, so much so that it was difficult to write a detailed biography about him.[13] Stoker wrote a total of 18 novels, but it is only *Dracula* that has stood the test of time and it is generally only by this single work that he is known to the public.[14]

What influenced Stoker to write the story, and under what circumstances he produced the work, are matters of considerable dispute.[15] Much scholarly attention has been directed to establishing the historical basis for the story of Count Dracula. It is now generally agreed that the figure of Vlad the Impaler, a fifteenth-century prince of Wallachia in what is now southern Romania, is the figure most likely to be behind it all.[16] It will come as no surprise to know that the association of Prince Vlad with the Dracula legend is something which post-communist Romania has been eager to exploit; sites associated with the Prince

12. Originally published by Archibald Constable and Company, Westminster.

13. This is now the standard biography of Stoker and replaces the other two inferior biographies by Ludlam (1962) and Farson (1975).

14. Although an increasing number of people are aware of his last novel *The Lair of the White Worm* (1911), largely through British director Ken Russell's film from 1989 which is based on the story.

15. The discovery in 1970 in the Rosenbach Library and Museum, Philadelphia, of Stoker's working notes for *Dracula* puts paid to the suggestion that the novel was a rush-job. It now seems clear that *Dracula* was meticulously planned and researched as a novel, in contrast to what was commonly assumed among earlier critics. Stoker spent at least six years researching and preparing the book. For further discussion along these lines, see Bierman (1977).

16. McNally and Florescu (1975); Leatherdale (1993: 13-44); Nandris (1966); and Porter (1992) all discuss this matter.

have now become tourist attractions and there are many travel companies which offer a Dracula tour to the relevant areas.[17] Yet whatever the historical anchors for them might be, vampire legends and myths have been around since the Middle Ages and stories of them became a standard feature of Gothic horror.[18] There is good evidence that Stoker was familiar with many of these stories, notably Joseph Sheridan Le Fanu's *Carmilla* (1872).[19]

The relationship between Bram Stoker and the celebrated actor Sir Henry Irving, with whom Stoker had a long and intimate association both as business manager of the Lyceum Theatre in London and as a personal friend, is sometimes said to be the inspiration behind *Dracula*.[20] In this sense, the relationship between Irving and Stoker is reflected in that of Count Dracula and his hapless business agent Jonathan Harker, and it is Irving/Dracula who sucks the life out of the devoted Stoker/Harker. In such a scenario Stoker's own wife Florence is reflected in the character Lucy Westenra, who is socially frivolous and seemingly unable to keep herself from seeking after and accepting the attentions of a myriad suitors. Nowhere is the power of Irving over Stoker more evident than in the fact that Stoker hurriedly wedded Florence and postponed his honeymoon with her in order to comply with Irving's demands that Stoker join him in Birmingham and begin the theatre season; in *Dracula* we find an echo of this in the fact that Jonathan Harker's wedding to Mina is postponed when Count Dracula demands that Harker come to Transylvania in order to finalize the arrangements for his move to England.

17. Elizabeth Miller, a Professor in the Department of English at the Memorial University in Newfoundland, Canada, manages an Internet site on the subject which is entitled 'Dracula's Home Page' (www.ucs.mun.ca/~emiller/). She includes colour photographs of most of the tourist spots in Romania.

18. One of the best treatments of the subject is Twitchell (1981). Also worth considering is Punter (1980). Several good anthologies of vampire stories are available which show the range and diversity of the subject. For example, consult Ryder (1987) and Haining (1995).

19. See Wilson (1983: ix-xii) on this point. Le Fanu was, like Stoker, an Irishman from Dublin. He was joint owner of the Dublin *Evening Mail* and thus was at one time Stoker's employer (when Stoker was writing theatre reviews for the paper).

20. A suggestion which is no doubt responsible for the decision to have a cover photograph of Henry Irving (as Mephistopheles) for the Penguin Classics edition of Stoker's *Dracula* (1993).

Both the narrative style and the structural design of *Dracula* have been focal points of investigation within recent years.[21] The novel is divided into 27 chapters but they are not as straightforward as one might expect.[22] The fact that the narrative throughout is conducted by means of a series of journals and letters, of diary entries and newspaper clippings, means that the way in which the story is communicated to the reader is somewhat unusual; there is always a sense of distancing involved, and there is no omniscient narrator to be found. The reader is never quite able to identify with the narrator of the story directly but is forced to engage with the narrative through a multiplicity of characters. The result is somewhat unexpected, yet spectacular: the reader encounters Dracula in a secondary sense. Count Dracula himself never assumes the role of the narrator in the novel; he is met only through the eyes and ears of the other characters in the story. Yet paradoxically this mediated encounter with the central figure of evil is all the more suspenseful as a result and the dramatic effect of the novel is enhanced by it.

The sexual imagery underlying the vampire story is generally recognized, and there have been many studies specifically given over to exploring this theme, perhaps the most discussed aspect of *Dracula* within the critical literature.[23] The illicit pursuit and capture of an unsuspecting victim, culminating in an intimate embrace and a bite to the throat, lies at the heart of the horror of the vampire story. Little wonder then that the marks left on the necks and throats of passionate lovers in Great Britain are commonly described as 'love bites' (the American equivalent of 'hickey' is rather lame in comparison). Given the thinly disguised sexual nature of the novel, it comes as no surprise that *Dracula* has been the happy hunting-ground for those pursuing a Freudian reading of the story. Many argue, for example, that it is the incest taboo that is foundational to the story and that the novel is best

21. See Senf (1979); Seed (1985); Johnson (1984b); and Miller (1994).

22. I shall cite passages from the novel by noting their chapter and page number (thus 1.5 denotes p. five of chapter 1). The edition used here is that within the Penguin Classics series (London: Penguin Books, 1993) and contains an introduction by Maurice Hindle.

23. See, e.g., Fry (1972); Weissman (1977); Griffin (1980); Wood (1983); Craft (1984); Stevenson (1988); Howes (1988); Hogan (1988: 138-63); Case (1991); Leatherdale (1993: 155-71); Krumm (1995); and Belford (1996: 5-9).

interpreted as a Victorian version of the Oedipus myth.[24]

The novel has been the focus of a number of other interpretative readings.[25] For example, it has been analysed by some feminist critics for what it contributes to the late Victorian view of the sexual roles of men and women, with Stoker being both hailed by some as an early feminist and condemned by others as a chauvinistic traditionalist.[26] The novel has also been subjected to various political interpretations, with the rich blend of metaphor and symbol inherent in the story readily lending itself to application. Thus it has been read as a text primarily concerned with political and economic matters arising out of the English imperial system and the role of England as an enlightened Western democracy in the face of the political chaos which threatened from the East.[27] The clash between gothic supernaturalism and Victorian science is also a key feature of the novel, particularly as it is non-scientific instruments (crucifixes, communion wafers, wooden stakes, garlic bulbs, etc.) which serve as weapons against the evil Count (Jann 1989). Some have detected in the novel echoes of the debate over Irish Home Rule which so dominated the domestic political agenda in Stoker's day. There has also been a school of thought which views *Dracula* as an illustration of the Marxist class struggle in which Count Dracula, as the personification of bourgeois capitalism constantly in search of new victims (or 'markets'?), preys upon the working-class and sucks them dry.[28] The interpretation of *Dracula* as an anti-Semitic work, in which Stoker employs the stereotypical nineteenth-century images of the Jew and sets these over against the virtues of Christianity, has also been put forward.[29] However, the theological dimensions of the novel have not received the attention that they are due, and these

24. Bentley (1972) is a case in point.

25. See Morrison (1994) for a helpful introduction to the ways in which Stoker's *Dracula* continues to challenge readers.

26. Demetrakopoulos (1977); Roth (1977); Senf (1982); Johnson (1984a); Williams (1991); and McDonald (1993) offer varying interpretations.

27. For discussion of the social and geo-political dimensions of the novel, see Wasson (1966); Hennelly (1977); Arata (1990); and Wicke (1992).

28. See Moretti (1983: 83-108); Hatlen (1980); and Jancovich (1992: 48-52) on this line of interpretation.

29. Halberstam (1993) offers some interesting ideas along these lines, calling attention to the possible influence of Henry Irving's portrayal of the Jew Shylock in Shakespeare's *The Merchant of Venice* upon Stoker's imagination.

promise much in terms of understanding the evolving nature of the religious mythology surrounding *Dracula*.

b. *Theological Imagery and Biblical Allusions in the Novel*
Dracula is a profoundly theological novel which contains a host of interlocking ideas commonly associated with historic Christianity. The novel contains a dozen or so clear allusions to biblical stories or texts that help to set the tone for the theological exploration that lies at its core. These come from a wide range of biblical strata, embracing both Old Testament and New Testament writings. For example, in 5.80, in one of Lucy Westenra's letters to Mina Murray, there is an allusion to the parable of the ten virgins (Mt. 25.1-10). This comes in the form of Lucy's recounting to her friend the proposal made to her by the Bowie-brandishing Texan Quincey P. Morris. Technically speaking, Morris is made to misquote the central image of the parable (he mentions the '*seven* young women with the lamps'), perhaps under the weight of seven as an image of perfection and the fact that in his eyes Lucy is the perfect woman. Similarly, in 10.156-57 there is an allusion to the parable of the sower (Mt. 13.1-9/Mk 4.1-9/Lk. 8.4-8), as Van Helsing explains to Dr Seward that they need to be patient in order to let the true nature of Lucy Westenra's vampiric condition be revealed in due course, like the slowly developing crop sown by the sower. Meanwhile, in 6.99 Mina Murray's journal contains an allusion to the story of the healing of the blind man of Bethsaida (Mk 8.24) when she offers a description of seeing people half-shrouded in the seaside mists of Whitby, and notes that they 'seem "like trees walking"'. In 8.133, within Dr Seward's diary, there is an allusion to the saying of Jesus recorded in Mt. 10.29-31/Lk 12.6-7 in which God's concern for the life of a sparrow (as compared to that for the life of an eagle) is asserted. The section of Dr Seward's diary also describes the religious mania of the lunatic patient Renfield in language which is reminiscent of Jn 3.29 where John the Baptist declares the imminent arrival of 'the Master' (the passage from John makes use of bridegroom imagery, perhaps building upon Isa. 62.5). In effect, this is to make Renfield something of an anti-type to John the Baptist and it carries the implication that Count Dracula is the anti-type to Jesus Christ himself. In 20.346 Dr Seward reports on a further conversation that he has had with his patient in which Renfield cites Gen. 5.24 ('Enoch walked with God') as part of how the lunatic perceives his relationship with Count Dracula.

He is to be rewarded with unending terrestrial life (as opposed to Enoch's unending spiritual life) from his Master and Lord—Count Dracula. In the next chapter this allegiance is tested in a passage which is a parody of the temptation of Christ in the wilderness. Here, in 21.360, the zoophagous Renfield, mortally wounded by Dracula for having attempted to protect Mina from him, relates to Dr Seward how Dracula had offered him thousands of rats to eat, as well as dogs and cats. Dracula promised him, 'All these lives I will give you, ay, and many more and greater, through countless ages, if you will fall down and worship me!' The parallel with Mt. 4.9/Lk. 4.7 is obvious. In 25.441 Van Helsing explains that Dracula's hypnotic power over Mina will be his undoing, alluding to Ps. 69.22 when he says 'The hunter is taken in his own snare'. The agelessness of Dracula is alluded to in 14.247 by comparing him with the biblical patriarch Methuselah who, according to Gen. 5.27, lived to be 969 years old. Meanwhile, the story of Noah's ark in Gen. 8.8-12 is alluded to in 4.64 where Jonathan Harker describes Dracula's castle in Transylvania as perched on a spot so high that it 'seemed to me as if the dove from the ark had lighted there'. In 19.333 there is an allusion to Exod. 40.34-38 with its mention of 'a pillar of cloud by day and fire by night' as part of 'Mina Harker's Journal'. Mina uses the image to describe her dream-like pseudo-sexual encounter with the Count in which he enters her bedroom as a thick and mysterious mist.

Even Dracula himself occasionally alludes to Scripture, as in 2.31 where he uses a phrase from Exod. 2.22, 'a stranger in a strange land', to describe how he fears he may feel when he makes the anticipated move to London. In the Old Testament story these are words on the lips of Moses and are used to denote his period of life in Egypt as an exile. There are several allusions to the passion and crucifixion of Christ which help to establish this as *the* key theological idea for the sub-text of the *Dracula* story-line. In 21.367 Mina declares 'God's will be done!' when she is informed of Renfield's death; arguably this is an allusion of Jesus' words in the garden of Gethsemane recorded in Mt. 26.39/Mk 14.36/Lk. 22.42. In all three Gospel accounts this prayer of Jesus that the Father's will might be done is linked to mention of the 'cup' of suffering which he must endure. In 18.305 there is an allusion to Christ's being pierced by the soldier's spear while hanging on the cross at Golgotha. This occurs in 'Mina Harker's Journal' when she mentions 'an arrow in the side of Him who died for man'. What is significant about this allusion is that it is recorded *only* in John's Gospel (Jn 19.34) and it is immediately followed by a mention of the '*blood* and water' which flowed from Christ's side—a fitting allusion considering the emphasis that blood has within the story-line of *Dracula* itself (the words 'blood' or 'bloody' occur a total of 117 times in the novel; only 5 out of 27 chapters omit reference to 'blood'). Meanwhile, in 19.321, as part of Jonathan Harker's journal, there is a recollection of how Professor Van Helsing bravely enters the lair of Count Dracula in London. As he crosses over the threshold of the home in which Dracula has hidden his earth-filled coffins, Van Helsing crosses himself and utters the Latin words '*In manus tuas, Domine!*', an adaptation of the final words of Jesus on the cross according to Lk. 23.46 ('Father, into your hands I commit my spirit').

Perhaps the most significant and best-known quotation of a biblical text within the novel appears in 11.184 where again in 'Dr Seward's Diary' the words of the maniac Renfield are cited. Following the knife attack by Renfield upon Seward, the attendants come to restrain Renfield and return him to his cell. As they do so Renfield repeats over and over again, 'The blood is the life! The blood is the life!', a line from Deut. 12.23 which could be described as one of the interpretative keys to the novel as a whole. The same line is repeated on other occasion by Renfield in 18.301.

What are we to make of all of this? Is there something significant about the frequent allusion to imagery drawn from the Bible? Many critics of *Dracula* think so. Leonard Wolf (1993: vii) describes *Dracula* as displaying 'the perpetual tension between the dark and the light; the wrestling match between Christ and Satan', a point which helps to account for the prevalence of crucifixion imagery within the novel. After all, in theological terms it is on the cross that the clash between good and evil might be said to reach a climax. The use of a crucifix as a means of fending off the vampire occurs frequently in the course of the story, a point that has been especially frequently used within the cinematic adaptations of Stoker's *Dracula* over the years.[30]

Other Christian rituals such as baptism and holy communion also appear at key points within the novel. These should not be overlooked, since they also contribute to the overall impression of the story as one which engages with the sacramental foundations of the Christian faith. For example, in 8.135 we find Seward remarking that Renfield 'thinks

30. This is explored more fully in Kreitzer (1997).

of the loaves and fishes even when he believes he is in a Real Presence'. The feeding of the five thousand is clearly alluded to in this comment, as is the eucharistic sub-text of the Gospel story (Mt. 14.13-21/Mk 6.32-44/Lk. 9.10-17/Jn 6.1-15). Similarly, the sacrament of baptism is alluded to at several points within the narrative: in 27.469 Van Helsing describes Mina Harker as having been tainted with the 'Vampire baptism', and in 24.414 this is expanded to 'the Vampire's baptism of blood'. Insofar as Mina has been joined to Dracula she sacramentally shares his existence, partaking of his very life-blood.

Charles S. Blinderman (1980: 427) associates this sharing of blood with eucharistic imagery, calling attention to the ominous reference in 21.370 to Mina as a 'wine-press'. He remarks:

> Dracula effects communion with his congregation through the sharing of blood, for instead of wine being blood, blood is substantiated into wine, Mina emerging from this ritual as Dracula's 'bountiful wine-press'.

One should perhaps also point out that the full declaration made to Van Helsing and his band of vampire hunters by Dracula about his 'wine-press' Mina is filled with phrases drawn from both Scripture (Gen. 2.23-24; Eph. 5.31) and from the *Book of Common Prayer*, which are traditionally associated with a Christian marriage ceremony. All of this supports the idea that the blood-sharing between Dracula and Mina is seen as an evil inversion of the relationship between Christ and the church which in itself is the theological underpinning of a marriage between a man and a woman. The fact that Mina has been contaminated via her blood-rites with Dracula means that she describes herself as 'Unclean! Unclean!' as if she were a leper (see Lev. 13.45-46). This sense of contamination is also mentioned in 21.366 and 22.381. However, perhaps the most celebrated instance in which the blood-based union between Mina and Dracula is detailed occurs in 21.363 within 'Dr Seward's Diary'. The evil Count has managed to overpower Jonathan Harker and isolate Mina from her other vampire-seeking protectors. He exerts his influence over her and, in a scene which is extremely suggestive of fellatio, forces her to drink blood from his breast. Van Helsing and his courageous band break down the door of Mina's room and find a hideous scene of seduction and blood-drinking intimacy before them. Dr Seward records Mina's plight, which is only brought to an end by the power of a communion host:

His [Dracula's] right hand gripped her by the back of the neck, forcing
her face down on his bosom. Her white night-dress was smeared with
blood, and a thin stream trickled down the man's bare chest which was
shown by his torn-open dress. The attitude of the two had a terrible
resemblance to a child forcing a kitten's nose into a saucer of milk to
compel it to drink. As we burst into the room, the Count turned his face,
and the hellish look that I had heard described seemed to leap into it. His
eyes flamed red with devilish passion. The great nostrils of the white
aquiline nose opened wide and quivered at the edge, and the white sharp
teeth, behind the full lips of the blood dripping mouth, clamped together
like those of a wild beast. With a wrench, which threw his victim back
upon the bed as though hurled from a height, he turned and sprang at us.
But by this time the Professor had gained his feet, and was holding
towards him the envelope which contained the Sacred Wafer.

At several other points the novel prominently displays the significance of holy communion as a weapon against Count Dracula and his
demonic powers. Theologically speaking, it is at Calvary that the
sacrifice of Christ, the shedding of *blood*, is most manifestly evident; it
is here on the cross of Christ that the sacredness of the eucharist host is
established. There is a deliberate and highly charged antithesis which is
being exacted here, one which Stoker builds creatively into his novel.
Indeed, James B. Twitchell (1985: 108)[31] has described this as 'an
elaborate allegory for the doctrine of transubstantiation in reverse'. He
states:

[T]he vampire myth explained the most difficult concept in the last of
the sacraments to be introduced—the Eucharist. It explained the doctrine
of transubstantiation in reverse. In the Middle Ages the Church fathers
found their congregation understandably hesitant about accepting that
the wafer and the wine were the actual, let alone the metaphoric, body
and blood of Christ. How better could the transubstantiation be
explained than on the more primitive level, the level the folk already
knew and believed in—namely, the vampire transformation. For just as
the devil-vampire drank the blood and then captured the spirit of a
sinner, so too could the penitent drink the blood, eat the body, and
possess the divinity of Christ.

More significantly, the use of the communion host as an effective
way to fend off Dracula frequently appears in the story. The conse-
crated communion host is also used as a means to seal doors and
windows, so as to protect against Dracula's entry. It is also employed

31. Also see Twitchell (1981: 13-16).

as the method of despoiling Dracula's earth-laden coffins. For example, the protective power of a communion wafer is mentioned in 19.321, and Van Helsing arms each of his intrepid band with a portion of the sacred wafer as they prepare to invade Dracula's Carfax property. Similarly, in 22.383 Van Helsing uses a communion host to 'desecrate' one of Dracula's coffins within the property. Jonathan Harker's journal records the words and actions of Van Helsing along these lines:

> Dr Van Helsing said to us solemnly as we stood before him, 'And now, my friends, we have a duty here to do. We must sterilize this earth, so sacred of holy memories, that he has brought from a far distant land for such fell use. He has chosen this earth because it has been holy. Thus we defeat him with his own weapon, for we make it more holy still. It was sanctified to such use of man, now we sanctify it to God.'
>
> As he spoke he took from his bag a screwdriver and a wrench, and very soon the top of one of the cases was thrown open. The earth smelled musty and close, but we did not somehow seem to mind, for our attention was concentrated on the Professor. Taking from his box a piece of the Sacred Wafer he laid it reverently on the earth, and then shutting down the lid began to screw it home, we aiding him as he worked.

In the same manner, a crumbled communion wafer is used by Van Helsing to seal the tomb of the vampiress Lucy Westerna in 16.269-70. It is also worth noting that Stoker's novel describes Professor Van Helsing's 'branding' of Mina's forehead by means of a communion wafer in 22.381. The 'mark' of this branding is strongly reminiscent of the 'mark of Cain' of Genesis 4, and suggestively invites a comparison along these lines.[32] The branding of Mina's forehead with the communion wafer is intimately connected with the ultimate destruction of Dracula himself, and Stoker cleverly alludes to biblical imagery of sacrificial purity to convey this. As Elisabeth Bronfen (1992: 319) puts it:

> The touch of the paternal sign—the holy wafer—leaves a 'red scar' on Mina's forehead to indicate that her body is tainted though her soul is pure. Killing the vampire will be coterminous with purifying her forehead, 'all white as ivory and with no stain.'

I turn now to consider some of the ways in which such communion imagery becomes transferred to cinematic adaptations of the Dracula myth.

---

32. Griffin (1980: 463) relates the image to Nathiel Hawthorne's *The Scarlet Letter* (1850): 'The scar, often referred to as a stain, of course duplicates Dracula's, but it is actually closer to Hester Prynne's red "A".'

3. *Communion Imagery in Some Film Adaptations of* Dracula

Representations of the Last Supper are staple items in most films depicting the life of Jesus of Nazareth, and many of them are quite good in portraying the sense of sacramental exchange which takes place between Jesus and his disciples in the course of the meal. Franco Zeffirelli's *Jesus of Nazareth* (1977) is a case in point, with a moving scene in which the Lord celebrates the Jewish feast with his 12 disciples. Jesus explains to Peter as they share together a cup of out-poured wine that 'It is for this Passover that I came into the world'. He then invites them all to drink from their cups of wine with the words: 'From now on this cup will not only be a memorial and sacrament of the covenant that God made with our fathers on Mount Sinai. This is my blood. The blood of the new covenant which is to be poured out for many.'

However, it is not only within 'lives of Jesus' films that we can find the importance of communion imagery. Any number of other films could be called upon to demonstrate the power that the idea of a communal meal has, particularly when it is shared by a group of followers as they are gathered around their leader and facing an uncertain future. The sequence contained in Kevin Reynolds's *Robin Hood: Prince of Thieves* (1991) where Robin and his band of merry men share a celebration meal in Sherwood Forest is an obvious case in point. The transformation that can be wrought within a community by sharing a meal together is one of the things that makes Gabriel Axel's Oscar-winning *Babette's Feast* (1987), based on a short story by Karen Blixen (Isak Dinesen), such a joy to watch.[33] However, not all such cinematic explorations of a community meal are as wholesome and uplifting as this, as the parodies of the Last Supper contained in Robert Altman's *M*A*S*H* (1970) and Mel Brooks's *History of the World Part One* (1981) serve only too well to illustrate. In any event, my task here is to explore some of the ways in which the idea of Christ's shedding of his blood for the sake of others, a central feature of the celebration of the eucharist in the Christian faith, has been portrayed within Dracula films.

Without doubt, the popularity of the figure of Dracula is due in no small measure to the various cinematic portrayals of him—a character

33. For more on the theological implications of this film see, Marsh (1997).

as mythologically rich and vibrant as this readily lends itself to such artistic expression. This was recognized very early on; even during Stoker's lifetime the novel *Dracula* was adapted for the London stage (Skal 1990). However, it was not until F.W. Murnau's film classic *Nosferatu: Eine Symphonie des Grauens* (1921) that the rich potential of Stoker's creation began to be explored cinematically, and even here it was not without controversy. The film, now regarded as a seminal work of German expressionism,[34] was an unauthorized adaptation of Bram Stoker's novel and Stoker's widow Florence vigorously pursued her legal rights through the courts. She eventually won her case in 1925 and all copies of the film were ordered to be destroyed, a legal injunction which fortunately, from the standpoint of cinematic history, was not successfully carried out since a few copies survived.[35] Given this inauspicious beginning, it is indeed remarkable that over 200 Dracula and vampire movies have now been made by film-directors from all around the world.[36] Perhaps most prominent among these, at least as far as shaping the popular understanding of the Dracula myth is concerned, are the various films produced by the British Hammer House of Horror films in the 1950s, 1960s and 1970s, films which made the actors Christopher Lee and Peter Cushing household names.[37] However, the vampire film remains a perennial favourite and it has experienced something of a revival in the past 15 years or so (particularly for the teenage audience). I shall concentrate my attention on three films, one from each of the past three decades. The films are quite diverse in their subject matter, each exploring the Dracula myth in its own unique way. Yet there is a common theme which unites them, for each film uses communion imagery—namely the 'drinking' of life-sustaining blood— to some extent within the story-line. I begin with the most recent of the three, one of the most ambitious efforts by the Oscar-winning director Francis Ford Coppola, perhaps best known for his *The Godfather* trilogy (1972, 1974 and 1990) and *Apocalypse Now* (1979).

34. This silent classic has been restored and is available through Redemption Films Ltd, London. The restoration contains English-text announcement panels and remains a must for anyone interested in the popular development of Dracula mythology. For more on this, see Wood (1979 and 1983).

35. Skal (1990: 40-63) discusses this.

36. A number of books catalogue this rich explosion of films. See Jones (1993); Silver and Ursini (1993).

37. See Eyles, Adkinson and Fry (1973); Hutchings (1993: 115-27).

a. *Bram Stoker's Dracula (1992)*

Francis Ford Coppola's *Bram Stoker's Dracula* (1992) has been the focus of considerable debate, not least because of the vision that it presents of Victorian England and the way in which it handles, or mishandles, the Gothic themes so central to the original novel.[38] Thus despite the brash claim of the film's title, in many ways this is barely recognizable as *Bram Stoker's* story of Count Dracula. To be fair, the major characters are all in place and the costuming is certainly reflective of the late-Victorian age in which Stoker lived, but the guts of the story—its pulse, as it were—is missing. The film boasts an all-star cast, including Gary Oldman as Count Dracula, Anthony Hopkins as Abraham Van Helsing, Winona Ryder as Mina Murray/Elizabeta, Keanu Reaves as Jonathan Harker, Richard E. Grant as Arthur Holmwood, and newcomer Sadie Frost as Lucy Westenra.[39]

Most damaging to the original plot of the novel is the way in which the relationship between Dracula and Mina Harker is transformed into a tale of lost love, as she becomes the reincarnation of Dracula's wife Elizabeta who committed suicide over four centuries before. Thus, promotional posters for the film proclaim it as a story whose major message is 'Love Never Dies'. In effect this makes the film into an overly sentimental love-story with *Aliens*-like special effects and bodily transformations galore gratuitously thrown in along the way. This substitution of romantic sentimentality for Gothic horror is all rather unfortunate. Nowhere in Stoker's novel is Count Dracula said to *love* Mina in this way; on the contrary, he is animalistic and predatory in his approach to the women he pursues. Coppola's film paints him as rather a noble figure, whose love for Mina eventually culminates in his own destruction as he sacrifices himself rather than contaminate the woman he loves with his vampirism. Indeed, even the erotic power of Stoker's work, his indirect association of vampiric activity with sexuality, is

38. The screenplay for the film was written by James V. Hart, who together with Coppola has produced *Bram Stoker's Dracula: The Film and the Legend* (1993), which contains a number of stills from the film together with the shooting script and some interesting interviews with people connected with the film. Fred Saberhagen's *Bram Stoker's Dracula* (1992) is a popular novel based on the screenplay as a movie tie-in. The book contains an afterword by Francis Ford Coppola and eight pages of colour photos from the movie.

39. A 30-minute supplemental video entitled *The Making of Bram Stoker's Dracula* is also available from Columbia Tristan Home Video (1993).

seriously undermined, for the film leaves nothing to the imagination and makes Mina and Dracula lovers. One wonders how much of the motivation behind this (mis)interpretation of Stoker's vision is due to the sexual climate of the 1990s and the ever-real threat of AIDS as a sexually transmitted disease; in effect vampirism becomes a thinly disguised cipher for HIV infection.[40] Unfortunately, the attempt to update the message of the film and make it relevant for the contemporary viewing audience has lost something essential, something mysterious, in the process.

Nowhere is the film more open to criticism than in the way in which it alters Stoker's conclusion to the novel. At the end of the story Mina gives birth to a son, symbolically named after the men who risked their lives to save her from Dracula's curse (see 27.485). Never in the film is there any mention of this. Instead, within the film we have the love between Dracula and Mina serving as the focus in the final confrontation at Dracula's castle in Transylvania. Indeed, it is Mina herself who rises to the awful demands of her love for Dracula as she challenges Van Helsing and the band of vampire hunters, and withdraws to the chapel with the wounded Dracula. There she dispatches him by driving Quincey Morris's Bowie knife through the Count's heart before retrieving the blade and decapitating him. All of this is said to be an expression of her love for him (more about this in a moment). This may be highly romantic, tear-jerking stuff, but it is certainly *not* Bram Stoker's *Dracula*.

Nevertheless, there are one or two interesting features of the film adaptation that contribute to the examination of the place that communion imagery has in the retelling of *Dracula*. The first of these occurs early in the film while Prince Vlad is away defending his homeland against the invading Turks. He has left his beloved wife Elizabeta back at home in his castle. She receives a false message that he has been killed in battle and, unable to contemplate going on without him, commits suicide. The Prince returns just as she is about to be interred without the church's blessing. She lies on the floor of the castle chapel, surrounded by a number of monks bearing crucifixes on standards. The

---

40. Thus Stewart (1995: 184-85) says, '[Dracula's] readiness to sacrifice comes across as a biomedical parable of tragic self-control in an age when the exchange of bodily fluids, blood or otherwise, is ruled by thanatos rather than eros'. Also, see Nixon (1997) for a stimulating discussion of Tony Scott's film *The Hunger* (1987) as an extended allegory of AIDS.

chief priest among them is named Chesare (played by Anthony Hopkins in a cameo role), and he informs Vlad that since Elizabeta was a suicide she is outside of grace, her soul damned. The dead body of Elizabeta lies on the floor of the chapel, the shadow of a cross falling across her face as Chesare pronounces her damnation (the same image is repeated in a flashback episode in the middle of the film wherein Mina Murray asks Dracula about his Princess Elizabeta). The injustice of this so incenses the Prince that he curses the Christian faith for which he had so bravely fought, and renounces God. Knocking over a baptismal font and spilling its sacred water on to the floor, he moves menacingly towards Chesare, who crosses himself in a futile gesture of defence. Vlad brutally brushes aside the crucifix which the priest holds up to protect himself and, drawing his sword, rushes across the chapel to stab the sword into the centre of a large cross which stands behind the chapel altar. Blood begins to flow from the cross and soon the chapel is engulfed in a torrent of free-flowing blood. Vlad grabs a chalice and, filling it with some of the blood which comes down from the cross, drinks it, declaring, 'The blood is the life ... and it shall be mine!' A river of blood flows everywhere, flooding the chapel, as the opening sequence shifts to the title credit, 'Bram Stoker's *Dracula*'. The scene is now set for a story of revenge and blood-lust, with a striking image of a perversion of Holy Communion at its heart.

Later on in the film, as Van Helsing attempts to discover the true story of what is taking place among them now that Dracula has arrived in London, he visits the British Museum and reads some forbidden records housed there relating to Dracula's background. As he reads, the arch vampire-hunter comes to an important realization. 'Ja, Draculea! The blood is the life!' he intones, recalling the earlier declaration by the Count himself as he drank blood from the chalice in his castle chapel. The crucifix-bearing Abraham Van Helsing is certainly integral to the novel, and there are several scenes in the film in which he uses communion hosts to protect himself or others against the advance of the evil Dracula. Sacred communion hosts thus figure prominently in his armoury, taking their place alongside such items as crucifixes, hawthorn bushes, holy water and garlic bulbs.

The scene where Jonathan Harker and Mina are married in the convent chapel in Romania also uses communion imagery to great effect. Interestingly, the ceremony is conducted in Romanian and is performed by an orthodox priest, a scenario which allows the inclusion of drinking from a communion cup as part of the proceedings. The complex sequence interweaves images of the wedding ceremony in Romania with images of Dracula's final and fatal vampiric attack upon Lucy Westenra in far-away London. As part of the wedding ceremony, the bride and groom drink from a communion chalice, each in turn as they gaze lovingly into each other's eyes. The wedding scene is framed by shots of Dracula making ominous declarations about his continuing presence in the life of the young married couple, most notably in Mina who is the reincarnation of his long-lost wife Elizabeta. Before the wedding vows are exchanged, we see the Count intone menacingly: 'Your impotent men with their foolish spells cannot protect you from my power!' The words are directed primarily against the vampirized Lucy who is being protected by Quincey Morris and Arthur Holmwood, who are armed with guns and knives. Yet Dracula's words could be more accurately construed as directed against Mina and the ritualistic 'spells' of the church, such as holy communion, in which she is partaking. Immediately before Jonathan and Mina drink from the communion chalice, a second shot of Dracula is given in which he declares: 'I condemn you to living death, to eternal hunger for living blood!' While Jonathan and Mina enjoy a long and lingering first kiss as a wedded couple, we see Dracula, in the form of a ravenous wolf, attack Lucy as she lies seductively awaiting the Count's violation in her bed. Her death at the hands of the blood-thirsty Count Dracula is graphically illustrated by a deluge of blood splashing upon her bed (a scene which is brilliantly parodied in Mel Brooks's spoof *Dracula: Dead and Loving It* [1995] in which Professor Van Helsing and Jonathan Harker attempt to 'stake' the vampiric Lucy).

One of the most celebrated images within Bram Stoker's novel involves Dracula slitting open a vein within his breast and inviting Mina to drink from it. The eucharistic implications of the passage, which occurs within the novel in 21.363 (see above), are clear. The conversation between Dracula and Mina that precedes this blood-drinking demonstrates an intriguing reworking of several key theological ideas from the New Testament, including eternal life, death to self, and rebirth.

Mina:	I want to be what you are, see what you see, love what you love.
Dracula:	Mina, to walk with me you must die to your breathing life and be reborn to mine.

Mina:	You are my love, and my life. Always!
Dracula:	Then, I give you life eternal ... everlasting love. The power of the storm and the beasts of the earth. Walk with me, to be my loving wife ... forever.
Mina:	Yes! I will, yes.
Dracula:	*(He caresses her, exposes her neck and inflicts the vampire's bite.)* I take you as my eternal bride.
Mina:	*(Moans in ecstasy as he drinks from her neck.)*
Dracula:	*(Slitting open a vein over his heart and pulling Mina to it.)* Mina, drink and join me in eternal life.
	(Mina begins to drink and Dracula throws back his head in delight. Suddenly a look of dread covers over his face as he realizes the enormity of what Mina's act might mean for her. He stops her drinking from his breast.)
Dracula:	No! I cannot let this be.
Mina:	Please, I don't care! Make me yours!
Dracula:	You will be cursed, as I am, to walk in the shadow of death for all eternity. I love you too much to condemn you!
Mina:	*(Pleading with him to allow her to continue.)* Take me away from all this death!
	(Mina forces her way back back onto his breast. Dracula yields and swoons in near orgasmic delight. He wraps his arms around her in an image of intimacy.)

The scene is certainly the most graphic use of the drinking of blood within the film. The dialogue is filled with language reminiscent of the New Testament descriptions of Christ's sacrificial shedding of blood as commemorated in the sacrament of holy communion. Indeed, in *Bram Stoker's Dracula: The Film and the Legend* (1993), issued by Francis Ford Coppola and screenwriter James V. Hart to accompany the release of the film, the scene is even described as 'The vampire wedding sacrament' (Coppola and Hart 1993: 135).[41]

---

41. The scene has long been a controversial one within the various theatrical and cinematic adaptations of Stoker's *Dracula*. For example, the version by playwright Charles Morrell, which had a brief run in 1927 at the Royal Court Theatre in Warrington, was the object of official censure. The British censor, the Lord Chamberlain, objected to both the breast drinking scene and one in which Mina is branded on the head by a communion wafer. These were deemed to be blasphemous. See Skal (1990: 77) for details. Occasionally modern *Dracula* films include a version of the scene within their story-line. A case in point is The Hammer Studio production entitled *Dracula Prince of Darkness* (1966), directed by Terence Fisher.

As a result of having drunk blood from Dracula's breast Mina falls increasingly under his spell. As Van Helsing says, 'The vampire has baptized her with his own blood'. Van Helsing and his band of vampire hunters travel to Dracula's home-country Romania, endeavouring to catch him before he is able to return to his castle and revive his waning energies. At one point the group divides into two, attempting to intercept Dracula's ship before it arrives in port or, failing that, to catch him in the mountain passes near his castle. Van Helsing travels with Mina in a carriage while Harker, Holmwood, Seward and Morris all travel by train and horseback. As Van Helsing and Mina draw near to the Count's castle Mina becomes increasingly under the influence of the Count and at one point attempts to seduce Van Helsing by using her vampiric powers. She very nearly manages to bite him on the neck, but he is able to fend her off with the aid of a communion host which he thrusts against her forehead. The host sears her flesh and she falls backward, her forehead bearing a scarlet brand.[42]

Mina's brand is prominently seen on her forehead until the final scenes in the chapel of the castle. The chapel offers a fitting setting for the conclusion of the film in that it was here that Dracula, outraged by the treatment of his beloved wife Elizabeta, stabbed his sword into the central crucifix and drank blood from the communion chalice (see above). The monster Dracula has been mortally wounded in his fight with Van Helsing and his band; his throat is cut and he has Quincey Morris's Bowie knife embedded in his chest. He is allowed by the vampire hunter to retreat with Mina to the chapel; the vampire hunters suspect that their work is over and that something decisive is about to happen. In this final sequence of the film, where Mina and Dracula lie together in the chapel of the castle in Transylvania, there is an interesting combination of two of Jesus' sayings from the cross. Dracula lies prostrate on the chapel floor, mortally wounded, and laments to Mina, 'Where is my God? He has forsaken me! It is finished!' These words allude to the words of Jesus from the cross recorded in Mt. 27.46/Mk 15.34 ('My God, my God! Why have you forsaken me?') and Jn 19.30 ('It is finished!'). The overall effect of this is to transform Dracula into something of a Christ-figure, one who has to undergo the abuse and misunderstanding of his fellow creatures as well as rejection by God.

42. In Stoker's novel the branding of Mina's forehead by Van Helsing takes place much earlier, just prior to the cleansing of Dracula's Carfax lair (*Dracula* 22.381).

This he willingly accepts out of love, *for Mina*. Mina, for her part, demonstrates her love for him. She professes her love, kissing his blood-stained mouth gently. Her voice-over explains: 'There in the presence of God, I understood at last how my love could release us all from the powers of darkness. Our love is stronger than death.' We see a brief shot of the central crucifix, in which the stab wound inflicted by Prince Vlad four centuries before is miraculously sealed. The monster is then suffused with a divine light from above and is changed in appearance back to the Prince Vlad we saw in the beginning of the film. He begs Mina to give him peace and she forces the Bowie knife through his heart. As he dies, the scarlet brand she bears on her forehead disappears in a puff of smoke.

Whatever else we might say about the way in which Francis Ford Coppola's film interprets the novel by Bram Stoker, whether we would choose to describe it as a creative adaptation of the book or as a seriously misguided reading of the work, it is clear that communion imagery has an important role to play in the film. Yet, the haunting thing about James V. Hart's screenplay is that it manages to build a consistent portrayal of Dracula as a man who has been forced to renounce the one thing that he held dear (the church and the cross of Christ) because of the all-consuming love that he has for another thing he holds dear (his wife Elizabeta and her reincarnation in the form of Mina).

b. *The Lost Boys* (1987)

Joel Schumacher's horror comedy *The Lost Boys* (1987) offers a vision of contemporary vampirism set in the picturesque coastal resort town of Santa Carla in California.[43] The film stars Kiefer Sutherland in the role of a vampire named David, and has become something of a cult-classic, particularly with teenage audiences who respond to the occultic theme, punctuated as it is by a pulsing rock soundtrack. The film is clearly aimed at a younger audience, with the film's promotional poster brashly declaring, 'Sleep all day, party all night. It's fun to be a vampire'.[44] David is the leader of a group of vampires who terrorize Santa Carla, killing its inhabitants and visitors to the town at will in order to satisfy their need for blood. He invites a recent arrival to the town, a young

43. The film was actually shot in the real resort town of Santa Cruz.
44. Latham (1997) discusses the vision of a consumer youth-culture which is portrayed within the film.

man named Michael (played by heart-throb Jason Patric), to join the group. This invitation is formalized by drinking from an ornate, bejewelled wine bottle, the content of which (Michael is warned) is blood. In effect, drinking from this bottle of blood turns Michael into a vampire; drinking of the blood is the sacramental rite of passage to a new way of life for him, the means whereby he joins the vampire community.[45] As one of the other vampires says to him after Michael has drunk from the bottle and is brought thereby to a near trance-like state, 'You are one of us, Bud!' The rest of the film is given over to an exploration of how the initiate vampire Michael deals with his status as a vampire. In short, he is both attracted to and repulsed by it. Catering to a younger audience, the film plays with many themes associated with teenage angst, including the pressures of a sex-crazed pubescence and the attempts to find identity within a like-minded peer group. Somewhat in keeping with the sexual imagery central to Stoker's original novel, there is an equation of the losing of one's sexual virginity with the making of a 'first kill' as a vampire, something which Michael barely manages to avoid in the end.[46] Although the film certainly panders to what might be described as the baser instincts of human beings, it nevertheless does explore the idea of the 'drinking of blood' in a highly original fashion. In this sense, *The Lost Boys* is an intriguing example of how the sacramental element of Dracula mythology, most notably the drinking of blood, in mock imitation of the Christian celebration of the eucharist, is portrayed by a modern film maker. Direct reliance upon the New Testament testimony concerning the Last Supper is certainly not overt; indeed it could be said to be subliminal at best, but it seems (arguably) to me to be present nonetheless. Such is the degree to which communion imagery has powerfully, but subtly, influenced our contemporary world.

c. *The Omega Man (1971)*

Finally, I turn to consider one of the most interesting cinematic interpretations of the Dracula myth. This is a science-fiction film which has included the idea of blood-sacrifice, and the salvation that it brings, as a prominent motif within it.

---

45. Zanger (1997: 18) notes that one significant change in modern presentations of vampires is that the 'new' vampire tends to live in communal settings.

46. Nixon (1997: 119-28) discusses the portrayal of sexuality offered within the film.

Boris Sagal's film from 1971 entitled *The Omega Man* starred Charlton Heston in one of his most mesmerizing roles.[47] This is a highly original adaptation of the ground-breaking novel by Richard Matheson entitled *I Am Legend* (first published in 1954).[48] Matheson's novel is clearly an updating of the *Dracula* story in that it is set in 1976–79 and chronicles the life of a man named Robert Neville who lives in a small town which is overrun with vampires. Everyone in the town, indeed, everyone in the world (as far as Neville is aware), has been infected with a bacterium that lives in the blood-stream and causes a vampire-like condition. Neville is unaffected by the vampire plague, perhaps because he was once bitten by a vampire bat and his blood developed antibodies to the disease. Neville lives a haunted and lonely existence, his wife and daughter having fallen victim to the disease some months before. He has turned his house into a fortress and he defends himself against the nightly attacks of the vampires who want to kill him. During the day, when the vampires are sleeping, Neville hunts them down, dispatching them with wooden stakes. In short, many of the basic elements of the Dracula mythology are included within Matheson's story, with the highly creative addition that vampirism is given a quasi-scientific explanation.

In Boris Sagal's film this scientific element is taken even further and is mixed with a political scenario to give it even greater plausibility. The setting for the film is the city of Los Angeles in the late 1970s, which allows for a powerful irony to be explored. Here we are presented with the tale of the survival of an individual in the midst of a modern city that has been all but emptied by the techniques of modern warfare. The basic story-line of Matheson's novel is followed, wherein the central character conducts a campaign during the daylight hours

47. Sadly, the tempermental Sagal was killed some years later while working on another film. He accidentally stepped into the whirling rear-rotor blades of a helicopter after disembarking from it. See Heston (1995: 442-43) for details.

48. This is not the first time that Matheson's novel was adapted for the cinema. A version was made in 1964, directed by Sidney Salkow, entitled *The Last Man on Earth* which starred Vincent Price. The has been enormously influential among horror writers, as Stephen King testifies: 'Richard Matheson is the guy who taught me what I'm doing. When I read *I Am Legend* I realized that horror... could appear in the suburbs, on the street, or even in the house next door' (cited on the back cover of a four-part graphic comic-book adaptation of the novel adapted by Steve Niles and illustrated by Elman Brown, published in Forestville, California by Eclipse Books in 1991).

against those who would destroy him at night. Yet there are also significant differences from Matheson's original novel. In *The Omega Man* humankind is afflicted not with vampirism as such, but with a plague arising out of a conflict between China and Russia in which biological weapons of mass destruction were used. The plague is invariably fatal, causing those infected to break out in boils, become albino-like in appearance and to develop an extreme sensitivity to light. Everyone succumbs to the plague in the end, although some do so more rapidly than others. Those afflicted with the plague live out the rest of their days with the spectre of death hounding them. They are led by Brother Matthias (brilliantly played by the character actor Anthony Zerbe) who has attempted to re-organize society by rejecting everything associated with the technological world which brought destruction to the human race. Members of 'The Family' wear black hooded robes, and give the appearance of belonging to a monastic order. Charlton Heston plays Colonel Robert Neville, a military scientist who was working on an experimental vaccine to combat the plague. He is involved in a helicopter crash (his pilot falls victim to the plague) but manages to inject himself with the vaccine just prior to passing out after the crash. This renders him immune to the effects of the plague and sets the stage for him being the redemptive agent against it. Neville's antibody-charged blood carries within it the hopes of an ever-dwindling number of humans who (so far!) have managed to survive the ravages of the plague. In this respect he may be regarded as something of a Christ-figure. Indeed, there are several scenes within the film which support just such an interpretation. Two short examples will serve to illustrate the essential point.

First, we note an exchange of dialogue between Robert Neville, Lisa, a young black woman whom he discovers one day during the daylight hours in a department store, and Dutch, a promising medical student who is the intellectual heart of the small group of people, mostly children, not yet fatally affected by the plague. They are all concerned that the younger brother of Lisa, whose name is Richie, is in danger of falling victim to the plague. Richie clearly has been infected and the immunity of Neville's blood becomes a critical issue as they discuss the fate of the young boy:

Neville:	I don't have it!
Lisa:	Have what?
Neville:	The plague! I'm immune.

Dutch:	Everybody has it!
Neville:	Everybody but me! There was a vaccine, just an experimental batch. We weren't sure it would work.
Dutch:	Why, if you're immune, you could...
Neville:	That's right! My blood might be a serum. The stage that boy's in, my antibodies could reverse the whole process. Stop it!
Dutch:	Christ, you could save the world!
Lisa:	Screw the world, let's save Richie!

Dutch's remark about Christ is, of course, not intended as a theological statement; rather it is uttered as a mild swear word prompted by the enormity of what Neville has revealed about his own blood. Yet, the irony of Dutch's declaration is not to be missed: there is a sense in which Neville (the new Christ) *could* save the world, or at least what is left of it. Indeed, one of the children, sensing the importance of what Neville is attempting to do in curing Richie, asks him, 'Are you God?' He does not answer her question directly, although the theological implication of it is left for the audience to contemplate. Neville goes about the business of offering transfusions of his blood to Richie, which eventually cure him of the disease.

The second scene is much more involved and demonstrates the rich religious symbolism of the film. On the strength of the success of the blood transfusions with Richie, Neville decides to use his blood to create a serum that can be used to cure Lisa, Dutch and the other members of their group. The famous line from Stoker's *Dracula*, that 'the blood is the life!' is here powerfully expressed, and Neville fills a transfusion bottle with his blood serum, declaring it to be 'genuine, 160-proof old Anglo-Saxon'. The bottle of blood figures in the final scenes of the film in which Neville is attacked by Matthias and other members of 'The Family' in his penthouse fortress. He manages to rescue the bottle of blood serum from the refrigerator in his laboratory and escapes from the building with Lisa. Unfortunately, Lisa has 'turned' and is beginning to show physical signs of the ravages of the plague; her hair has become white and she wears sunglasses to protect her light-sensitive eyes. Neville and Lisa retreat to the front of the building where there is a large fountain bathed in the spotlights of the now-compromised penthouse fortress. Matthias appears above on the balcony of Neville's apartment beckoning Lisa to return to him and 'The Family'. He hurls a spear at Neville down below, striking him in the chest. Neville falls backward into the fountain, struggling to remove the protruding spear. He manages to remove it and pull himself to a standing position, leaning heavily on an ornament at the centre of the fountain, but he is fatally wounded. A few minutes later Dutch arrives in a truck with the small group of surviving children. Neville pulls the bottle of blood serum out from beneath his shirt and passes it on to Dutch before slumping against an ornament in the centre of the fountain. The final scene shows Neville in what can only be described as a crucifixion pose, arms outstretched, head bowed. He has died, but not before providing a way of salvation through his blood. The water in the fountain is red, coloured by the blood of the Christ-like Neville. This closing scene offers a striking visual representation of the fountain image from Zech. 13.1, which I noted at the beginning of the study was so influential in the work of William Cowper. Here there is indeed 'a fountain filled with blood', and while the blood may not have been 'drawn from Immanuel's veins', it certainly comes from an all-too-human saviour figure, albeit an unlikely one, Robert Neville.[49]

4. *Summary*

I began this study by noting the place that eucharistic imagery has within the Pauline letters, particularly as an expression of the apostle's teaching concerning the reconciliation brought about by the shedding of Jesus Christ's blood on the cross. The use of the cup of wine as a metaphor for 'the new covenant in Jesus' blood' was highlighted as an illustration of the importance that eucharistic imagery has in Paul's thought.

I then recorded the extensive use that Bram Stoker's novel *Dracula* makes of such imagery, with the author creatively interweaving it with allusions to biblical themes and stories in the novel. These all help to illustrate how theologically profound a book *Dracula* really is. In particular, I noted that communion hosts served as one of the primary

49. Heston (1995: 443-44) briefly discusses the Christ analogy of the film. Interestingly, he notes that Warners, the film studio, altered the end of the film, dropping a scene which could be interpreted as a version of the Gospel story of the women at the tomb of Christ. Heston relates: '[Warners] asked us to cut a very short, silent scene I was sorry to lose: a ten-year-old girl bicycles up during the safe daylight hours to the fortified building where I live, leaves on the doorstep an offering of a few wilted flowers and some fruit, and pedals away. Even with the scene gone, I'm surprised at how often people mention the Christ analogy in the film.'

weapons used against the evil Count Dracula by his arch-rival, the vampire-hunter Van Helsing. I also noted how the idea of drinking blood builds upon the eucharistic texts of the New Testament and transforms such ritual drinking into a demonic perversion of the Christian sacrament. This is seen not only through Dracula's drinking of the blood of his various victims, but also in the Prince's invitation that Mina Murray drink blood from his breast and thereby become united with him in a sacred pact.

Finally, I discussed three cinematic interpretations of the Dracula story, especially calling attention to the ways in which they made use of the shedding of blood and related eucharistic imagery within their re-telling of the vampire myth. No doubt the infinite adaptability of the Dracula myth, together with the sexual innuendo which lies just beneath the surface of the neck-biting and blood-sucking, means that film-makers will continue to find it to be a vein which is worth further exploration (and exploitation!).

Chapter 4

UNCLE TOM'S CABIN:
THE LIBERATION OF SLAVERY?

It may come as a surprise to discover that Harriet Beecher Stowe's *Uncle Tom's Cabin*[1] was the best-selling novel in the nineteenth-century, outselling anything written by Robert Louis Stevenson, Jane Austen or even Charles Dickens. In fact, during that century the only book to sell more copies worldwide than *Uncle Tom's Cabin* was the Bible. Stowe's masterpiece was the first novel by an American author to sell more than a million copies; approximately 300,000 were sold in the United States alone within the first year, and an estimated 2,500,000 worldwide. It was quickly translated into a number of European languages and was widely read in France and Britain. English reviewers described it as 'the Iliad of the Blacks', a title that recognizes the work as a major player in what Virginia Woolf has described as the 'epic age' of women's writing.[2]

More importantly, the novel helped to form popular conceptions of the slave South, many of which endure to the present day.[3] In the words of William R. Taylor (1979: 307):

> [*Uncle Tom's Cabin*] probably did more than any book ever published to alter the American image of the South and, once it had appeared, no one could hope to write about the plantation and ignore or slight the Negro.

The same could be said about some of the characters of the novel who take on an existence far beyond the pages of the novel itself.

---

1. I shall cite passages from the novel by noting their chapter number, title and page number (thus, *UTC* 1.5 denotes p. 5 of chapter 1). The edition used here is that within the Penguin Classics series (London: Penguin Books, 1986). The edition contains an introduction by Ann Douglas.

2. See Moers (1976: 15) on this point.

3. See Gerster and Cords (1977) for a brief discussion of Stowe's contribution on this issue.

Indeed, *Uncle Tom's Cabin* is one of the few American novels of the nineteenth century which could legitimately be said to have generated a complicated mythology which continued to be adopted and adapted for decades after its publication. The backdrop of this mythology is the institution of slavery as it was practised in the United States prior to the Civil War, and it is this so-called 'peculiar institution' which concerns us within this study. Thus, I shall examine the curious passage contained in 1 Cor. 7.20-24 in which Paul offers some advice about how Christian slaves and slave-owners are to act with respect to one another, particularly in the face of prevailing eschatological expectations about the imminent parousia of the Lord. In this regard, the highly controversial meaning of 1 Cor. 7.20-24 shall occupy my attention. In these verses Paul writes:

> ²⁰ἕκαστος ἐν τῇ κλήσει ᾗ ἐκλήθη, ἐν ταύτῃ μενέτω. ²¹δοῦλος ἐκλήθης, μή σοι μελέτω· ἀλλ᾽ εἰ καὶ δύνασαι ἐλεύθερος γενέσθαι, μᾶλλον χρῆσαι. ²²ὁ γὰρ ἐν κυρίῳ κληθεὶς δοῦλος ἀπελεύθερος κυρίου ἐστίν, ὁμοίως ὁ ἐλεύθερος κληθεὶς δοῦλός ἐστιν Χριστοῦ. ²³τιμῆς ἠγοράσθητε· μὴ γίνεσθε δοῦλοι ἀνθρώπων. ²⁴ἕκαστος ἐν ᾧ ἐκλήθη, ἀδελφοί, ἐν τούτῳ μενέτω.

> ²⁰Every one should remain in the state in which he was called. ²¹Were you a slave when called? Never mind. But if you can gain your freedom, avail yourself of the opportunity. ²² For he who was called in the Lord as a slave is a freedman of the Lord. Likewise he who was free when called is a slave of Christ. ²³You were bought with a price; do not become slaves of men. ²⁴So, brethren, in whatever state each was called, there let him remain.

What does Paul mean by this cryptic advice? How *does* one 'remain in the state in which one was called'? Does Paul mean that Christian slaves should actively pursue their legal freedom or not? It is at precisely this juncture that Harriet Beecher Stowe's novel affords us an unusual entry-point for a fresh consideration of Paul's words. Ironically, Stowe's picture of life lived under slavery in the American antebellum South contains a duality which, on the surface at least, is remarkably similar to that commonly suggested by Paul's teaching in this extract from 1 Corinthians 7. The stage is thus set for a creative exploration of slavery as it is contained in these two distinct but overlapping works of literature. On the one hand we have a highly personal letter written nearly 2000 years ago by the apostle Paul to a particular congregation in order to answer specific questions raised by them about the nature of their lives as Christian believers. On the other hand we have a widely published novel written nearly 150 years ago by a strong-minded woman whose avowed aim was to prick the consciences of her (largely) Christian readership and effect a change in the political stance of the nation over the issue of slavery. What unites the work of these two very different writers is a shared commitment to the importance that the Christian message had in resolving the debate over slavery as a socio-economic institution. They both also have in common a long history of diverse interpretation as to the central message about slavery that their authors intended to convey.

In keeping with the interpretative approach of this volume, I shall establish a three-way conversation between Paul's letter to the Corinthians, Harriet Beecher Stowe's highly influential novel and some recent cinematic interpretations of *Uncle Tom's Cabin*. Thus, I shall pursue my study in four parts: (1) 1 Cor. 7.20-24 and Paul's attitude to slavery; (2) Harriet Beecher Stowe: the crusading pen of God almighty; (3) slavery and liberation in *Uncle Tom's Cabin*: various responses to emancipation; and (4) film adaptations of *Uncle Tom's Cabin*.

I begin by noting how 1 Cor. 7.20-24, one of the few passages that discusses the matter of slavery within the undisputed Pauline corpus,[4] has been recently interpreted.

1. *1 Corinthians 7.20-24 and Paul's Attitude to Slavery*

Theological arguments have often been used to justify the practice of slavery, with key passages from the Bible interpreted in such a way as to support a pro-slavery position.[5] A good example of this is the way that Old Testament texts which mention divine curses were applied along racial lines and taken to mean that being black was a part of the curse of God (Bradley 1971). This in itself constitutes a major break with the way in which slavery was viewed within the ancient world, for the question of a person's race or colour was not automatically a factor in determining whether he or she was destined to be a slave.[6]

Investigations into slavery as it was practised in the Graeco-Roman

4.   1 Cor. 12.13, Gal. 3.28 and Phlm. 10-19 are the only other undisputed texts that discuss slavery directly.

5.   Swartley (1983: 31-64); Cannon (1989); Giles (1994); and Meeks (1996) all address this matter.

6.   For more on this issue, see Snowden (1983).

world have long been a favourite topic for classicists, particularly in the last century or so.[7] In large measure this has been under the influence of Marxist theory, which sought to ground the assessment of the class struggle between slaves and masters within the pages of ancient history.[8] The collapse of communism in the 1980s has meant that such ideologically driven interpretations have also been found wanting. A more methodologically sound approach is needed if we are to attempt to understand how the institution of slavery functioned within the ancient world. However, there are enormous difficulties in comparing what the New Testament has to say about slavery with how the institution has been viewed in subsequent periods of history, including the antebellum South of the United States, not to mention our own day. For one thing, it must be recognized that slavery was an almost universally accepted phenomenon within the first-century world, with as many as one-third of the population in a city such as Rome or Corinth technically falling into the category of slaves. At the same time, it is actually quite rare to find any voices raised against slavery as a way of structuring society; the days of the slave-revolutions had long passed by the time that Paul was writing to the church at Corinth.[9] Following an extensive survey of what ancient writers had to say about slavery, including the attempts to justify it on the basis of 'natural law', or to qualify it as financially expedient, or to concentrate attention on the abuses of the slave-system rather than on the institution itself, Peter Garnsey (1996: 10-11) remarks:

> All this adds up to much less than a lively, open debate over the existence and legitimacy of slavery such as was waged in the antebellum South, but also rather more than a universal, passive acceptance of the institution.

Within this part of the study I would like to focus on two books by New Testament scholars which have been especially concerned with the question of slavery as it is addressed within Paul's letters. The first

7.   Standard texts include: Barrow (1928); Westermann (1955); Finley (1960; 1980); Zeitlin (1962–63); Urbach (1964); Jeremias (1969: 312-16); Hopkins (1978); Wiedemann (1981); Garlan (1988); Bradley (1987); Kirschenbaum (1987); Yavetz (1988).

8.   Wiedemann (1997) offers a helpful summary on the point.

9.   The best study of this topic is Bradley (1989). Also worth consulting is Vogt (1974: 39-92); and Cartledge (1985) which discusses slave-revolts (or more precisely, the *absence* of them) in both classical Greece and the American South.

was written some years ago and focuses on the many interpretative problems surrounding 1 Cor. 7.21. I speak of S. Scott Bartchy's *ΜΑΛΛΟΝ ΧΡΗΣΑΙ: First-Century Slavery and 1 Corinthians 7.21* (1973), an oft-cited work which approaches the task at hand from what we might call the 'micro' level. That is to say, it is predominantly a text-based study, patiently building a case from the bottom up. In contrast, the second book approaches the task at hand from a much more theoretical level, addressing the question of slavery in the thought of Paul on what we might call the 'macro' level. I speak of Dale B. Martin's *Slavery as Salvation* (1990), an extremely creative effort which explores how slavery was used as a theological metaphor of salvation within the Pauline epistles. Taken together these two books provide us with an intriguing basis upon which to investigate the place that slavery had within Paul's thought, what he expected of the Corinthian church with respect to delicate master–slave relationships, and how this was conceived in terms of Christian theology. Let us turn now to consider the contributions of Bartchy and Martin, both of whom address one of the most perplexing topics within Pauline studies: exactly what was Paul's teaching regarding slavery and what did he expect the members of the congregation at Corinth, both slave and free, to do in light of it?

a. *S. Scott Bartchy: A New Way of Reading a Problem Text*
One of the exegetical difficulties of 1 Cor. 7.21 is the fact that the crucial aorist imperative χρῆσαι in the verse does not have a grammatical object (a noun in the dative case has to be supplied to complete the thought).[10] Scholars over the years have tended to suggest one of two possible options: either τῇ ἐλευθερίᾳ ('freedom') or τῇ δουλείᾳ ('slavery'). The two possibilities yield contrasting explanations of the verse as a whole, which have been described as the 'take freedom' and the 'use slavery' interpretations respectively.[11] S. Scott Bartchy suggests that there are difficulties with both of these traditional approaches to the verse and therefore puts forward a third alternative, namely τῇ

10. Harrill (1994) offers a philological study of the phrase μᾶλλον χρῆσαι within ancient Greek literature. Dodd (1925) cites the evidence of two Greek papyri from the sixth-century CE which use the crucial aorist imperative χρῆσαι in support of his translation: 'If you actually have before you the possibility of becoming free, avail yourself of it by preference'.

11. Bartchy (1973: 1-27) offers a history of the interpretation of the verse.

κλήσει ('calling'). This, he contends, makes better sense of Paul's overall argument in 1 Corinthians 7 (which is primarily concerned with marital relationships within the church)[12] and also accords with what we know about the practices of slavery in the Graeco-Roman world at the time. The use of the unusual term ὁ ἀπελεύθερος ('freedman') in 1 Cor. 7.22 is also somewhat striking (the term appears only here within the Pauline letters) (Bartchy 1973: 57).[13] The verse is generally taken to be an indication that Paul was familiar with the legal practices governing the manumission of slaves by their owners.[14] It appears that there were no legal grounds upon which slaves could refuse manumission should their masters want to set them free. This has implications for the meaning of 1 Cor. 7.21, especially as it is commonly assumed that a slave could *do* something to effect his or her manumission ('if you can gain your freedom, *take it*'). Crucial to Bartchy's case is his contention that 'calling' in 7.17, 20, 24 always means for Paul the calling of Christ, the Christian calling, rather than one's status in society. The result is that 7.21 cannot be said either to carry the force of an exhortation to the Christian slave that he should 'stay in slavery', or that he should 'pursue freedom'. Thus Bartchy (1973: 183) gives the sense of the contentious verse as:

> Were you a slave when you were called? Don't worry about it. But if, indeed, you become manumitted, by all means, as a freedman live according to God's calling.

The scholarly response to this very imaginative suggestion has not been entirely favourable. Despite the very helpful insights about the

---

12. Dawes (1990) refines Bartchy's argument along these lines. Shaw (1983: 77) remarks on Paul's teaching here: 'It is no accdent that in a passage on marriage he can easily include a digression on slavery.' Interestingly, Origen (c. 185–c. 254 BCE) interprets the exhortation μᾶλλον χρῆσαι to refer to marriage rather than slavery ('take freedom from marriage'). See Jenkins (1908: 507-508).

13. Jones (1987: 29-37) discusses Paul's use of the term ἀπελεύθερος κυρίου. One of the most unusual accounts of a 'freedman' in antiquity is contained in Finley (1968: 154-66). This concerns a man named Aulos Kapreilios Timotheos, a first-century slave who obtained his freedom and then turned to slave-trading as an occupation.

14. The literature on the manumission of slaves within the Roman world is extensive. For more on the subject see Lyall (1970–71; 1984); Massey and Moreland (1978); Wiedemann (1985); Bradley (1987: 81-112; 1994: 154-65); Kyrtatas (1987: 25-74); Watson (1987: 23-45); Gardner (1991: 205-231). The manumission of Christian slaves by the church is discussed in Harrill (1993).

practice of manumission, and the attempt to place 7.20-24 sensibly within the argument of ch. 7 as a whole, Bartchy's solution to the *crux interpretum* of 7.21 is, in the minds of many, a forced and unnatural reading of Paul's words. At the same time, it is only fair to note that since the publication of Bartchy's interpretation in 1973, no scholarly consensus about the meaning of 1 Cor. 7.21 has emerged. Most commentators agree that Bartchy's interpretation of Paul's words is wrong (or at least misleading), but they cannot agree on what is right. Competent arguments continue to be put forward within the scholarly discussion, in favour of both the 'take freedom' and the 'use slavery' options (with the former much more often asserted).[15]

b. *Dale B. Martin: A New Way of Interpreting a Theological Metaphor*
At first it may seem quite strange to think that the early Christians expressed their experience of salvation by using terminology and concepts drawn from the world of slavery. Is there not something degrading and unhealthy in being another's slave? Is not the idea of slavery contrary to the spirit of freedom and liberty that lies at the centre of the Christian's religious experience, and therefore something from which one hoped and prayed to be delivered? Does not Paul himself describe the pre-Christian condition as 'slavery to sin' (Rom. 6.6-9, 16-23; 8.12-17; 21-23; Gal. 4.1-9; 24-25; 5.1)?[16] Is not he primarily concerned with the moral and ethical conduct of the Corinthians and invoking language of slavery to that end?[17] Why, then, does Paul use the metaphor of slavery *positively* to declare faith in what God has done through Christ, and even go so far as to describe himself as a 'slave of Christ'? It is precisely these kinds of questions that Dale B. Martin's *Slavery as Salvation* explores.

15. On the side of the 'take freedom' option, see Trummer (1975); Baumert (1984: 114-21); Prior (1985: 132); Fee (1987: 306-22); Talbert (1987: 41-42); Brauch (1990: 118-23); Watson (1992: 73-74); Kistemaker (1993: 231-33); Elliott (1994: 32-40); Deming (1995); Witherington (1995: 181-85); Horrell (1996: 160-67); Hays (1997: 125-26); Dunn (1998: 698-701); Meggitt (1998: 181-83); Wallace and Williams (1998: 141). For the 'use slavery' side, see Crouch (1972: 122-29); Barrett (1975); Gayer (1976: 154-68); Keck (1979: 94-98); de Ste Croix (1983: 419-20); Kyrtatas (1987: 33); Mitchell (1992: 121-25). MacDonald (1998: 171-72) suggests that Paul might have been deliberately ambiguous in writing to the Corinthians about this delicate subject.
16. So Rollins (1987) argues.
17. As Malan (1981) suggests.

Methodologically Martin is attempting to give due weight to the social context of early Christian communities, and in this sense he could be classified as a social historian. He is not primarily concerned with determining Paul's stance on the institution of slavery as such, and offers precious little discussion of 1 Cor. 7.20-24, the passage (as we have noted above) upon which Bartchy's interests were so concentrated. Rather, Martin is interested in how the metaphor of slavery would have been heard and understood within Paul's world, what the members of the congregation at Corinth would have made of it, and what inferences they would have drawn about the nature of the Christian experience based upon it.

That is not to say that Martin's discussion does not have a textual focal point—1 Corinthians 9 serves in this capacity for much of the book. The reason for this is that this chapter contains an extended discussion of Paul's thought about his own apostolic ministry, the fact that he declares his willingness to surrender his life in service of Christ and the church. Such an understanding of ministry clearly overlaps with the practices of slavery wherein the slave becomes obedient to his or her master. It is this 'enslavement for others', particularly as it is discussed in 1 Cor. 9.19-23, that attracts Martin's attention. In addition, two other aspects of the slavery metaphor are explored for what they might reveal about the Christian experience of salvation. These are: (1) the use of the term 'slave of Christ' as a term for leaders within the church; and (2) the way in which the slavery image lent itself to expectations of upward mobility and promoted social change within the life of the church. The latter point is perhaps the most difficult for contemporary readers to appreciate, for slavery is almost universally viewed as an oppressive force in society, one that is deeply destructive within human relationships. However, it must be remembered that slavery was an acknowledged means by which people of the ancient world could climb the social ladder. There are many examples of slaves of prominent figures within society who were themselves, by virtue of their association with their masters, forces to be reckoned with. Thus, Martin is quick to point out that it is the *social status* of Christian slaves, rather than their *individual state* as Christians, that lies at the heart of Paul's use of the slavery metaphor. This has tremendous implications for how 1 Cor. 7.22-23 is interpreted, for example, because as modern readers we tend to misunderstand the meaning of the all-important term 'freedman'

(ἀπελεύθερος) and take it to be the equivalent of 'free man'.[18] We too
readily assume that the first century '*freed* man' is the same as the
twentieth century '*free* man', thereby confusing a Graeco-Roman
socio-economic classification with a post-Enlightenment philosophical
one. Martin suggests that throughout 1 Corinthians 9 Paul employs the
slavery metaphor as a means of challenging the more wealthy and powerful members of the Corinthian congregation to take seriously the fact
that they were 'slaves of Christ', as Paul frequently declared himself to
be (Rom. 1.1; Gal. 1.10; Phil. 1.1—although curiously *not* in 1 or 2
Corinthians!). In this sense, Paul leads by example, refusing to accept
their financial assistance and continuing to support himself by his own
labour, as befits a proper slave. Indeed, Paul extends the range of his
own status as a slave, presenting himself as one who is enslaved not
only to Jesus Christ but to the church at large. According to Martin, this
is the essential point of Paul's argument in 1 Cor. 9.19-23, and in so
arguing Paul relies upon an alternative vision of political leadership
which was well established within the ancient world (although admittedly a minority view). This alternative vision Martin describes as 'a
populist model' which stresses the enslavement of the leader to the
people he serves. Such a model would have been particularly impres-
sive to the lower-class members of the Corinthian society (the 'weak')
who would have understood Paul to be identifying himself with their
position and status.[19] In summary, in 1 Corinthians 9 Paul presents
himself as a slave whose allegiances are to two distinct but related
masters: he is a slave to Christ (9.16-18) and he is a slave to all (9.19-
23). The connection between the two is intimate, as intimate as the relationship between Christ and his body, the church. In being willing to be
a slave in this manner, Paul demonstrates that he moves beyond the
Stoic sentiments about the 'free slave', a fascinating strand of ancient
philosophy which stressed the paradox at the heart of slavery. As
Martin (1990: 34) remarks:

> Paul does not use the philosophical commonplace of the paradoxically
> free slave or the enslaved free man; rather, his argument effects a linear

18. Martin (1990: 63-65) demonstrates this misunderstanding to be a fatal flaw
in the interpretation of Hans Conzelmann (1975).

19. Martin follows the lead of Gerd Theissen's influential assessment of the
Corinthian situation, but he does suggest some refinements. See Martin (1990: 126-
29); the influence of Meeks (1983: 63-64) upon Martin is also clearly in evidence
here.

movement from high status to low status. The movement from high to
low is indicated within verse 19 by the movement from 'free from all' to
'enslaved to all'.

In the end, Martin's interpretation of Paul is an adaptation of Gerd
Theissen's influential ideas about 'love-patriarchialism' within the early
church (Theissen 1982). Martin suggests Paul is using traditional categories of masters, freedmen and slaves to construct a potent challenge
to his Corinthian audience. He reverses the existing master–slave relationships and thereby revolutionizes the perceptions of social status
within the congregation. And yet Paul does all of this (seemingly)
without rejecting the institution of slavery itself! Ultimately it is the
unity of the church that he wishes to preserve, and (Martin argues) it is
his deep and abiding commitment to this that drives Paul to write as he
does to the troubled church at Corinth.

Bearing in mind these two innovative approaches to the question of
slavery in Paul's thought, I now turn to consider Harriet Beecher
Stowe's *Uncle Tom's Cabin*.

2. Harriet Beecher Stowe: The Crusading Pen of God Almighty

Harriet Beecher Stowe's bestseller was first published between June
1851 and April 1852 as a serial within the weekly *The National Era*
based in Washington, DC. The story was told in 40 installments of this
influential anti-slavery newspaper. It was then issued in 1852 in two
volumes by the Boston-based publisher John P. Jewett and Company.
Many abolitionists from the North viewed *Uncle Tom's Cabin* to be a
valuable contribution in their struggle against slavery and hailed it as a
great literary achievement. Included among these was the prominent
black leader Frederick Douglass, who unashamedly appropriated sections of the novel in his own high-profile speeches and much-publi-
cized writings.[20] At the same time, the novel caused a storm of
controversy, particularly among Southerners who objected to the high-
handed moralizing which they felt it contained. The work was critically
reviewed by a number of prominent newspapers and journals of the day
who felt that the characterization was unrealistic, the plot implausible
and overly sentimental, and the description of slavery harsh and misleading. Many Southerners were outraged by Stowe's work and considered it a scandalously inaccurate presentation of the institution of

20. See Levine (1992) and Banks (1993) for more on this.

slavery. One of the most outspoken critics was George F. Holmes, whose review of the novel in the pro-slavery *Southern Literary Messenger* was published on 18 October 1852.[21] Holmes's critique slides into sexist sarcasm, as he not only exhorts the devoutly religious Stowe to abide by the scriptural injunction about women not usurping the authority of men and maintaining silence (1 Tim. 2.13), but accuses her of deliberately lying and closes his article with a quotation from Exodus 20 about bearing false witness against one's neighbour.[22] Stowe countered criticism such as this with a follow-up book entitled *The Key to Uncle Tom's Cabin* (1853) wherein she sought to document her story with background documents, letters, testimonies of former slaves, and so on.[23] A number of fictional spin-offs were quickly produced by writers from both the North and the South, which sought to refute the assertions of *Uncle Tom's Cabin* about the injustice of slavery and preserve the union of the nation which Stowe's book threatened to undermine.[24] In short, the appearance of *Uncle Tom's Cabin* was certainly a publishing phenomenon the like of which the world has rarely since seen. What do we know about its author, and how important is this in understanding the public reaction to the work?

Harriet Beecher Stowe (1811–96) was born on 12 June in Litchfield, Connecticut. She was the seventh of what were to be 13 children within the household of her father Lyman Beecher (her mother Roxanna died

21. See Holmes (1994). Gossett (1985: 164-211) provides an overview of some of the critical reviews of Stowe's novel.

22. Another good example is William Gilmore Simms, a prolific and influential writer from Charleston, South Carolina, who even went so far as to write a fictional reply to *Uncle Tom's Cabin* which was entitled *Woodcraft* (1852). For more on his assessment of Stowe's novel, see Duvall (1958–59); Ridgely (1959–60); and Watson (1976–77).

23. From this and other sources it is now known that the major inspiration for the character of Uncle Tom was a slave from Maryland named Josiah Henson. For more on his story, see Nichols (1954); Henson (1994); Stowe (1994). Richman (1997) discusses what remains of the actual plantation site upon which Henson lived. Hovet (1979–80) suggests a woman slave who may have helped contribute to Stowe's characterization of Uncle Tom. The characterization of George and Eliza Harris is almost certainly based upon the figures of Henry and Malinda Bibb, as Stepto (1986) argues. Also see, Canady (1973) and Brandstadter (1974) for discussions of earlier literary precursors to Stowe's work.

24. Tandy (1922: 41-58, 170-78); Hayne (1968); Gardiner (1978); Hirsch (1978); Yarborough (1986); Roberts (1994: 55-76); and Gossett (1994) provide some details.

in 1816 when Harriet was only five years old and her father quickly remarried). She came from a family whose service to the Christian church is now the stuff of legend. Her father was a well-known Presbyterian minister, as were her seven brothers, one of whom was Henry Ward Beecher, perhaps the most famous preacher of his day. In addition, Harriet was married to an ordained clergyman, Calvin Stowe, who at the time when she began writing *Uncle Tom's Cabin* was a teacher of biblical languages at the Lane Theological Seminary in Cincinnati, Ohio (where Harriet's father was President). At the time, Cincinnati was a thriving city with some 300,000 inhabitants, one of the fastest growing cities in the country (by 1850 it was the sixth largest city in the nation). In March 1851 Calvin Stowe went on to accept a post as professor of Ancient Languages at Bowdoin College in Brunswick, Maine, at a rather paltry salary of $1000 per annum, an appointment which meant that Harriet was relieved of the pressures of helping to support the family financially by means of her writing. Religious conventions of the day prohibited Harriet from becoming a minister, but as her biographer Joan D. Hedrick (1988: 307) puts it: 'Like many another nineteenth-century woman, she turned to writing and used her pen as her pulpit'.

She was probably most influenced by her oldest sister Catharine, one of the most important figures in the movement to establish schools for women and an influential personality for others who would become active in feminist causes (Catharine was the driving force in the establishment of the Hartford Female Seminary, one of the first such institutions to be founded in the United States). The line separating Stowe's interest in the abolitionist movement and her interest in the women's movement is exceedingly thin, although she probably would not have described herself as a feminist.[25] Nevertheless, she was an active participant in the political debates about the role and legal status of women and in the writing of her masterpiece was inspired by many feminists of the day, including the black activist Sojourner Truth (1797–1883) and the radical abolitionist sisters Sarah Grimké (1792–1873) and Angelina Grimké (1805–79) (Lebedun 1974–75; Yellin 1986). *Uncle Tom's Cabin* quickly became a focal point for debate about the rising tide of feminism in the mid-1800s as more and more women writers entered the world of published authors. Many of the debates about the place of

25. See Sundquist (1986); Sánchez-Eppler (1988); and Romero (1989) on this point.

Uncle Tom's Cabin as a worthy example of American literature have continued well into the present century, especially given that the so-called 'literary canon' was largely determined by men, and almost exclusively consisted of works written by men (Baym 1981).[26] As a result, *Uncle Tom's Cabin* has long been at the centre of a debate about the nature of 'classic' American literature, and the continuing success of the novel is something which continues to confound many literary critics of the modernist school. Such critics point out its artistic shortcomings as well as its tendency to collapse into sentimentalism, particularly with respect to the portrayal of the deaths of two central characters, Little Eva and Uncle Tom.[27] The portrayal of the death of Little Eva as a victory (Stowe calls it 'the crown without the conflict' [*UTC* 27.429]) is especially contentious, given the fact that her death is theologically presented as an extension of the death of Jesus Christ himself. However, there remains some difficulty in making a straightforward connection between Eva's death and that of Jesus Christ. In the insightful words of Elisabeth Bronfen (1992: 90-91):

> Of course the question remains open whether her death is too fundamentally decorative to be morally effective, whether it is morally effective as a citation of its culture's central myth—the story of the crucifixion—or whether it fails to lead to concrete political action because the fact of death can never fully be denied and so a general helplessness underlies any call for action induced by death.[28]

In any event, *Uncle Tom's Cabin* remains the subject of critical assessments, many of which focus on the racism inherent within the book. Thus, James Baldwin (1994: 498) charges that the Negro characters of Stowe's novel are 'as white as she can make them' and contends that the central figure of Uncle Tom is the only black man in the book and that he 'has been robbed of his humanity and divested of his sex'.[29] While some have sought to defend, or at least understand, Stowe's

---

26. Sundquist (1986: 1-7) also discusses this.

27. See Tompkins (1994); Joswick (1984); Fluck (1992); and White (1994). Stories relating the death of a little child formed a popular literary genre within fiction of the day, as Smith (1997) shows.

28. Also see Douglas (1977: 1-12).

29. Baldwin's caustic comments are often cited, but they have themselves been the subject of criticism. See Strout (1968); Gossett (1985: 388-90); and Meyer (1994).

views on racial matters,[30] others have lamented that the characterization of Uncle Tom as a passive slave who is resigned to his fate has severely harmed the movement toward racial equality.[31] Stowe is also frequently charged with political naivete, particularly in connection with the colonization movement, that is, the setting up of an African state for freed slaves. Stowe shows little awareness, or indeed any interest in, the diversity of African culture and appears to assume that all freed slaves would want to live in the utopian paradise of Liberia.[32] The fact that *Uncle Tom's Cabin* seems to conclude with a vision of a Christianized Africa is frequently cited as further evidence of Harriet Beecher Stowe's religious and elitist ideas which were out of touch with reality.

However, we should not think that the idea of a novel about the injustices and the human tragedy implicit within the slave system is to be rejected outright simply because Harriet Beecher Stowe reflects some of the prejudices of her time. Nor should we assume that the inspiration for *Uncle Tom's Cabin* came upon her only in mid-life as she became more and more involved with the emerging abolitionist and feminist movements. There is ample evidence to suggest that a concern for those caught up in the tragedy of slavery preoccupied Harriet's mind for much of her life. As a young girl of 12 or 13 she wrote a short story entitled *Cleon* which was set in the days of the Emperor Nero. The title character is a wealthy Greek lord who embraces Christianity and finds that his decision brings him into conflict with the Emperor. Nero has him tortured and executed, but not before Cleon professes his faith in Christ and prays for the salvation of the Emperor, as well as offering forgiveness to his torturers.[33] The story-line clearly anticipates much that is within *Uncle Tom's Cabin*.

Moreover, other personal factors also had an important bearing on the production of the novel which was to rocket Harriet Beecher Stowe on to the national political scene and make her a household name. Several of these factors are worth noting in passing, including a personal

30. Hudson (1963); Levy (1970); Cassara (1973); Graham (1973); Gossett (1985: 64-86); Yarborough (1986); Riss (1994); Ducksworth (1994); Meyer (1994); Nuernberg (1994) and Donovan (1995) discuss this controversial topic.

31. Notably, Furnas (1956: 8-10), whose rather caustic work is often cited. Also see Chaput (1964); Gossett (1985: 388-96); and Yarborough (1986).

32. McPherson (1965) discusses how controversial this subject was in the period immediately following the publication of *Uncle Tom's Cabin*.

33. Grinstein (1983: 123) discusses this.

tragedy in her life, a legislative enactment by Congress and her abiding personal commitment to the Christian faith. Let us take each of these in turn. First, we note that in July 1849 Harriet's 18-month-old baby son Charley died during a cholera epidemic; this tragedy gave Stowe a sense of compassion which was to bear fruit within *Uncle Tom's Cabin*. As she wrote to a correspondent from London, a woman named Eliza Cabot Follen who had inquired about the circumstances surrounding the writing of the novel,

> It was at his dying bed and at his grave that I learnt what a poor slave mother may feel when her child is torn from her… I have often felt that much that is in that book had its root in the awful scenes and bitter sorrows of that summer. It has left now, I trust, no trace on my mind, except a deep compassion for the sorrowful, especially for mothers who are separated from their children.[34]

It is no wonder that tensions between the social and moral dimensions of society are skilfully exposed within *Uncle Tom's Cabin* and the family is presented as the only means of healing such tensions. In this regard Stowe castigates slavery as an evil, primarily because it destroys families and separates mothers from their children. Her own loss sensitized her to the plight of others.

Second, the immediate political backdrop for the writing of *Uncle Tom's Cabin* was the government's passing of the Fugitive Slave Act in September 1850, a law which required that all citizens, whether they were Northerners or Southerners, turn in runaway slaves. Effectively this made all Americans, regardless of their stance on abolition, complicit in 'the peculiar institution' of slavery. Cincinnati, the city in which Stowe lived for 18 years from 1832 to 1850 and in which the ideas for *Uncle Tom's Cabin* took shape, was a flash-point for the abolitionist movement, being strategically located on the Ohio River, a boundary between the 'free' North and the 'slave' South.[35] In a letter dated 6 January 1853 to Anthony Ashley Cooper, the seventh Earl of Shaftesbury (1801–85), Stowe stated that one of her primary aims in writing the novel was to 'awaken conscience in the slaveholding States

---

34. The text of the letter is given in Stowe (1889: 197-204). It is dated 16 February 1853 and was written from Andover, Massachusetts. White (1987) provides some additional primary source material about how women slaves were treated. Also see Hedrick (1994: 192-93).

35. Middleton (1987) provides some historical background. Also see Hedrick (1994: 102-109, 202-204).

and lead to emancipation' (Stowe 1889: 172). Meanwhile, she claimed that the immediate inspiration for the novel came to her in 1851 during a communion service at the First Parish Church in Brunswick when she had the vision of a death scene of a Negro slave (the vision was later transformed within the novel into Uncle Tom's death at the hands of Simon Legree).[36]

Third, we must consider the importance of Stowe's own religious commitments within any assessment of the drive to produce the novel. So convinced was Stowe of the hand of providence in *Uncle Tom's Cabin* that later in life she downplayed her role in the production of the novel, describing it as having been 'written by God'.[37] The novel's sub-title was 'Life among the Lowly', and in this we see something of Stowe's intentions within the book. Clearly the passage from Mt. 25.31-46 in which Jesus is said to identify with the downtrodden and the outcast peoples of society is in mind here (the passage is alluded to at several points within the story). James H. Smylie (1973: 72) comments on the importance of the text from Matthew: 'The passage is a hermeneutical key to the novel, and the novel is a commentary on the passage'.

In many ways Harriet Beecher Stowe's religious faith is perfectly in line with the evangelicalism of the mid-nineteenth century (Kimball 1982). She saw personal conversion to Christ as a necessary precondition for bringing about any social, political and economic changes within society. Thus, Stowe's religious heritage serves her well as the tradition of Puritan typology is brought into service within her writing. In this sense, the novel is a re-enactment of the biblical drama of redemption, with the liberation of the people from Egypt being recast as the liberation of Negroes from slavery,[38] and the vicarious death of Jesus Christ being recast in such noble acts as the self-sacrifice of Little Eva and the martyrdom of Uncle Tom.[39] Throughout the novel it is the

36. Hedrick (1994: 155-56) mentions this incident in passing.

37. Wilson (1942: 294-95); Wilson (1962: 32-4); Crozier (1969: 3-33); Gossett (1985: 93-97); and Kazin (1997: 74-85) all discuss this.

38. Hedrick (1994: 214-17) notes how the crossing of the Ohio river is equated with the Old Testament stories of the Israelites crossing the Jordan river to enter the promised land. Also see Lowance (1994) on the use of this Old Testament typology.

39. Szczesiul (1996) suggests that Stowe may have been more ecumenical in her understanding about the Christian faith than is sometimes appreciated. He suggests that the death of her infant son Charley in 1849 left Stowe open to Catholic

injustices of the institution of slavery which are being addressed and the reader is exhorted to examine his or her own conscience against the truth of the coming kingdom of God.

But what *is* the proper Christian response to that institution? In what sense is the Christian message about the liberation of slavery to be brought about within the lives of believers? It is in exploring these kinds of questions that *Uncle Tom's Cabin* shows a remarkable similarity to the explorations of 1 Cor. 7.20-24 and 1 Corinthians 9 which we noted above. All of these texts are concerned with some of the practical issues raised by the emancipation of slaves, the effects that such a move would have not only in the church but in the society at large, and the implications for future master–slave relationships within the life of the church at Corinth.

3. *Slavery and Liberation in* Uncle Tom's Cabin: *Various Responses to Emancipation*

For all her political activism, Stowe was quite conservative when it came to her understanding of the place of the family within society. Within her written work she stressed the role of the wife and mother within the home, effectively defining domesticity as *the* personification of Christian virtue.[40] The characterization of the central figure Uncle Tom himself can even be read in this light, as many feminist critics have demonstrated. Such readings of the novel tend to stress the connection between Stowe's feminism and her presentation of Uncle Tom

traditions about the intercession of the departed. He further suggests that the portrayal of Uncle Tom and Eva within the novel reflects aspects of Catholicism, particularly as both characters are put forward as people who are venerated for their self-sacrifice. Also see Ammons (1986: 163-70) for more on the portrayal of Eva and Uncle Tom as Christ-figures.

40. The matter of Stowe's feminism and her vision of domesticity has been the subject of much recent research and remains the most discussed topic within criticism of *Uncle Tom's Cabin*. See Welter (1966); Douglas (1977: 3-5, 244-56); Fiedler (1982: 168-78); Crumpacker (1982); Brown (1984); Railton (1984); Fisher (1985: 87-127); Lang (1986; 1987: 161-92); Jehlen (1989); Korg (1990); Jenkins (1992); Wardley (1992); Tompkins (1994); Shaw (1994); Roberson (1994); and Wolff (1995). Smith-Rosenberg (1977) provides some useful background material. Stowe's novel has also been assessed from the standpoint of Freudian psychology, particularly as an illustration of Oedipal theory. For a helpful introduction to this, see Van Buren (1986).

as a figure who embodies the self-sacrifice of Christianity, a man who does not resort to violence and revenge, but endures all that is placed upon him with gentleness and meekness, prompting descriptions of him as a figure of maternalistic forbearance. Stowe's 'feminization' of Uncle Tom is one of the most frequent assertions within criticism of *Uncle Tom's Cabin*,[41] and arises, in part, as a result of Stowe's presentation of slavery as 'the *patriarchal* institution', the only cure for which is outright abolition as brought about through the agency of conscience-driven women.[42] Yet even here there is some room for diversity of interpretation, since Tom can also be read as the supreme example of patriarchy within the novel (Leverenz 1989: 171-204; Zwarg 1994). In short, the genius of Stowe's novel is the way in which such weighty matters as a devoutly Christian faith and a commitment to abolitionist politics are set against a backdrop of traditional domestic arrangements in which women took precedence.

At the same time, such a balancing act means that many of the interpretative questions raised within 1 Cor. 7.20-24 and, to a lesser extent, 1 Corinthians 9 are again placed in sharp relief. Should slaves acquiesce and accept their slavery as a matter of course, or should emancipation from slavery be something which is actively sought? To what extent is it legitimate for slaves to live within the bounds of their slavery yet harbour passive resistance against it as an institution? These remain the kinds of questions delicately posed within the novel, and Stowe offers what are, in effect, two possible solutions to them. Gillian Brown (1984: 515) addresses the problem when she says:

> Domestic conventions in Stowe's abolitionism work in two directions, simultaneously pointing to the sentimental solution of the afterlife in heaven and to a radical plan of immediate action to secure better temporal conditions. Tom and Eva die in set pieces that memorialize their Christian virtues; Eliza, Harry, George, and Cassy rebel and escape to Canada in a dramatic and often melodramatic narrative that affirms the necessity of active protest.

Before we move to consider further how Stowe juxtaposes the two approaches to the question of slavery (which we might term 'active

41. Ammons (1977–78) offers a good summary discussion of the point.

42. For more on the term 'patriarchy', see Duvall (1963). In discussing the challenge that Harriet Stowe's effort represented to the status quo, Duvall (1984: 141) says that *Uncle Tom's Cabin* 'reflects a kind of Mason-Dixon line between the sexes'. Also see Hovet (1981) and Kisthardt (1994).

protest' and 'passive resistance') within the story-line, it is worth noting how the structure of the novel itself is designed to facilitate their contrast. In this respect Stowe proves herself to be an extremely clever writer who makes use of the writing conventions of the day and turns them to good effect within her story.

Not surprisingly, *Uncle Tom's Cabin* has been explored from the standpoint of its use of accepted literary patterns, including the employment of Gothic categories within the story-line.[43] A complex colour scheme is also in evidence within the novel as people are classed as blacks and whites, or varying mixtures of these two opposing categories (mulattos, quadroons, etc.), with their respective fates played out accordingly. In addition, the novel contains a number of interesting uses of geographical metaphors which help to give structure to the narrative.[44] The most obvious use of a geographical metaphor in *Uncle Tom's Cabin* concerns the directional points on a compass; the freedom of the states of the *North* is contrasted with the slavery practices in the states of the *South*. In this connection to be sold 'down river' means to travel south along the Mississippi river toward New Orleans in Louisiana and thereby enter, stage by stage, deeper and deeper into the cruelty that was slavery. Going 'down river' is a veritable descent into the hell of slavery; slaves sold 'down river' embark on a journey from which they almost never return.

The result is that a deliberate pattern is presented within the novel in which geographical descent is equated with moral depravity, and geographical ascent is equated with freedom and the realization of personhood. This is clearly seen in the carefully crafted juxtaposition of the lives of the two men whose struggle with slavery is at the centre of the narrative within the novel, namely George Harris and Uncle Tom. The differing responses of these two characters has received the lion's share of the critical discussion, although there are other figures who deserve attention as well. For example, we need to consider instances

43. The Gothic undercurrents of this rich mythology are explored in Fiedler (1966: 262-65); Gilbert and Gubar (1979: 533-35); Halttunen (1986); Roberts (1994: 23-54); and Hedrick (1994: 213).

44. Showalter (1991: 153-55) makes a rather bizarre attempt to argue that structurally *Uncle Tom's Cabin* is a 'metanarrative marker' of a particular quilting pattern known as the 'Log Cabin Quilt'. Showalter suggests that Stowe stitches her novel together in such a way that suggests conformity to this basic sewing pattern. Surely this is taking the idea of domesticity in Stowe's work a stage too far!

wherein emancipation of slaves is offered by the slave owners but not taken up by the slaves themselves, as a further illustration of the complexities involved in master–slave relations and a factor in establishing the pros and cons of emancipation. There are two instances in *Uncle Tom's Cabin* in which slaves choose *not* to accept their emancipation and voluntarily continue their lives as slaves in service to their masters. The first concerns a slave named Scipio, who was owned by Augustine St Clare and whose story is related in a brief flashback scene in '19: Miss Ophelia's Experiences and Opinions Continued'; the second concerns the slaves on the Shelby plantation who are offered their freedom by George Shelby at the end of the novel in '44: The Liberator'.

It is on the differing reactions which these various characters exhibit to their enslavement that I shall next concentrate my attention. I shall begin with the juxtaposition of the central figures George Harris and Uncle Tom before I move to consider the often-overlooked episode involving the slave Scipio, and its counterpart involving slaves of the idealistic George Shelby.

As *Uncle Tom's Cabin* opens we find the fates of George Harris and Uncle Tom intertwined on the Shelby plantation in the 'mild' slave state of Kentucky. Their destinies take radically different directions, however, and they quickly come to represent two opposing reactions to the slavery which entraps them and threatens to destroy both men and their families. Hard times have fallen on the Shelby plantation and Mr Shelby is forced to sell some of his slaves to pay off some debts; the two are Uncle Tom and George Harris's young son Harry. George Harris is owned by another master and works on a neighbouring plantation, but his wife Eliza and their son Harry are part of the Shelby household. Eliza hears of the decision to sell their little Harry and she determines to run away with him before the boy can taken from her. As the story unfolds the volatile George Harris decides to run away towards Canada, refusing to face the humiliation and abuse meted out to him by his cruel master. Meanwhile, Eliza and Harry make their escape across the frozen Ohio river into the free state of Ohio with a view to joining George in Canada (they meet in a Quaker community in Ohio and eventually make it to Canada). On the other hand, Uncle Tom is sold to the slave-trader Mr Haley and is taken further and further south to Louisiana, into the very heart of the inferno of slavery itself. There he has two masters, Augustine St Clare and Simon Legree, each of whom, in turn, buys him and puts him to work on the home plantation. Uncle Tom, however, does not survive the transition to the South, at least not physically. In short, a richly textured geographical motif is used by Stowe to convey what is at heart a *spiritual* journey, particularly for Tom as he enters into the area of the *Red* River—it is red as a symbol of hell and it is red as an emblem of Tom's life-blood.[45]

a. *George Harris: The Active Revolutionary*

To what extent did Harriet Beecher Stowe accept the use of violence as a legitimate means of abolishing slavery?[46] This is a fascinating question, one which has engendered differing responses. Interestingly, following the publication of *Uncle Tom's Cabin* in 1852, Stowe turned to expound the violent approach to the abolition of slavery in her novel *Dred* based on the slave uprising led by Nat Turner in Southampton County, Virginia in 1831 (Hedrick 1994: 258-59). This, her second anti-slavery novel which was published in 1856, gives greater weight to the question of the so-called 'natural rights argument' against slavery and shows Stowe demonstrating her awareness that domestic sentimentality has important legal implications which must be worked out politically. In effect, Stowe shows herself to be in the tradition of such figures as John Locke and Thomas Jefferson when it comes to matters of the individual's right to challenge the law of the land. This raises important questions about obedience to unjust or immoral laws of the state and invokes the principles of the American Constitution which speaks of the 'inalienable right of life, liberty and the pursuit of happiness'.[47] Hints of this engagement with political thought also appear in

45. Hovet (1979: 269) notes Stowe's use of a 'spiritual landscape' in her portrayal of the South. The geographical metaphor is even extended to include bodies of water which serve as boundaries separating one area from another; within the novel, bodies of water are key transitions of narrative which must be crossed despite the danger involved. Thus, the Ohio river is the boundary between the slave state of Kentucky and the free state of Ohio and Eliza's successful crossing of it by skipping and hopping across the ice floes, with her baby son Harry in her arms, is an important scene within the overall story-line. So, too, is George, Eliza and Harry's crossing of Lake Erie into the freedom of Canada, where the laws of the United States governing slavery have no jurisdiction over them.

46. The use of violence in the cause of abolition was a hotly contested issue. See Demos (1964).

47. This is a complex issue which has become something of a bone of contention among feminist interpreters of Stowe's work and those who challenge what are perceived to be the excesses of that interpretative movement. For more on the

Uncle Tom's Cabin, especially in connection with the decision by George Harris to break the law, run away from his master and claim his freedom as a birth right. In this sense, George Harris is certainly not content to follow Paul's advice 'to remain in the state in which he was called'. Indeed, he finds it offensive that it is suggested that he does so.

The only explicit reference to 1 Cor. 7.20-24 within the novel comes in '11: In Which Property Gets into an Improper State of Mind'; this occurs in the midst of a conversation between George Harris and Mr Wilson (a white businessman not unsympathetic to the plight of slaves) in which precisely these matters are discussed. Note, too, within the following excerpt the way in which Paul's advice to Philemon concerning the runaway slave Onesimus (Philemon 10-19) is worked into the discussion between the two men (*UTC* 11.183-84):

> 'Well, George, I s'pose you're running away—leaving your lawful master, George—(I don't wonder at it)—at the same time, I'm sorry, George—yes, decidedly—I think I must say that, George—it's my duty to tell you so.'
>
> 'Why are you sorry, sir?' said George, calmly.
>
> 'Why, to see you, as it were, setting yourself in opposition to the laws of your country.'
>
> '*My* country!' said George, with a strong and bitter emphasis; 'what country have I, but the grave,—and I wish to God that I was laid there!'
>
> 'Why, George, no—no—it won't do; this way of talking is wicked—unscriptural. George, you've got a hard master—in fact, he is—well he conducts himself reprehensibly—I can't pretend to defend him. But you know how the angel commanded Hagar to return to her mistress, and submit herself under the hand; and the apostle sent back Onesimus to his master.'
>
> 'Don't quote Bible at me that way, Mr. Wilson', said George, with a flashing eye, 'don't! for my wife is a Christian, and I mean to be, if ever I get to where I can; but to quote Bible to a fellow in my circumstances, is enough to make him give it up altogether. I appeal to God Almighty;—I'm willing to go with the case to Him, and ask Him if I do wrong to seek my freedom.'
>
> 'These feelings are quite natural, George', said the good-natured man, blowing his nose. 'Yes, they're natural, but it is my duty not to encourage 'em in you. Yes, my boy, I'm sorry for you, now; it's a bad case—very bad; but the apostle says, "Let everyone abide in the condition in which he is called". We must all submit to the indications of Providence, George,—don't you see?'

matter, see Cox (1984); Sundquist (1985); Camfield (1988); Whitney (1993); O'Connell (1994); and Crane (1996).

George stood with his head drawn back, his arms folded tightly over his broad breast, and a bitter smile curling his lips.

'I wonder, Mr. Wilson, if the Indians should come and take you a prisoner away from your wife and children, and want to keep you all your life hoeing corn for them, if you'd think it your duty to abide in the condition in which you were called. I rather think that you'd think the first stray horse you could find an indication of Providence—shouldn't you?'

In one important respect George Harris represents the highest point of moral argument against slavery contained within the novel, in so far as he gives voice to the abolition of slavery as a matter of principle, as an essential means of self-determination. As Thomas P. Joswick (1984: 269) puts it:

[George] is the one least bound by the conventions of either slavery or domestic influences ... [he] is the only one who takes questions about the rights of the individual and the obligations to authority beyond what is defined either by the slave laws or the ethics of right feeling in the novel's ideal community.[48]

Yet, we should not assume that George Harris is the only example of a slave who adopts a revolutionary stance to enslavement. There are other scattered figures who also take extreme measures in rebelling against their slave status. Perhaps the best example is the slave Cassy, the battered and abused mistress of Simon Legree whose whole life has been an up-and-down affair within the slave system. Significantly, at one point in the narrative ('34: The Quadroon's Story') she admits to having killed one of her children by forcing it to drink laudanum rather than allow it to grow up under slavery, a powerful image which has been given renewed circulation in the form of Nobel prize-winning authoress Toni Morrison (1987) whose slave character Sethe also commits infanticide.[49]

48. Joswick describes George Harris as 'the most troubling figure in the novel'. There is some evidence that Stowe was influenced by the Hungarian Revolution of 1848 in her portrayal of George Harris. See Van Hoy (1973) on this point.

49. There are many important parallels between Morrison's novel and Harriet Beecher Stowe's *Uncle Tom's Cabin*, not least of which is the fact that both stories have a connection with Cincinnati, a city on the borderlands of the 'free' North and the 'slave' South. There is also an interesting reaction within Morrison's novel to the work of Nathaniel Hawthorne, who was writing at exactly the same time as Stowe but much less directly about slavery as such. See Arac (1986); Yellin (1989: 75-97); Fleischner (1991: 96-106); Askeland (1992); Wiodat (1993); and Robbins

Yet in terms of the overall structure of the novel, it is clear that Uncle Tom is really the hero of the story in a way that the volatile revolutionary George Harris is not. The two characters are clearly juxtaposed and as such represent world views that are ultimately incompatible. As Richard Yarborough (1986: 253) puts it:

> [T]hey inhabit different worlds, parallel dimensions that never intersect. A full-blood Clark Kent and a mulatto Superman, they are never on the stage at the same time. One can imagine that, like matter and antimatter, if they were forced into contact, the result would be an explosion of immeasurable force that would leave only Tom, for he, not George, is Stowe's real hero.

b. *Uncle Tom: The Passive Christian Martyr*

The main story-line of the novel traces Uncle Tom's fate as he is sold from one slave-master to another. Tom's three slave-masters (Shelby, St Clare and Legree) represent three ways in which slavery treats slaves: the three men embody a kindly, but somewhat detached concern, a well-meaning but ultimately ineffective benevolence, and an outrightly destructive malevolence, respectively. Ironically, Uncle Tom's second master, Augustine St Clare, the father of Little Eva and the person to whom the slave is closest within the novel, is the harshest critic of the system of slavery within the novel. At one point he even offers an economic assessment of slavery which is suggestive of the Marxist critique of capitalism. St Clare argues that workers are exploited by the Southern institution of slavery, just as they are by the Northern wage system (Gossett 1985: 139-41). Yet, despite this criticism of slavery, St Clare is caught up in the midst of it and does not see a way to extract himself from it. Ultimately his inability to do so is fatal to Uncle Tom. If Augustine St Clare can be described as a well-intentioned man whose actions are in the end ineffective, Uncle Tom can be described as someone who appears to accept whatever comes, all the while keeping his eyes firmly fixed on his risen Saviour, and assessing

---

(1997) for more on the connection between the three writers. For additional material on Morrison's *Beloved* as a re-conceptualization of American history through the experiences of African American slaves, see Lange (1983); Thurman (1987); Crouch (1987); Fields (1989); Horvitz (1989); Otten (1989: 81-98); Ferguson (1991); Henderson (1991); Scarpa (1991–92); Krumholz (1992); Rushdy (1992); Keenan (1993); Malmgren (1995); Rody (1995); Weinstein (1996: 66-74); Corey (1997); Hogan (1997); and Parrish (1997).

everything on the basis of his Christian beliefs about the rewards of the heavenly life. In this sense, Uncle Tom is presented as someone who has taken the declaration of Paul recorded in Phil. 4.11 to heart. Thus in '22: "The Grass Withereth—the Flower Fadeth"', we have this interesting paragraph offered as part of the description of Uncle Tom's adjustment to life on the St Clare plantation. Tom's love of Scripture comes through:

> Tom read, in his only literary cabinet, of one who had 'learned in what-soever state he was, therewith to be content'. It seemed to him good and reasonable doctrine, and accorded well with the settled and thoughtful habit which he had acquired from the reading of that same book (*UTC* 22.378).

Needless to say, such a response to slavery is in stark contrast with that of the hot-headed George Harris. What effect does the central juxtaposition of George Harris and Uncle Tom as representing two opposing ways of dealing with slavery have in the novel overall? Is the fact that the rebellion of George Harris comes *before* Uncle Tom's passive resistance significant? Some critics of *Uncle Tom's Cabin* have argued that this is indeed the case. Thus, Elizabeth Ammons suggests (1977–78: 171) that Stowe structures the novel in such a way as to associate Tom more firmly with female characters and present his passivity as a Christian alternative to the violent approach adopted by Harris. There is much to be said for such an assessment of Stowe's work.

Uncle Tom is commonly regarded by critics of Stowe's work as something of a Christ-figure, with many parallels being identified between his life and the life of Jesus of Nazareth, who also undergoes suffering on behalf of others.[50] Even the Lord's temptation in Gethsemane has a parallel, namely the trial Tom undergoes on Legree's plantation in which he is tempted to rebel against the wicked slave-master (Brown 1969: 1334). Yet it is important to note that while Tom does not rebel, he never ceases to desire his freedom and is even made to speak of it three times within the novel. A good example of this occurs in the midst of a conversation between Augustine St Clare and Uncle Tom. St Clare decides that it is time for the deathbed request of Little Eva to be put into motion; she had specifically asked that Uncle Tom be set free. In '28: Reunion' we read:

---

50. Steele (1972) and Lowance (1994) are cases in point.

'Well, Tom', said St. Clare, the day after he had commenced the legal formalities for his enfranchisement, 'I'm going to make a free man of you;—so have your trunk packed, and get ready to set out for Kentuck.'

The sudden light of joy that shone in Tom's face as he raised his hands to heaven, his emphatic 'Bless the Lord!' rather discomposed St. Clare; he did not like it that Tom should be so ready to leave him.

'You haven't had such very bad times here, that you need be in such a rapture, Tom', he said drily.

'No, no, Mas'r! 'tan't that,—it's bein' a *freeman*! that's what I'm joyin' for.'

'Why, Tom, don't you think, for your own part, you've been better off than to be free?'

'*No, indeed*, Mas'r St. Clare', said Tom, with a flash of energy. 'No, indeed!'

'Why, Tom, you couldn't possibly have earned, by your work, such clothes and such living as I have given you.'

'Knows all that, Mas'r St. Clare; Mas'r's been too good; but, Mas'r, I'd rather have poor clothes, poor house, poor everything, and have 'em *mine*, than have the best, and have 'em any man's else,—I had *so*, Mas'r; I think it's natur, Mas'r.'

'I suppose so, Tom, and you'll be going off and leaving me, in a month or so', he added, rather discontentedly. 'Though why you shouldn't, no mortal knows', he said, in a gayer tone; and, getting up, he began to walk the floor.

'Not while Mas'r is in trouble', said Tom. 'I'll stay with Mas'r as long as he wants me,—so as I can be any use.'

'Not while I'm in trouble, Tom?" said St. Clare, looking sadly out of the window… 'And when will *my* trouble be over?'

'When Mas'r St Clare's a Christian', said Tom.

'And you really mean to stay by till that day comes?' said St Clare, half smiling, as he turned from the window, and laid his hand on Tom's shoulder. 'Ah, Tom, you soft, silly boy! I won't keep you till that day. Go home to your wife and children, and give my love to all' (*UTC* 28.441-42).

What is significant about this particular exchange is the way in which Uncle Tom's own desire to be out from under the yoke of slavery is certainly voiced, but it is overruled by an even deeper concern on the part of the slave—a desire to fulfil his Christian commitment of helping to evangelize his master St Clare.

Most critics of *Uncle Tom's Cabin* agree that one of its coordinating motifs is the faith of Uncle Tom himself. Despite all of the trials and tribulations that the man endures he holds fast to his belief in the Bible and his Christian faith (Anderson 1991). While in the clutches of the evil Simon Legree, he refuses to betray his fellow slaves Cassy and Emmeline, or deny his commitment to Jesus Christ, even when it is clear that this conduct will probably cost him his life. Indeed, at several key points within the novel Uncle Tom declares that he is willing to sacrifice his own life in order that his slave-master might come to faith in Christ. Such a declaration is made to Augustine St Clare following the death of Eva, as the two men read the Bible together and discuss the theological implications of her death. Thus in '27: 'This is the Last of Earth', Uncle Tom says: 'I's willin' to lay down my life, this blessed day, to see Mas'r a Christian' (*UTC* 27.436). A similar declaration is made to Simon Legree in the face of his threat to kill Uncle Tom unless he reveals what he knows concerning the whereabouts of Cassy and Emmeline. In '40: The Martyr' we read:

> Tom looked up to his master, and answered, 'Mas'r, if you was sick, or in trouble, or dying, and I could save ye, I'd *give* ye my heart's blood; and, if taking every drop of blood in this poor old body would save your precious soul, I'd give 'em freely, as the Lord gave his for me. O, Mas'r! don't bring this great sin on your soul! It will hurt you more than 't will me! Do the worst you can, my troubles'll be over soon; but, if ye don't repent, yours won't *never* end!' (*UTC* 40.582-83).

In summary, the characters of George Harris and Uncle Tom are used in such a way as to highlight the intertwining of political and spiritual concerns, as well as a means of contrasting the ultimate fate of two very different men whose responses to slavery are just as different. As Lisa Watt MacFarlane (1990: 137) perceptively comments:

> George Harris' quest for political autonomy as he travels towards the Canadian border reverses Tom's pilgrimage towards spiritual completion as he descends into the swamplands of the Red River. But although George and Tom succeed in achieving the freedoms they seek, neither example resolves the spiritual and political oppression of the slave system.[51]

It appears that Stowe has to turn to another character to provide the way forward in resolving the oppression of the slave system—the

---

51. Similarly, Fiedler (1964: 125-26) says: 'There is a curious pessimism in Mrs. Stowe; for though her book may have provided an ideology for abolitionism, it does not really foresee such a solution, but closes just short of any happy ending, even the rescue of Uncle Tom by the white boy who loved him. For her, love comes too late, here on earth at least; and the reconciliation of black and white must be remanded to heaven.'

radical George Shelby, whose solution to the problem of slave owner-
ship she relates in the provocatively entitled penultimate chapter of the
book, 'The Liberator'. George Harris's way of handling the question of
slavery does have an echo earlier in the novel, namely the short episode
involving the slave Scipio. I turn now to examine the responses that
these two characters provide to the perplexing question of freedom
from slavery.

c. *The Slave Scipio and the Slave-Master George Shelby: Models of Christian Behaviour*

The short little story about the slave Scipio in '19: Miss Ophelia's
Experiences and Opinions Continued' is rarely discussed within the
critical literature (and does not appear in either of the films discussed
below).[52] Yet the passage is an excellent means of exploring some of
the various dynamics that the emancipation of a slave may have
entailed; in this sense it provides a helpful starting-point for a comparison with Paul's advice in 1 Cor. 7.20-24. So does the story of George
Shelby's treatment of his slaves in '44: The Liberator' following the
death of Uncle Tom. Taken together these two incidents provide us
with narrative pictures of how Stowe felt Christian slaves and masters
could relate to one another, and invite us to consider how much such a
vision was dependent upon Paul's teaching on such things.

We enter the story of Scipio as Augustine St. Clare explains to his
wife Marie and his cousin Ophelia about the limitations of corporal
punishment as a means of disciplining slaves. St. Clare tells of how he
came to know Scipio through his brother Alfred, who once owned the
slave:

> 'I broke a fellow in, once', said St. Clare, 'that all the overseers and
> masters had tried their hands on in vain.'
>
> 'You!' said Marie; 'well, I'd be glad to know when *you* ever did any-
> thing of the sort.'
>
> 'Well, he was a powerful, gigantic fellow,—a native-born African;
> and he appeared to have the rude instinct of freedom in him to an
> uncommon degree. He was a regular African lion. They called him
> Scipio. Nobody could do anything with him; and he was sold round from
> overseer to overseer, till at last Alfred bought him, because he thought
> he could manage him. Well, one day he knocked down the overseer, and

---

52. Joswick (1984: 264) and Brodhead (1988: 83-84) contain brief discussions
of the episode.

was fairly off into the swamps. I was on a visit to Alf's plantation, for it was after we had dissolved partnership. Alfred was greatly exasperated; but I told him that it was his own fault, and laid him any wager that I could break the man; and finally it was agreed that, if I caught him, I should have him to experiment on. So they mustered out a party of some six or seven, with guns and dogs, for the hunt. People, you know, can get up as much enthusiasm in hunting a man as a deer, if it is only customary; in fact, I got a little excited myself, though I had only put in as a sort of mediator, in case he was caught.

'Well, the dogs bayed and howled, and we rode and scampered, and finally we started him. He ran and bounded like a buck, and kept us well in the rear for some time; but at last he got caught in an impenetrable thicket of cane; then he turned to bay, and I tell you he fought the dogs right gallantly. He dashed them to right and left, and actually killed three of them with only his naked fists, when a shot from a gun brought him down, and he fell, wounded and bleeding, almost at my feet. The poor fellow looked up at me with manhood and despair both in his eye. I kept back the dogs and the party, as they came pressing up, and claimed him as my prisoner. It was all I could do to keep them from shooting him, in the flush of success; but I persisted in my bargain, and Alfred sold him to me. Well, I took him in hand, and in one fortnight I had him tamed down as submissive and tractable as heart could desire.'

'What in the world did you do to him?' said Marie.

'Well, it was quite a simple process. I took him to my own room, had a good bed made for him, dressed his wounds, and tended him myself, until he got fairly on his feet again. And, in process of time, I had free papers made out for him, and told him he might go where he liked.'

'And did he go?' said Miss Ophelia.

'No. The foolish fellow tore the paper in two, and absolutely refused to leave me. I never had a braver, better fellow,—trusty and true as steel. He embraced Christianity afterwards, and became as gentle as a child. He used to oversee my place on the lake, and did it capitally, too. I lost him the first cholera season. In fact, he laid down his life for me. For I was sick, almost to death; and when, through the panic, everybody else fled, Scipio worked for me like a giant, and actually brought me back into life again. But, poor fellow! he was taken, right after, and there was no saving him. I never felt anybody's loss more.'

Eva had come gradually nearer and nearer to her father, as he told the story,—her small lips apart, her eyes wide and earnest with absorbing interest.

As he finished, she suddenly threw her arms around his neck, burst into tears, and sobbed convulsively.

'Eva, dear child! what is the matter?' said St. Clare, as the child's small frame trembled and shook with the violence of her feelings. 'This child,' he added, 'ought not to hear any of this kind of thing,—she's nervous.'

'No, papa, I'm not nervous', said Eva, controlling herself, suddenly, with a strength of resolution singular in such a child. 'I'm not nervous, but these things *sink into my heart*' (*UTC* 19.345-47).

The story of Scipio is inspiring, particularly for Little Eva. Just as Scipio is willing to tear up his freedom papers in the hopes that he might save the life of his master, so too is Little Eva motivated to surrender her life if it would save the slaves of the St Clare plantation from further pain and anguish.[53]

The second example of slaves willing to forsake emancipation occurs toward the end of the novel. It describes Master George Shelby's attempt to set right some of the injustices that have been inflicted upon the slave families of the Shelby plantation which he inherits after the death of his father. The haunting death of Uncle Tom clearly hangs over the scene. In '44: The Liberator' we read:

> About a month after this, one morning, all the servants of the Shelby estate were convened together in the great hall that ran through the house, to hear a few words from their young master.
>
> To the surprise of all, he appeared among them with a bundle of papers in his hand, containing a certificate of freedom to every one on the place, which he read successively, and presented, amid the sobs and tears and shouts of all present.
>
> Many, however, pressed around him, earnestly begging him not to send them away; and, with anxious faces, tendering back their free papers.
>
> 'We don't want to be no freer than we are. We's allers had all we wanted. We don't want to leave de ole place, and Mas'r and Missis, and de rest!'
>
> 'My good friends', said George, as soon as he could get a silence, 'there'll be no need for you to leave me. The place wants as many hands to work it as it did before. We need the same about the house that we did before. But, you are now free men and free women. I shall pay you wages for your work, such as we shall agree on. The advantage is, that in case of my getting in debt, or dying,—things that might happen,—you cannot now be taken up and sold. I expect to carry on the estate, and to teach you what, perhaps, it will take you some time to learn,—how to use the rights I give you as free men and women. I expect you to be

---

53. See Joswick (1984: 264) for a comment about how this story is used as a basis for emphasizing the self-sacrifice that Little Eva is willing to make in order to end the misery of suffering that slavery brings.

good, and willing to learn; and I trust in God that I shall be faithful, and willing to teach. And now, my friends, look up, and thank God for the blessing of freedom' (*UTC* 44.616).

Here we see another instance in which slaves are depicted as rejecting their freedom. In this case their desire to remain slaves is not explicitly connected in any way with a Christian commitment on their part, as we saw was the case with Uncle Tom. However, the actions of the slave-owner George Shelby are certainly presented as those of a conscientious Christian. In the end, through the characters of Uncle Tom and George Shelby, Stowe presents us with powerfully drawn examples of how slaves and masters ought to act and fulfil their Christian callings. What is remarkable is the way in which Stowe's fictional story anticipates the interpretations of slavery offered by both S. Scott Bartchy and Dale B. Martin. Not only is the decision by Scipio and Uncle Tom about whether to choose freedom or to remain in slavery set against the backdrop of Christian calling, but the decision to follow Paul's example and become a 'slave to all' is reflected in the person of George Shelby (and through him, the rest of the slaves on the Shelby plantation), as the meaning of true slavery and emancipation is brought to a higher plain.

I turn now to consider how Stowe's *Uncle Tom's Cabin* has been handled within two recent film adaptations. As we shall see, the films offer intriguing interpretations of several of the novel's critical episodes which describe the difficulties that emancipation brings to the problem of slavery.

4. *Film Adaptations of* Uncle Tom's Cabin

Several dramatized versions of *Uncle Tom's Cabin* were produced immediately after the publication of the novel and did much in helping to make it the publishing phenomenon that it was, promoting sales by increasing public awareness (Furnas 1956: 259-84; Gossett 1985: 260-83, 367-87; Henderson 1994). The first theatrical version of the novel was produced by Charles Western Taylor and premiered at the National Theatre in New York City on 23 August 1852. It was effectively an adapted minstrel show with a happy ending (here Tom returns to his cabin rather than dying at the hands of Sambo and Quimbo, the death-dealing instruments of the wicked Simon Legree). Several other adaptations of Stowe's novel appeared in the years 1852–60, including one by the master showman P.T. Barnum. However, by far the most influential and long-running of the theatrical versions of *Uncle Tom's Cabin* was that written by George Aiken, a 22-year-old abolitionist from Boston, for the theatre company managed by his cousin George C. Howard (this version is sometimes known as the Aiken–Howard production). The play contained an unprecedented six acts, eight tableaux and thirty scenes, and starred Cordelia Howard (the four-year-old daughter of George C. Howard) as Little Eva.[54] It opened at a theatre in Troy, New York, on 15 November 1852.[55]

Other theatrical versions appeared around the nation and on the international scene, often with their own particular slant in relating the story. For example, the British versions tended to emphasize the anti-slavery cause by stressing the wicked character of Simon Legree and downplaying the role of St Clare. In addition, many different film versions of *Uncle Tom's Cabin* are known from the days of silent film.[56] The character of Little Eva, in particular, proved to be irresistible and actresses made their careers on the role. The attraction continued into the early days of sound films, as Shirley Temple's appearance as Little Eva in *The Littlest Rebel* (1935) and *Dimples* (1936), to cite but one example, illustrates.

However, it is with two more recent films given over to adapting Stowe's story that we shall concern ourselves here. The first was a European enterprise made at the height of the Civil Rights movement in America, and designed to capitalize on that market; the second was a made-for-TV adaptation first aired on the ABC network in the United States in the summer of 1987.

a. *Géza von Radványi's* Onkel Toms Hütte *(1965)*

The Hungarian director Géza von Radványi filmed his version of *Uncle Tom's Cabin* entirely in Europe. The film was first released in West Germany and France in 1965 with a subsequent release on 1 January 1969 in the United States. The film exists in a number of language versions, including French, Italian, German, Serbo-Croatian and English. Most of the cast are lesser known actors and actresses; the only really recognizable name is that of Herbert Lom who plays the role of Simon Legree. The credits list John Kitzmiller in the role of Uncle Tom, with O.W. Fisher as Pierre Saint-Claire, Thomas Fritsch as George Shelby,

54. Gerould (1980: 14-18) discusses Aiken's play.
55. Williams (1996) provides details.
56. Slout (1973) offers a survey of the matter.

Catana Cayetano as Eliza, Gertraud Mittermayr as Little Eva, Eleonora Rossi-Drago as Marie Saint-Claire, Olive Moorefield as Cassy, and Harold Bradley as Harris. The film plays fast and free with the story-line of the novel, at times so much so that it is difficult to see it as an adaptation of Harriet Beecher Stowe's classic at all. The names and spellings of some of the central characters are altered and new relation-ships between them are asserted: Augustine St Clare becomes *Pierre* Saint-Claire, George Harris becomes *Jim* Harris, Cassy is made the *sister* of Jim Harris rather than the long-lost *mother* of Eliza, and so on.

With regard to plot, other changes of a more serious nature are made as well. Thus the character Simon Legree is conflated with that of the slave-trader Haley (who appears in the opening chapter of the novel, but nowhere in this film adaptation). Similarly, the character of Eliza is conflated with that of the young slave-girl Emmeline who appears in the closing chapters of the novel as the object of Simon Legree's lusts, but is completely written out of the screenplay, and Pierre Saint-Claire is shot by Simon Legree for threatening to set his slaves free (in the novel he is knifed by an anonymous brawler in a beer-hall fight). Even more astonishing is the fact that other characters who do not exist within the novel are interjected into the film, notably a young and beautiful woman named Harriet (played by Mylène Demongeot). Harriet serves as the obligatory love-interest of the plantation owner Pierre Saint-Claire, whose relationship with his cold and self-obsessed wife Marie is strained to say the least.

Extra scenes are inserted into the novel's story-line, some seemingly with no other purpose than to provide opportunities for set action-scenes commonly associated with Westerns, or to confirm cinematic stereotypes about the South. For example, at one point there is a bar-room brawl between abolitionists and pro-slavers, as well a final shootout between Simon Legree and his cronies on the one side, and gun-toting Quakers (!) who help to shelter escaping slaves in a Francis-can monastery on the other. We see scenes of a paddle-boat steamer cruising lazily down the Mississippi river, and of slaves singing Negro spirituals while they work in the cotton fields. Rich baritone versions of such songs as 'Go Down Moses', 'Let my People Go' (with which the film opens), 'Ole, Ole Mississippi' and 'Joshua Fit de Battle of Jericho' are provided.[57] The songs are performed by an un-credited

57. Levine (1979: 143-72) offers a full-bodied discussion of the importance of singing in the life of Negro slaves.

Paul Robeson and terribly lip-synched by Uncle Tom as he leads the slaves in song.

Completely unexpected scenes, which are either factually inaccurate or out of keeping with the publication date of the novel, also appear. Thus we are treated to a scene of rather gratuitous violence in which one of the slaves jumps overboard into the Mississippi river only to be eaten by *alligators*, without a thought as to whether there *are* alligators in the Mississippi (this scene takes the place of the incident described within the book in '14: Evangeline', in which Eva falls into the river and is rescued by Uncle Tom). Also, the 1852 publication date of the novel is forsaken in favour of presenting a scene within the Shelby household in which the presidency of Abraham Lincoln is anticipated. The conversation revolves around what Lincoln might do as President to help the abolitionist cause, and recalls a promise that the young George Shelby makes to Uncle Tom in the beginning of the film about redeeming him from the clutches of Simon Legree as soon as he is in a position to do so. Note the following conversation between the two Shelby men, father and son, Mrs. Shelby, and Virginia (George's fiancée) as the four of them drink coffee before a roaring fire in the Shelby home:

Mr Shelby:	The way things are going, it's just possible that Uncle Tom may not need your help, George.
George Shelby:	Why is that?
Mr Shelby:	*(Handing his son a newspaper.)* Here, read it for yourself. There's a lot of talk going on about abolition. This backwoodsman made quite a speech at Cooper Union.
Virginia:	Backwood?
Mr Shelby:	Rail-splitter. Lincoln. *(He points to an article within the newspaper.)* Abraham Lincoln. After that speech in New York he stands a good chance of becoming the Republican candidate for President.
Mrs Shelby:	Are you voting for him?
Mr Shelby:	Yep!
Mrs Shelby:	Good! I am against slavery.
George Shelby:	John Brown is too, but violence isn't the answer. Eventually slavery must go.

The point here is that the references to Lincoln's speech at Cooper Union and the allusion to the abolitionist extremist John Brown (who led a massacre of pro-slavers in Kansas) both point to a date some years later than the appearance of Stowe's *Uncle Tom's Cabin*. In fact, Lincoln's speech was made in February 1860 and John Brown was executed on 2 December 1859. At one level, George Shelby's words serve as an ominous warning about the future, but they prove to be something of a false prophecy. In the end (at least as far as this film is concerned), slavery *does* 'go', but it is not by non-violent means (as we shall see in a moment).

Perhaps the best part of the film is the portrayal of Eliza's escape across the river on the ice floes, clutching little Harry to her breast.[58] The action is realistically portrayed and is fairly faithful to the novel. The only real difficulty with the scene concerns what river it is that Eliza is crossing to gain her freedom. In the novel it is, of course, the Ohio River, which separates the free State of Ohio from the slave State of Kentucky, which Eliza and Harry cross. Within the film we are never told explicitly that it is the Ohio river which Eliza braves, and are left with the impression that it might even be the Mississippi river (the only river which is explicitly named within the film). Yet there is room for considerable confusion about this point because later on we discover that Cassy comes to the aid of Eliza and little Harry, sneaking away from Simon Legree's plantation to do so. This plantation is said to be near Natchez, Mississippi (another change from the novel), which means that somehow Eliza crosses the (Ohio?) river to escape from slavery only to find that she is somehow transported hundreds of miles south along the Mississippi river. Here she is in hiding, crouched in a barn in the middle of a Mississippi plantation of the man who tried to separate her from her husband in the first place. This may all be convenient in terms of the plot, but it makes no sense to anyone with any sense of the geography of the United States. It is as if the *idea* of Eliza escaping across a river is what was fastened upon within the film, and any adherence to Stowe's carefully constructed geographical motif was sacrificed in the process.

The film begins with a rewriting of the novel's opening scene in which Mr Shelby is discussing with the slave-trader Haley about the fate of the slaves on the Shelby plantation. In the film this is replaced by a sequence in which the slave-trader Simon Legree visits the plantation and forces the hapless Mr Shelby to exchange ten male slaves for

58. Warhol (1986: 814) discusses the importance of this incident within Stowe's overall purposes in writing the novel.

the promissory notes he holds for the property. Thus the character Simon Legree is imported to the beginning of the story and the drama is built around him and his treatment of the slaves he purchases from Shelby. This is in contrast to the novel wherein Simon Legree does not come into the story until '30: The Slave Warehouse' following the death of Augustine St Clare and the auctioning off of his plantation by his widow. In effect, Legree is made to carry the role of the villainous slave-trader on his own within the film. He is presented as a heartless man with no concern for the impact of his slave-trading activities on the lives of others. Legree is further vilified within the film by being portrayed as having the left side of his face disfigured by a large and hideous scar.

Legree is also brought into the depiction of the slave Jim Harris and his decision to run away from his bondage in pursuit of freedom. Here we have a scene in which one of Simon Legree's slave-owning friends, a Mr Morrison, decides to sell Harris to the unscrupulous slave-trader. Morrison fetches Harris from his place of work at Mr Wilson's cotton-factory and ties him behind his horse. He then mounts the horse and rides off, dragging the bound slave behind. Harris tries to keep up with the galloping horse for a while, but eventually trips and ends up being dragged behind the horse. He manages to cut himself free with a knife and runs off into the woods, with a furious Mr Morrison drawing a pistol, firing at him and shouting 'Run! Tomorrow there will be a reward notice on every tree from here to Kentucky!' Harris makes it to the cabin where his wife Eliza and their young son are anxiously wait-ing for him. Harris explains that he must run away quickly, 'before Morrison comes' and the family is broken up. There is no conversation between Harris and Mr. Wilson over the rights and wrongs of rebellion, such as is contained within the novel in '11: In Which Property Gets into an Improper State of Mind', although Harris does return to face Legree again later in the film and to attempt to buy Eliza and his son Harry from the slave-trader.

What of Uncle Tom's response to his slavery? How is his reaction to the breakup of his family portrayed? Uncle Tom's passivity in accept-ing the life of a slave is brought through in several early scenes in the film. For example, note the exchange between Mr Shelby and Tom as the master of the plantation visits Uncle Tom and his wife Chloe in their cabin and tries to explain the situation that has arisen with regard to Simon Legree. Rumours have begun to circulate among the slaves on the Shelby plantation that some of them have been sold and Uncle Tom has been trying to calm their fears.

Shelby: Tom, suppose that this isn't just a rumour. I've been obliged... I've sold some of you. *(Shelby sits wearily at a table in the middle of the room; Uncle Tom stands beside him.)*

Uncle Tom: Then ... Then I know dis must be hard times fo' sure. Why else would you sell any of us off the plantation? I know lessun' you had to, you would *never* do anything like that! *(Tom walks across the room toward some clothes which are hung on nails in the wall.)*

Shelby: Where are you going?

Uncle Tom: Gettin' my other shirt.

Shelby: But Tom, there is no question of *your* going! Why, you're as much a part of the Shelby plantation as I am myself.

Uncle Tom: All of us is part of the Shelby plantation, like one big ole family. Mr. Shelby, if you gotta sell anyone, please sir, I want you to sell me. *(He walks to the table and picks up a copy of the Bible which is before Shelby.)* It say here in the Bible, 'No one has greater love than this: to lay down his life for a friend.' If you don't want me to do it for you, then I'll do it for Master George, sir.

Chloe: *(Entering the shot.)* Don't listen to what he's a'saying! Please sir, don't let him go away. Ain't nothing about 'going' in the Bible! *(She snatches the Bible out of Tom's hands and begins to trace the words on a page with her finger as if she is reading.)* Know what it says here? It says, 'Tom, stay where you're at.'

Uncle Tom: It don't say one word about that.

Chloe: *(In despair.)* Then what it is? *(She slams the Bible back into Tom's hands and storms away.)*

Tom's passivity is not carried through to the end of the film, however. His experience of living under the iron rod of Simon Legree eventually pushes him to the point that he advocates violent revolution as the way to deal with slavery. In fact, the slaves on Legree's plantation are inspired by Uncle Tom himself to rise up and seize their freedom by force. On this specific point the film offers an interpretation of the character of Uncle Tom, which is wholly at odds with how he is portrayed within the novel. The crucial scene in which this pro-rebellion stance is given comes as Uncle Tom lies in the barn mortally wounded (he has been trampled by horses in the act of saving Cassy from the vicious temper of Simon Legree who drives a horse-drawn wagon at her).

Some of the plantation slaves are gathered around the dying figure of Uncle Tom as Cassy tries to nurse him. Tom, however, is desperate to get his final message to the surrounding slaves:

Uncle Tom:	*(Labouring to speak.)* There's a saying I remember hearing once. I never understood it before. It's very, very important. I must tell you, Cassy. I must tell you. I haven't very much longer. The saying is, 'God helps those who helps themselves.'
One of the slaves:	There's only one thing wrong; that's a saying for white people.
Uncle Tom:	No! Listen to me. God sees black and white the same. He will help you. You *must* run away!
Another slave:	They have guns, Uncle Tom. And animals.
Uncle Tom:	Dogs can't follow tracks in water. Open the levy. You *must* run away. God will help you then, if no one else will.
Another slave:	But *you* can't run, Uncle Tom.
Uncle Tom:	Don't worry about me. I'd just be a burden to you. Go on without me.
Another slave:	*(Speaking for the rest.)* We ain't gonna do it, Uncle Tom.
Uncle Tom:	You must! I'm gonna be free soon in God's heaven. Go! Go, I beg you.

By contrast, the later response of Jim Harris to his slavery is much more conventional and non-violent. In this sense the roles that he and Uncle Tom have are reversed from those they have in the novel. Jim Harris *buys* his freedom, aided by the royalties he receives from inventing the cotton gin (making Jim Harris the inventor of the machine is another historical oddity of the film!). Jim, although he is depicted as rebelling and running away from his wicked master, eventually becomes the man who works the economics of the slave system to his own advantage and purchases his freedom. In contrast, Uncle Tom becomes the violent revolutionary, or at least the man who serves as the catalyst for such an uprising. He dies, eager to enter the heavenly realm which his Christian faith promises, but does so knowing that he has fomented a revolt among the slaves which will mean the end of Simon Legree's tyranny. We are left to infer that the revolt on this one plantation is replicated throughout the South as the institution of slavery itself is dismantled and freedom demanded by the slaves who have long been held in bondage.

Two other scenes that appear within the film are worth mentioning briefly. The first concerns a depiction of the Christian church (as represented by the Franciscan monks who live in a nearby monastery) and its abiding role in facing the evil of slavery. This interesting, almost comic, scene occurs as the climactic gun battle erupts between the plantation owners and the Franciscan monks and Quakers who are protecting the runaway slaves within the monastery. A leader of the monks goes out of the front gates of the monastery waving a white flag. He makes his way to Simon Legree and engages him in conversation:

Monk:	A message! I have a message. I have a message for the planters.
Legree:	Give the slaves back to us!
Monk:	And your cotton? Your beautiful cotton, my son? Are you aware that they opened the levies as they ran? You really *ought* to see to your fields.
Legree:	And you really ought not to lie.
Rider:	*(Arriving on horseback to confirm the Monk's words.)* Legree, they are drowning our cotton fields! The sluice-gates are open!
Legree:	*(Turning to leave.)* We're coming back later!
Monk:	*(With a mischievous smile on his face.)* We'll still be here!

The second concerns an intriguing vision of the future based on the slave revolution which we saw had begun on the Legree plantation. The final scenes of the film are shown with the chorus of 'Joshua Fit de Battle of Jericho' being sung once again. We see several concluding images, including one of a group of slaves in a covered wagon (presumably heading off to a better future out West), as well as a final shot of a paddleboat steamer on the Mississippi. The voice of a narrator comes in over the sound of the music. He says:

> Only God fully understands these United States. Soon after Lincoln gave the Negro freedom from slavery, the President was shot. God alone guides our destiny.

After this is said, the final phrase of the chorus of the song comes through: 'And the walls came tumbling down!' It is difficult to think of a more fitting phrase to describe the collapse of the institution of slavery. Harriet Beecher Stowe would almost certainly have approved.

b. *Stan Lathan's* Uncle Tom's Cabin *(1987)*
Stan Lathan's adaptation of *Uncle Tom's Cabin* offers an all-star cast including Avery Brooks as Uncle Tom, Phylicia Rashad as Eliza

Harris, Samuel L. Jackson as George Harris, Bruce Dern as St Clare, and Edward Woodward as Simon Legree. The screenplay for this made-for-TV film is by John Gay. It was first broadcast in the United States in June 1987. Much of it was filmed in Natchez, Mississippi, which adds greatly to the sense of realism which pervades the production. This is especially true when it comes to the scenes depicting the plantations of both Augustine St Clare and Simon Legree.

In the main, this is a high-quality effort which offers a sensitive version of Stowe's novel and cleverly interweaves the two contrasting stories involving George/Eliza on the one hand and Uncle Tom on the other. Several important scenes within the novel which are rarely depicted within film adaptations are found here, including George Harris's defiant speech of self defence and his shooting of the bounty-hunter Tom Loker who has been hired to recapture him. The scene where Ophelia St Clare is given the little slave-girl Topsy is also present here (there is no Ophelia in the 1965 film version discussed above!). However, there are several points at which the film departs from the story-line of the original book and offers its own distinctive interpretation of the tale. Some of the characters' first names are changed from those contained within the novel, no doubt in an attempt to clarify what can be a confusing feature of Stowe's book. Thus, the name of George and Eliza's son is Jimmy (rather than Harry) and George Shelby becomes *Christopher* Shelby, while the central character is generally known as Tom rather than *Uncle* Tom (probably because of the negative associations with the epithet 'Uncle Tom' among African Americans).

The film opens with a chase scene in which George Harris is running through the woods, trying to escape from his master; we are told by an on-scene graphic that the setting is Kentucky in 1852. The threat to the Harris family lies behind the decision of George to flee; it also prompts Eliza to take her young son Jimmy and escape to the North. Eliza goes to Tom's cabin and relays the news that Tom too has been sold by Master Shelby. As Tom and his wife Chloe argue about what they should do we get our first glimpse into the moral dilemma that must be faced:

Chloe:	You got to go too, Tom!
Tom:	I can't go.
Chloe:	You *got* to!
Tom:	If I go, then everybody here gets sold. And I *can't* do that. I can't let that happen!

Somewhat surprisingly, one of the most famous episodes of *Uncle Tom's Cabin*, the highly improbable escape of Eliza skipping across the ice floes of the Ohio River, is not portrayed within the film, at least not in the manner we might expect. Rather, in this version a more realistic escape is shown as Eliza flees with Jimmy on a raft which is conveniently found to be in place on the southern shore. As she makes it safely to the other side of the river, one of the Negro slaves charged with chasing Eliza is made to exclaim, 'Praise the Lord!' Eliza and Jimmy do eventually meet up with George and the family ultimately make it to Canada where they establish a home in freedom. Somewhat disappointingly, the internal struggle that George Harris has over his slavery, so graphically portrayed in the novel, is not explored at much depth within this film. Neither is George here presented as quite the violent revolutionary that he is in the book. The only scene in which we see anything like the revolutionary George of the novel is his act of self-defence against Tom Loker (mentioned above). In this film George is presented as a reasonable man, reacting as any sensible person would when his life, or the lives of members of his family, are threatened. In fact, the burden of exploring what the Christian response should be to slavery falls on the shoulders of the character Tom within this film. It is to the portrayal of him that we now turn.

One of the most important scenes in which we see Tom's desire for freedom occurs in connection with his enslavement on the St Clare plantation. Tom has proven himself a loyal and hard-working slave, and the affection between him and Little Eva is sensitively handled. Her death is a blow to everyone on the plantation, including Tom who took care of her in the final stages of her life. This kindness is noticed by Augustine St Clare and the two men grow quite close. The scene in which St Clare tells Tom that he will set him free is one of the most moving within the film. St Clare is seated at a table in the drawing room of his mansion as Tom enters and addresses his master:

Tom: Miss Ophelia said you wanted to see me.
St Clare: Tom! Please, come in. *(Tom steps up to the table as St Clare rises.)* I've started proceedings to grant you your enfranchisement. In other words, I'm going to make you a free man.
Tom: *(In astonishment.)* Lord God!
St Clare: I'll sign the papers on Friday and that will be the end of the matter. You can pack your bag and head on back to Kentucky.

Tom:	Oh, my God! *(He begins to cry, his face a mixture of disbelief and joy.)*
St Clare:	Don't look in such rapture! Have ... have I really been that bad?
Tom:	*(Shaking his head.)* It's being free. Don't you see? A free man!
St Clare:	It was Eva, Tom. When she died she made me promise that I would let you go. And I would never, ever break that promise as long as I live.
Tom:	Miss Eva was a messenger from the Lord.
St Clare:	*(Nodding in agreement.)* Yep. I truly think she was. *(Ophelia enters the room, interrupting the men in the midst of this intimate conversation.)*
Ophelia:	Oh! I am sorry.
Tom:	I'm just leaving, Miss Ophelia. *(He departs from the room, pausing to stop and whisper in Ophelia's ear.)* I'm free!
Ophelia:	*(Addressing St Clare.)* What's that he said?
St Clare:	He said he was free.
Ophelia:	You mean you...?
St Clare:	I mean, I've known two genuine saints in my life. I've lost one, and I'm about to lose the other.
Ophelia:	Oh my dear cousin! Thank you! *(She moves to embrace him.)* *(The camera cuts to Tom in the hallway outside the drawing room; he is looking in a mirror.)*
Tom:	Free, Lord! Free! *(He bursts into laughter.)*

However, this brief glimpse of impending freedom is short-lived, as short-lived as the man who intended to bring it to pass. Following the murder of Augustine St Clare, the conversation between Marie St Clare and Ophelia about the freedom of Tom highlights the insensitivity of the (supposedly) grieving widow. Marie is lounging on a divan, a slave-girl making a frenzied attempt to cool her mistress with a broad fan. Ophelia enters the room and the following conversation takes place:

Ophelia:	I must talk with you about Tom.
Marie:	Tom?
Ophelia:	Augustine promised Tom his freedom before he died.
Marie:	If Tom told you that, he's lying.
Ophelia:	No! Augustine told me himself.
Marie:	*(Obviously disappointed.)* Oh, well. *(She pauses for a moment of false contemplation.)* It's absolutely impossible. Tom's the most valuable servant we've got. Besides, what does he want with liberty? He's better off as he is.

| Ophelia: | *(She paces the room for a few moments.)* He does want his freedom. He was promised it! |
| Marie: | He simply doesn't know what is best for him. |

Marie sells Tom to the wicked Simon Legree and we are quickly given a scene depicting the clash of personality between the master Legree and the slave-hand Tom. At the slave auction Legree strikes Tom in the face with the back of his hand. Tom does not resist; he remains controlled and passive, but there is a fire in his eyes. The contrast between the genteel, well-managed estate of Augustine St Clare and the run-down, dilapidated plantation of Legree is striking. In many ways it personifies the difference between the two men, not least with regard to their attitude to the slaves that they own. Tom has to wrestle intensely with his Christian beliefs and whether he should take an active role in claiming his freedom, particularly when the wicked Simon Legree tries hard to break his spirit. The matter comes to a head when Legree attempts to force Tom to whip another slave named Lucy (the incident is related in '33: Cassy'):

Legree:	I want you to take that Lucy and flog her. Go!
Tom:	That's not a thing for me to do. I never could and never did. No way possible.
Legree:	*(Laughing.)* Are you telling me 'No!'?
Tom:	No, sir. What I am trying to say to you…
Legree:	*(Striking Tom in the face with his fist.)* Boy, are you trying to tell me what is right and what is wrong?
Tom:	That poor woman is sick. And there's no way that I'm going to beat her. If you mean to kill me for it, then I can't stop you. But, no, I'm not going to raise my hand against that woman. It's a sin.
Legree:	*(Beginning to rant and rave.)* Sin? *(He turns to the crowd of on-looking slaves and addresses them.)* Do you hear that? He called us sinners! *(Legree turns back to Tom.)* Well now, haven't we got ourselves a powerful, holy critter here? You read your Bible, boy? You read the Bible? The Bible says, 'Obey thy master.' Well, ain't I your master? Didn't I pay good money for you, boy? Heh? Well, didn't I? *(He strikes Tom again, knocking the man to the ground.)* Now you gonna answer me, boy?
Tom:	*(Rising defiantly.)* Nobody … Nobody can buy my soul!
Legree:	Your *soul*?

Two other incidents are used within the film to emphasize the struggle that goes on within Tom about how he should react to the wickedness of the slave-master Legree. The first of these involves the quadroon Cassy and her own efforts to gain some self-respect and free herself from the evil master. She hatches a plot to murder Legree and attempts to entice Tom to assist her. Surreptitiously she engages Tom in conversation:

Cassy:	Tonight!
Tom:	What?
Cassy:	When he's sound asleep. I'm going to give him enough brandy to keep him out all night. There's an axe in the cellar and I'll have the door to his room open. You can do it, Tom.
Tom:	*(Shaking his head no.)*
Cassy:	He deserves to die!
Tom:	Would you sell your soul to the devil for *that*?
Cassy:	What would you have me do? Pray some more? Well, I can't! Eat or pray? Sing? All I can do is hate and cuss. Don't you see, Tom? That's all that's left inside me. That's all I got. That's *all* I got.
Tom:	Be still daughter. *(He pauses, reflecting for a moment.)* You run. Run for your life. Because without faith you'll not survive this hell. God will be with you.

The second incident is the emotional and theological climax of the film. It relates how Legree again tries to break Tom, only to find that the man's faith is enough to sustain him through the threats and beatings. Tom is brought before Legree by the henchmen Sambo and Quimbo so that Legree can question him about the disappearance of Cassy and Emmeline.

Legree:	I have made up my mind that I am gonna kill you, lessen you tell me what happened to them. Now maybe you don't believe me. Now, maybe you think that yo' Massa wouldn't throw away that kind of money. But I assure you, boy, I am sincere. *Sincere!* So, you hear me? So now. You speak up! Come on, speak up now!
Tom:	Nothing to tell.
Legree:	Boy, I have counted the cost. And I am determined to break you once and for all, right now. I am gonna take every drop of blood you got! I ask you. Do you hear me? Well?
Tom:	*(Defiantly.)* You take my blood. That is nothing. No! You can hurt me no more!
Legree:	Well, now. We'll see, huh?

In the next scene we see Tom being flogged by Sambo and Quimbo with Legree sitting nearby on a stump. Tom is tied to a T-form cross with his arms outstretched in a crucifixion pose. The whipping has been going on for some time and Legree finally leaves, thinking that Tom is dead. The two slaves, like the two thieves flanking the dying Christ on the cross, are increasingly fearful as they begin to realize what they have done. Sambo says, 'Quimbo, I think we done did a wicked thing, cause I ain't never felt like this before. O Lord Jesus, forgive us!' They cut him down from the flogging tree and carry him away to a nearby barn. Here the saintly man eventually dies, just as the young Master Shelby arrives on the scene intending to buy his freedom.

In the end, Tom is the supreme example of passive resistance within the film. He desires his freedom intensely, but will not compromise his Christian ideals and take up violence to get it, even though he is understanding of others, such as Cassy, who take the path of active revolution. There is in this film no figure comparable to the novel's character Scipio, who voluntarily renounces his freedom and remains in slavery in order to serve his master. Neither are the slaves of the Shelby plantation portrayed here when, following Uncle Tom's death, George Shelby attempts to emancipate them only to find his intentions rejected. In this sense, the variety of responses to slavery which are contained within Stowe's novel are somewhat curtailed in the film. Instead, the powerfully presented inner strength of Uncle Tom, which in Stowe's novel is energized by his deep spirituality, becomes heavily politicized within Lathan's film. This extends to the point of equating the thread of apocalypticism, so much a part of Stowe's *Uncle Tom's Cabin*, with the American Civil War and its aftermath, up to and including the Civil Rights movement of the 1960s.[59] This is most evident by the way in which the film ends.

The last scenes of the film show Christopher Shelby driving away with the body of Tom in his wagon. A narrator's voice offers an interpretation of the death of Tom:

59. Stowe reflects the millennialism of her Calvinistic heritage and shows herself in *Uncle Tom's Cabin* to be deeply influenced by her father's theological stance on the matter. Yet she radically adapts the millennial vision of her father and transforms it into a Christian moral vision whose essence is a message of anti-slavery. For more on this fascinating topic, which has important connections with how Paul's own apocalyptic vision of the imminent arrival of Christ is commonly thought to shape his ethical teaching about slavery, see Strout (1968); Reed (1968); MacFarlane (1990); Bellin (1993); Westra (1994); Lowance (1994); Shaw (1994); Tompkins (1994).

> Uncle Tom was right. Only his body died at the hands of Simon Legree. Tom's spirit rose out of the pages of Harriet Beecher Stowe's novel to agitate the conscience of a nation. A war was fought; the black people were legally freed. Today, 120 years later, the battle for true freedom still continues.

This epilogue by the narrator not only serves to update Harriet Beecher Stowe's story for the original viewing audience (the Americans who watched the film in 1987, some 124 years after Lincoln's signing of the Emancipation Proclamation in 1863), but it also conceals an important break with Stowe's novel. That is to say, by ending the adaptation of *Uncle Tom's Cabin* on this highly politicized note, the film avoids having to engage with that most troublesome idea contained in Stowe's novel—the matter of colonialism and the establishment of the state of Liberia in Africa for freed slaves. Nothing is ever mentioned about this within the film, even though it figures prominently in the novel.[60] In fact, within the book George, Eliza and Harry are said to go to Liberia out of deliberate choice, seeing the work among the African peoples as a matter of destiny, not to say their Christian commitment. So, too, does Topsy, who serves in Africa as a missionary following her education in Vermont.

It is significant that not one of the slave characters in the book *Uncle Tom's Cabin* remains in the United States to carry on the abolitionist cause. Clearly, resolving one of the difficulties of the slavery issue along these lines (shipping all the freed slaves to a foreign land without consideration of their own desires and sense of nationhood) was completely unacceptable for a 1987 audience, and Stan Lathan's film wisely avoids it. In so doing, a break with Harriet Beecher Stowe's own vision of what the abolition of slavery entails is made, but given the circumstances, this cannot but be a good thing. At the end of the day, we have a most interesting adaptation of Stowe's *Uncle Tom's Cabin* on offer here, even if it does come to some predictable conclusions about the politics of slavery. An atmosphere of 'political correctness' seems to pervade here, which means that some of the more unpleasant dimensions of Stowe's novel, as well as some of the ambiguities of Paul's own advice to slaves and masters, get lost in the shuffle.

---

60. It is interesting that the ending of Aiken's play adaptation of *Uncle Tom's Cabin* likewise does not pursue the idea of colonization in Africa. Neither do the other major plays of the era. See Gossett (1985: 269, 272) for details on this point.

5. *Summary*

One of the central moral dilemmas that Stowe wrestles with throughout her influential novel concerns the Christian response to slavery. How *are* Christian slaves and Christian slave-masters to react to one another and yet remain true to their religious beliefs? A good example of this wrestling is placed on the lips of the slave Eliza Harris early in the story. Eliza is in earnest discussion with her husband George about how to reconcile her Christian faith with the threat that slavery presents to their family, a threat made real by the economic difficulties on the Shelby plantation which mean some slaves will have to be sold. Stowe has Eliza voice one side of the moral dilemma, the side of the slaves: 'Well', said Eliza, mournfully, 'I always thought that I must obey my master and mistress, or I couldn't be a Christian' (*UTC* 3.61).

Similar thoughts must have arisen in the minds of many first-century Christians, if the exhortations contained in Col. 3.22-25, Eph. 6.5-8 and 1 Tim. 6.1-2 are anything to go by. Yet the advice that Paul offers to slaves in 1 Cor. 7.20-24 is much less specific than these exhortations, and scholarship has come to something of an impasse with respect to its interpretation. Precisely what Paul meant by declaring that Christians should 'remain in whatever state they were at the time of their calling' (7.20, 24) is a hugely contentious matter as we have noted, and the advice in 7.21 about gaining freedom (or not!) is anything but unambiguous.[61] Striking too is the way that Paul uses the metaphor of slavery in 1 Corinthians 9 as a way of saying something distinctive about the Christian experience of salvation. Together these two sections of 1 Corinthians provide us with an open window through which we can explore issues concerning slaves and masters, freedom and responsibility, self-sacrifice and willingness to submit to bondage.

Harriet Beecher Stowe's *Uncle Tom's Cabin* serves as a valuable point of comparison on matters such as these, offering us a memorable picture of the complexities of slavery as it was practised in the American antebellum South. Through its characters the novel invites us to

---

61. Rowland (1985: 275) remarks on the tension within the Pauline materials between presenting Christianity as a liberating force in society and presenting it as concerned with maintaining the status quo: 'This ambivalence in the Pauline ethics is one of the most important features of early Christian tradition and helps us to understand some of the varied features of the Christian religion through the centuries.'

explore a number of responses to enslavement. Should one pursue active revolution and rebel against the system? Or is passive resistance the more prudent response? Or is there something in between, a position in which the sense of a higher calling both tames the abolitionist urge as well as transforms the tendency blandly to accept the status quo. In this chapter I have had occasion to examine how Stowe's novel addresses each of these responses to slavery, as well as the way in which they are carried through, adapted and curtailed, within two of the film treatments of her novel. The temptation in dealing with a novel like *Uncle Tom's Cabin* is to view it solely as a work preoccupied with concerns of the nineteenth century and to file it away as concerned with what is now deemed a 'dead issue'—slavery. Yet the degree to which Stowe's *Uncle Tom's Cabin* helped to set the agenda for race relations for subsequent generations, particularly in the United States is remarkable. To illustrate: one of the best examples of someone who embodies the struggle which slavery continued to present for blacks within the period of reconstruction following the American Civil War is Booker T. Washington (1856–1915), who first published his autobiography *Up from Slavery* in 1901. The work chronicles his life from slave beginnings (his mother was a slave on a Virginia plantation) to the great work of his career as a pioneering educationalist. He is perhaps best known for his part in the establishment of Tuskegee College in Alabama, a school dedicated to the education of African Americans. Yet for all his achievements, it is interesting to note that Washington was, during his lifetime, accused of selling out to the white establishment. In the eyes of many he was an 'Uncle Tom', an epithet which is taken from Harriet Beecher Stowe's novel (Flynn 1969),[62] which in itself is something of a demonstration of how significant her influence was in re-shaping the public perception of race relations.

While it may be true that 'chattel' slavery, as it were, is no longer a problem that must be faced in the modern world, there certainly are any number of socio-economic equivalents that plague us today. More to the point, the debate about how such injustices are addressed remains as much a concern now as it was 150 years ago. Is violent revolution an answer? Is passive resistance the solution? Do we follow the examples of Karl Marx and Che Guevara, or are we to emulate Mahatma Gandhi and Martin Luther King, Jr? And how relevant is the model which Paul

62. For more on the use of the term 'Uncle Tom' as an epithet, see Gossett (1985: 365).

invokes in 1 Cor. 9.19, the declaration that he willingly becomes 'the slave of all', to the present situations in which people find themselves? It is these kinds of questions that make a study of Harriet Beecher Stowe's *Uncle Tom's Cabin* a valuable way of re-considering Paul's advice about master–slave relationships.

CONCLUSION

We come now to the conclusion of this investigation of Pauline images in fiction and film. The creative experiment in hermeneutics which I suggested within the two earlier books on fiction and film from 1993 and 1994 is thus extended to include a more specific strand of the New Testament materials, those associated with Paul the apostle.

The studies offered here cover literature from a wide time-span, from the initial stages of English novel-writing in the early 1700s through to the time when horror/Gothic stories were beginning to give way to detective fiction at the end of the 1800s. I have also taken time to consider one of the most successful novels of the nineteenth century—success measured not only in terms of the sheer number of copies sold, but in terms of helping to bring about social and political change by popularizing the abolitionist cause in the American antebellum South. Admittedly, it is a long way from *Robinson Crusoe* to *Dracula* to *The Picture of Dorian Gray* to *Uncle Tom's Cabin*, but the journey has not been without its rewards. The writers whose work has formed the basis of my literary investigations (Defoe, Stowe, Stoker and Wilde) are four quite distinctive artists, and it might seem difficult at first to find a point of commonality between them. However, the thread which has been identified as tying them together for the purposes of this study has been the way in which they use or adapt ideas or images either contained within the Pauline epistles or associated with the New Testament witness about Paul.

More specifically, each of the four chapters has some connection with the letters that Paul wrote to the church at Corinth; in this connection we noted 1 Cor. 5.7; 7.17-24; 9; 11.23-26; 13.12; 2 Cor. 3.18; 11.22-28 (and Acts 27.1–28.16) within the course of discussion. In one sense, this is corresponds to a subtle, but not imperceptible, shift in focus which has begun to take place within Pauline studies in recent years. For so long, the way into any discussion of Paul's place within the life and thought of the New Testament has been through his contribution to the theological debate involving the doctrine of justification by faith, the juxtaposition of law and grace. Inevitably this has meant that Romans and Galatians have been *the* great focal points of Pauline theology. However, recent studies seem to show a growing sensitivity to and awareness of the importance of the sociological dimensions of Pauline Christianity, and this has meant that 1 and 2 Corinthians have begun to come to the forefront of critical discussion. This is not to suggest that important studies of Romans and Galatians are no longer being produced (they certainly are), but it does mean that those two epistles no longer can be *assumed* to occupy the centre stage of Pauline studies. Perhaps the fact that Paul writes the Corinthian letters to a church that he knows well, while the epistles to Rome and to the churches in the region of Galatia are directed to congregations with which he is less intimate, has something to do with this. In any event, in the minds of many interpreters the Corinthian letters seem more personal, revealing the human side of the apostle as he wrestles with a congregation that he knows and loves deeply.

In addition to noting the Pauline connections in each of the four literary classics, we have also been exploring how modern film adaptations of these works can in their own way contribute to our understanding of the interpretative process. Several interesting books and articles have recently been published which demonstrate a growing awareness of the importance of cinema within the study of theology. Included among these are Bruce Babington and Peter William Evans, *Biblical Epics: Sacred Narrative in the Hollywood Cinema* (1993); Joel W. Martin and Conrad E. Ostwalt, Jr (eds.), *Screening the Sacred: Religion, Myth, and Ideology in Popular American Film* (1995); the various contributions in *Semeia* 74 (1996) edited by Alice Bach; Clive Marsh and Gaye Ortiz (eds.), *Explorations in Theology and Film: Movies and Meaning* (1997); and Peter Fraser, *Images of the Passion: The Sacramental Mode in Film* (1998). Students who are interested in exploring the borderlands of theology and film can rest assured that their chosen field of study is not viewed with quite the same suspicion that it once was. Film and media studies is a growth industry in the educational market with many colleges and universities offering degree courses specializing in various aspects of the subject. Cinematic studies is also a booming business, if the recently increased shelf-space dedicated to 'Cinema' in Blackwell's bookstore in Oxford is any guide to the matter! We can anticipate that the volumes listed above will be but the tip of the iceberg and that many more will follow.

To my mind, such developments as these are very much welcomed, even if one may quibble over whether they be technically described as *cross*-disciplinary or *inter*-disciplinary in nature.[1] My aim throughout has been to stimulate thought and encourage discussion between those interested in theology, those committed to reading literature, and those fascinated by film. If I have managed to persuade a single curious reader to undertake such a discussion with others, then the task of producing this book has been well worth the effort.

---

1.   Plate (1998: 17) discusses this question. He suggests: 'Religion and film scholarship has generally borrowed the methodologies of theology, religious studies, and/or literary studies, and ignored the importance of film studies and the medium of film itself. In other words, it remains cross-disciplinary, simply borrowing rather than fully engaging with another field of inquiry'.

BIBLIOGRAPHY

Ackroyd, P.
    1985   'Introduction', in Wilde 1985: 7-15.
    1983   *The Last Testament of Oscar Wilde* (London: Penguin Books).
Acworth, A.
    1973   'Where Was St. Paul Shipwrecked? A Re-Examination of the Evidence',
         JTS 24: 190-93.
Albert, J.
    1988   'The Christ of Oscar Wilde', *ABR* 39: 372-403.
Alexander, L.
    1996   ' "In Journeyings Often": Voyaging in the Acts of the Apostles and in
         Greek Romance', in C.M. Tuckett (ed.), *Luke's Literary Achievement:*
         Collected Essays (JSNTSup, 116; Sheffield: Sheffield Academic Press):
         17-49.
Alkon, P.K.
    1979   *Defoe and Fictional Time* (Athens, GA: University of Georgia Press).
Allen, W.
    1954   *The English Novel: From The Pilgrim's Progress to Sons and Lovers*
         (London: Penguin Books).
Ammons, E.
    1977–78 'Heroines in *Uncle Tom's Cabin*', *AL* 49: 161-79.
    1986   'Stowe's Dream of the Mother-Saviour: *Uncle Tom's Cabin* and Ameri-
         can Writers before the 1920s', in E.J. Sundquist (ed.), *New Essays on*
         Uncle Tom's Cabin (Cambridge: Cambridge University Press): 155-95.
Ammons, E. (ed.)
    1994   *Harriet Beecher Stowe's Uncle Tom's Cabin* (Norton Critical Edition;
         New York: W.W. Norton).
Anderson, B.A.
    1991   'Uncle Tom: A Hero at Last', *ATQ* 5: 95-108.
Arac, J.
    1986   'The Politics of *The Scarlet Letter*', in S. Bercovitch and M. Jehlen (eds.),
         Ideology and Classic American Literature (Cambridge: Cambridge Uni-
         versity Press): 247-66.
Arata, S.D.
    1990   'The Occidental Tourist: *Dracula* and the Anxiety of Reverse Coloniza-
         tion', *VS* 33: 621-45.
Armstrong, D.
    1992   'The Myth of Cronus: Cannibal and Sign in *Robinson Crusoe*', *ECF* 4:
         207-20.

Armstrong, K.A.
    1996   *Defoe: Writer as Agent* (Victoria, BC: University of Victoria).
Askeland, L.
    1992   'Remodeling the Model Home in *Uncle Tom's Cabin* and *Beloved*', *AL*
             64: 785-805.
Ayers, R.W.
    1967   '*Robinson Crusoe*: Allusive Allegorick History', *PMLA* 82: 299-407.
Babington, B., and P.W. Evans
    1993   *Biblical Epics: Sacred Narrative in the Hollywood Cinema* (Manchester:
             The University of Manchester Press).
Bach, A. (ed.)
    1996   'Biblical Glamour and Hollywood Glitz', *Semeia* 74.
Backscheider, P.R.
    1982   'Defoe's Prodigal Sons', *SLI* 15: 3-18.
    1989   *Daniel Defoe: His Life* (Baltimore: The Johns Hopkins University Press).
Baine, R.M.
    1968   *Daniel Defoe and the Supernatural* (Athens, GA: University of Georgia
             Press).
Baker, H.A.
    1969–70   'A Tragedy of the Artist: *The Picture of Dorian Gray*', *NCF* 24: 349-55.
Baldwin, J.
    1994   'Everybody's Protest Novel', in E. Ammons (ed.), *Harriet Beecher
             Stowe's Uncle Tom's Cabin* (Norton Critical Edition; New York: W.W.
             Norton): 495-507.
Banks, M.
    1993   '*Uncle Tom's Cabin* and Antebellum Black Response', in J.L. Machor
             (ed.), *Readers in History: Nineteenth-Century American Literature and
             the Contexts of Response* (Baltimore: The Johns Hopkins University
             Press): 209-27.
Barrett, C.K.
    1975   'Review of Bartchy's *ΜΑΛΛΟΝ ΧΡΗΣΑΓ*, *JTS* 26: 173-74.
    1985   *Church, Ministry and Sacraments in the New Testament* (Carlisle: Pater-
             noster Press).
    1987   'Paul Shipwrecked', in B.P. Thompson (ed.), *Scripture: Meaning and
             Method. Essays Presented to Anthony Tyrrell Hanson* (Hull: Hull Uni-
             versity Press): 51-64.
Barrow, R.H.
    1928   *Slavery in the Roman Empire* (London: Methuen).
Bartchy, S.S.
    1973   *ΜΑΛΛΟΝ ΧΡΗΣΑΙ: First-Century Slavery and 1 Corinthians 7.21*
             (SBLDS, 11; Atlanta: Scholars Press [repr. 1985]).
    1992   'Slavery (Graeco-Roman)', in *ABD*, VI: 65-73.
Barton, S.
    1986   'Paul's Sense of Place: An Anthropological Approach to Community
             Formation in Corinth', *NTS* 32: 225-46.
Bassett, S.E.
    1928   '1 Cor. 13.12, βλεπόμεν γὰρ ἄρτι δι᾽ ἐσόπτρου ἐν αἰνίγματι', *JBL* 47:
             232-36.

Bastian, F.
    1981   *Defoe's Early Life* (London: Macmillan).
Baumert, N.
    1984   *Ehelosigkeit und Ehe im Herrn: Eine Neuinterpretation von 1 Kor 7* (Würzburg: Echter Verlag).
Baym, N.
    1981   'Melodramas of Beset Manhood: How Theories of American Fiction Exclude Women Authors', *AQ* 33: 123-39.
Beckson, K.
    1984   'Oscar Wilde and the Masks of Narcissus', *PSS* 10: 249-67.
    1986   'Wilde's Autobiographical Signature in *The Picture of Dorian Gray*', *VN* 69: 30-31.
Begam, R.
    1994   'Silence and Mut(e)ilation: White Writing in J.M. Coetzee's *Foe*', *SAQ* 93: 111-29.
Belford, B.
    1996   *Bram Stoker: A Biography of the Author of Dracula* (London: Weidenfeld & Nicolson).
Bell, I.A.
    1985a   'Narrators and Narrative in Defoe', *Novel* 18: 154-72.
    1985b   *Defoe's Fiction* (Totowa, NJ: Barnes and Noble).
    1996   'Crusoe's Women: Or, the Curious Incident of the Dog in the Night-Time', in L. Spaas and B. Stimpson (eds.), *Robinson Crusoe: Myths and Metamorphoses* (London: Macmillan): 28-44.
Bellin, J.D.
    1993   'Up to Heaven's Gate, Down in Earth's Dust: The Politics of Judgment in *Uncle Tom's Cabin*', *AL* 65: 275-95.
Bender, J.
    1994   'The Novel and the Rise of the Penitentiary: *Robinson Crusoe*', in M. Shinagel (ed.), *Daniel Defoe's Robinson Crusoe* (Norton Critical Edition; New York: W.W. Norton): 390-402.
Benjamin, E.B.
    1951   'Symbolic Elements in *Robinson Crusoe*', *PQ* 30: 206-11.
Bentley, C.F.
    1972   'The Monster in the Bedroom: Sexual Symbolism in Bram Stoker's *Dracula*', *LP* 22: 27-34.
Bergson, K. (ed.)
    1970   *Oscar Wilde: The Critical Heritage* (London: Routledge & Kegan Paul).
Berne, E.
    1956   'The Psychological Structure of Space with Some Remarks on *Robinson Crusoe*', *PsyQ* 25: 549-67.
Bierman, J.S.
    1977   'The Genesis and Dating of "Dracula" from Bram Stoker's Working Notes', *NQ* 24: 39-41.
Birdsall, V.O.
    1985   *Defoe's Perpetual Seekers: A Study of the Major Fiction* (London: Associated University Presses).

Blackburn, T.C.
    1984–85   'Friday's Religion: Its Nature and Importance in *Robinson Crusoe*', *ECS*
              18: 360-82.
Blewett, D.
    1979   *Defoe's Art of Fiction: Robinson Crusoe, Moll Flanders, Colonel Jack &
              Roxana* (Toronto: University of Toronto Press).
    1995   *The Illustration of Robinson Crusoe (1719–1920)* (Gerrards Cross: Colin
              Smythe).
Blinderman, C.S.
    1980   'Vampurella: Darwin and Count Dracula', *TMR* 21: 411-28.
Boardman, M.M.
    1983   *Defoe and the Uses of Narrative* (New Brunswick, NJ: Rutgers Univer-
              sity Press).
Bogle, D.
    1997   'Black Beginnings: From *Uncle Tom's Cabin* to *The Birth of a Nation*',
              in V. Smith (ed.), *Representing Blackness: Issues in Film and Video*
              (London: Athlone Press): 13-24.
Boreham, F.W.
    1955   *The Gospel of Robinson Crusoe* (London: Epworth Press).
Bradley, K.R
    1987   *Slaves and Masters in the Roman Empire: A Study in Social Control*
              (Oxford: Oxford University Press).
    1989   *Slavery and Rebellion in the Roman World, 140 B.C.–70 B.C.* (London:
              B.T. Batsford Ltd).
    1994   *Slavery and Society at Rome* (Cambridge: Cambridge University Press).
Bradley, L.R.
    1971   'The Curse of Canaan and the American Negro', *CTM* 42: 100-110.
Brandstadter, E.
    1974   'Uncle Tom and Archy Moore: The Antislavery Novel as Ideological
              Symbol', *AQ* 26: 160-75.
Brauch, M.
    1990   *Hard Sayings of Paul* (London: Hodder & Stoughton).
Braverman, R.
    1986   'Crusoe's Legacy', *SN* 18: 1-26.
Brînzeu, P.
    1994   'Dorian Gray's Rooms and Cyberspace', in C.G. Sandulescu (ed.), *Redis-
              covering Oscar Wilde* (Gerrards Cross: Colin Smythe): 21-29.
Bristow, J.
    1997   '"A Complex Multiform Creature": Wilde's Sexual Identities', in
              P. Raby (ed.), *The Cambridge Companion to Oscar Wilde* (Cambridge:
              Cambridge University Press): 195-218.
Brodhead, R.H.
    1988   'Sparing the Rod: Discipline and Fiction in Antebellum America', *Repre-
              sentations* 21: 67-96.
Bronfen, E.
    1992   *Over her Dead Body: Death, Femininity and the Aesthetic* (Manchester:
              Manchester University Press).

Brown, D.S.
    1969   'Thesis and Theme in *Uncle Tom's Cabin*', *EJ* 58: 1330-34, 1372.
Brown, G.
    1984   'Getting in the Kitchen with Dinah: Domestic Politics in *Uncle Tom's Cabin*', *AQ* 36: 503-524.
Brown, H.O.
    1971   'The Displaced Self in the Novels of Daniel Defoe', *JELH* 38: 562-90.
Brown, J.P.
    1997   *Cosmopolitan Criticism: Oscar Wilde's Philosophy of Art* (London: The University Press of Virginia).
Budgen, F.
    1960   *James Joyce and the Making of Ulysses* (Oxford: Oxford University Press).
Bultmann, R.
    1952   *Theology of the New Testament*, I (London: SCM Press).
Burgess, A.
    1980   'Making de White Boss Frown', in E. Ammons (ed.), *Critical Essays on Harriet Beecher Stowe* (Boston: G.K. Hall): 122-27.
Burnett, P.
    1996   'The Ulyssean Crusoe and the Quest for Redemption in J.M. Coetzee's *Foe* and Derek Walcott's *Omeros*', in L. Spaas and B. Stimpson (eds.), *Robinson Crusoe: Myths and Metamorphoses* (London: Macmillan): 239-55.
Cadbury, H.J.
    1956–57   '"We" and "I" Passages in Luke–Acts', *NTS* 3: 128-32.
Camfield, G.
    1988   'The Moral Aesthetics of Sentimentality: A Missing Key to *Uncle Tom's Cabin*', *NCF* 43: 319-45.
Camus, A.
    1960   *The Plague* (Harmondsworth: Penguin Books [1947]).
Canady, Jr., N.
    1973   'The Antislavery Novel Prior to 1852 and Richard Hildreth's *The Slave* (1836)', *CLAJ* 17: 175-91.
Cannon, K.G.
    1989   'Slave Ideology and Biblical Interpretation', *Semeia* 47: 9-23.
Carroll, J.T., and J.B. Green
    1995   *The Death of Jesus in Early Christianity* (Peabody, MA: Hendrickson).
Carter, E.
    1960   'Cultural History Written with Lightning: The Significance of *The Birth of a Nation*', *AQ* 12: 347-57.
Cartledge, P.A.
    1985   'Rebels & Sambos in Classical Greece: A Comparative View', in P.A. Cartledge and F.D. Harvey (eds.), *Crux: Essays in Greek History presented to G.E.M. de Ste Croix on his 75th Birthday* (London: Gerald Duckworth): 16-46.
    1989   'The Importance of Being Dorian: An Onomastic Gloss on the Hellenism of Oscar Wilde', *Hermathena* 147: 7-15.

Case, S.E.
    1991   'Tracking the Vampire', *Differences* 3: 1-20.

Cassara, E.
    1973   'The Rehabilitation of Uncle Tom: Significant Themes in Mrs. Stowe's Anti-Slavery Novel', *CLAJ* 17: 230-40.

Cervo, N.
    1985   'Wilde's Closet Self: A Solo at One Remove', *VN* 67: 17-19.

Chaput, D.
    1964   'Uncle Tom and Predestination', *NHB* 27: 143.

Charlesworth, B.
    1988   'Oscar Wilde', in D.L. Lawler (ed.), *Oscar Wilde's The Picture of Dorian Gray* (Norton Critical Edition; London: W.W. Norton): 381-405.

Coetzee, J.M.
    1986   *Foe* (London: Secker & Warburg).

Cohen, E.
    1987   'Writing Gone Wilde: Homoerotic Desire in the Closet of Representation', *PMLA* 102: 801-813.

Cohen, W.A.
    1989–90   'Willie and Wilde: Reading *The Portrait of Mr. W.H.*', *SAQ* 88: 219-45.

Coleridge, S.T.
    1936   *Coleridge's Miscellaneous Criticism* (ed. Thomas M. Raysor; London: Constable).

Conzelmann, H.
    1975   *1 Corinthians* (Hermeneia; Philadelphia: Fortress Press).
    1987   *Acts of the Apostles* (Hermeneia; Philadelphia: Fortress Press).

Coppola, F.F., and J.V. Hart
    1993   *Bram Stoker's Dracula: The Film and the Legend* (London: Pan Books).

Corcoran, P.
    1996   '*Foe*: Metafiction and the Discourse of Power', in L. Spaas and B. Stimpson (eds.), *Robinson Crusoe: Myths and Metamorphoses* (London Macmillan): 257-66.

Corey, S.
    1997   'The Religious Dimensions of the Grotesque in Literature: Toni Morrison's *Beloved*', in J.L. Mayo and W. Yates (eds.), *The Grotesque in Art and Literature: Theological Reflections* (Grand Rapids: Eerdmans): 227-42.

Cottom, D.
    1981   '*Robinson Crusoe*: The Empire's New Clothes', *ECTI* 22: 271-86.

Cowper, W.
    1934   *The Poetical Works of William Cowper* (ed. H.S. Milford; London: Oxford University Press, 4th edn).

Cox, J.M.
    1984   'Harriet Beecher Stowe: From Sectionalism to Regionalism', *NCF* 38: 444-66.

Craft, C.
    1984   '"Kiss Me with Those Red Lips": Gender and Inversion in Bram Stoker's *Dracula*', *Representations* 8: 107-133.

Crane, G.D.
1996   'Dangerous Sentiments: Sympathy, Rights and Revolution in Stowe's Anti-Slavery Novels', *NCF* 51: 176-204.

Crouch, J.E.
1972   *The Origin and Intention of the Colossian Haustafeln* (Göttingen: Vandenhoeck & Ruprecht).

Crouch, S.
1987   'Aunt Medea', *NR* (19 October): 38-43.

Crozier, A.C.
1969   *The Novels of Harriet Beecher Stowe* (Oxford: Oxford University Press).

Crumpacker, L.
1982   'Four Novels of Harriet Beecher Stowe: A Study in Nineteenth-Century Androgyny', in F. Fleishmann (ed.), *American Novelists Revisited: Essays in Feminist Criticism* (Boston: G.K. Hall & Co.): 78-105.

Curtis, L.A.
1984   *The Elusive Daniel Defoe* (London: Vision Press).

Dale, P.A.
1995   'Oscar Wilde: Crime and the "Glorious Shape of Art" ', *VN* 88: 1-5.

Dalzell, F.
1998   'Dreamworking *Amistad*: Representing Slavery, Revolt, and Freedom in America, 1839 and 1997', *NEQ* 71: 127-33.

Damrosch, Jr., L.
1994   'Myth and Fiction in *Robinson Crusoe*', in M. Shinagel (ed.), *Daniel Defoe's Robinson Crusoe* (Norton Critical Edition; New York: W.W. Norton): 373-90.

Danker, F.W.
1960   'The Mirror Metaphor in 1 Cor. 13.12 and 2 Cor. 3.18', *CTM* 31: 428-29.

Danson, L.
1991   'Oscar Wilde, W.H., and the Unspoken Name of Love', *ELH* 58: 979-1000.
1997   *Wilde's Intentions: The Artist in his Criticism* (Oxford: Clarendon Press).

Davis, L.J.
1996   *Factual Fictions: The Origins of the English Novel* (Philadelphia: University of Pennsylvania Press).

Dawes, G.W.
1990   ' "But if you can gain your freedom" (1 Corinthians 7.17-24),' *CBQ* 52: 681-97.

Defoe, D.
1985   *Robinson Crusoe* (ed. Angus Ross; London: Penguin Books).

Dellamora, R.
1988   'Representation and Homophobia in *The Picture of Dorian Gray*,' *VN* 73: 28-31.

Demetrakopoulos, S.
1977   'Feminism, Sex Role Exchanges, and Other Subliminal Fantasies in Bram Stoker's *Dracula*', *FAJWS* 3: 104-113.

Deming, W.
1995   'A Diatribe Pattern in 1 Cor. 7.21-22: A New Perspective on Paul's Directions to Slaves', *NovT* 37: 130-37.

Demos, J.
1964   'The Antislavery Movement and the Problem of Violent "Means"', *NEQ*
            37: 501-526.

Dibelius, M.
1956   *Studies in the Acts of the Apostles* (London: SCM Press).

Dickson, D.R.
1983   "In a mirror that mirrors the sour": Masks and Mirrors in *Dorian Gray*',
            ELT 26: 5-15.

Dodd, C.H.
1925   'Notes from Papyri', *JTS* 26: 77-78.

Donovan, J.
1995   'A Source for Stowe's Ideas on Race in *Uncle Tom's Cabin*', *NWSAJ* 7:
            24-32.

Doody, M.A.
1997   *The True Story of the Novel* (London: HarperCollins).

Dottin, P.
1928   *The Life and Strange and Surprising Adventures of Daniel Defoe*
            (London: Stanley Paul & Co.).

Douglas, A.
1977   *The Feminization of American Culture* (New York: Alfred A. Knopf).
1982   'Introduction: The Art of Controversy', in Stowe 1982: 7-36.

Ducksworth, S.S.
1994   'Stowe's Construction of an African Persona and the Creation of White
            Identity for a New World Order', in M.I. Lowance, Jr, E.E. Westbrook
            and R.C. De Prospo (eds.), *The Stowe Debate: Rhetorical Strategies in
            Uncle Tom's Cabin* (Amherst: University of Massachusetts Press): 205-
            235.

Dunn, J.D.G.
1974   'Paul's Understanding of the Death of Jesus', in R. Banks (ed.), *Reconcil-
            iation and Hope: New Testament Essays on Atonement and Eschatology
            Presented to L.L. Morris on his 60th Birthday* (Grand Rapids: Eerd-
            manns): 125-41.
1996   *The Acts of the Apostles* (EC; London: Epworth Press).
1998   *The Theology of Paul the Apostle* (Edinburgh: T. & T. Clark).

Duvall, R.
1984   'Mothers, Husbands, and Uncle Tom', *GR* 38: 129-44.

Duvall, S.
1963   '*Uncle Tom's Cabin*: The Sinister Side of the Patriarchy', *NEQ* 36: 3-22.

Duvall, S.P.C.
1958–59   'W.G. Simms's Review of Mrs. Stowe', *AL* 30: 107.

Earle, P.
1976   *The World of Defoe* (London: Weidenfeld & Nicolson).

Edwards, O.D.
1998   'Impressions of an Irish Sphinx', in J. McCormack (ed.), *Wilde the Irish-
            man* (New Haven: Yale University Press): 47-70.

Egan, J.
1973   'Crusoe's Monarch and the Puritan Concept of the Self', *SEL* 13: 451-60.

Elliott, N.
1994   *Liberating Paul: The Justice of God and the Politics of the Apostle* (Sheffield: Sheffield Academic Press).

Ellis, F.H.
1969   'Introduction', in F.H. Ellis (ed.), *Twentieth Century Interpretations of Robinson Crusoe: A Collection of Critical Essays* (Englewood Cliffs, NJ: Prentice–Hall): 1-18.

Ellis, M.
1993   'Crusoe Cannibalism and Empire', in L. Spaas and B. Stimpson (eds.), *Robinson Crusoe: Myths and Metamorphoses* (London: Macmillan): 45-61.

Ellmann, R.
1970   'Introduction: The Critic as Artist as Wilde', in Richard Ellmann (ed.), *The Artist as Critic: Critical Writings of Oscar Wilde* (London: W.H. Allen).
1977   'A Late Victorian Love Affair', in R. Ellmann and J. Espey (eds.), *Oscar Wilde: Two Approaches* (Los Angeles: University of California): 1-21.
1988   *Oscar Wilde* (London: Penguin Books).

Emerton, J.A.
1955   'The Aramaic Underlying τὸ αἷμά μου τῆς διαθήκης in Mark XIV.24', *JTS* 6: 238-40.

Engelibert, J.-P.
1996   'Daniel Defoe as Character: Subversion of the Myths of *Robinson Crusoe* and of the Author', in L. Spaas and B. Stimpson (eds.), *Robinson Crusoe: Myths and Metamorphoses* (London: Macmillan): 267-81.

Erickson, R.A.
1982   'Starting Over with Robinson Crusoe', *SLI* 15: 51-73.

Espey, J.
1977   'Resources for Wilde Studies at the Clark Library', in R. Ellmann and J. Espey (eds.), *Oscar Wilde: Two Approaches* (Los Angeles: University of California): 23-48.

Eyles, A., R. Adkinson and N. Fry (eds.)
1973   *The House of Horror: The Story of Hammer Films* (London: Lorrimer Publishing Ltd).

Farson, D.
1975   *The Man Who Wrote* Dracula (New York: St Martin's Press).

Fee, G.D.
1987   *The First Epistle to the Corinthians* (NICNT; Grand Rapids: Eerdmans).

Ferguson, R.
1991   'History, Memory and Language in Toni Morrison's *Beloved*', in S. Sellers (ed.), *Feminist Criticism: Theory and Practice* (Toronto: University of Toronto Press): 109-27.

Fiedler, L.A.
1964   *Waiting for the End* (New York: Stein & Day).
1966   *Love and Death in the American Novel* (New York: Stein & Day).
1979   *The Inadvertent Epic: From Uncle Tom's Cabin to Roots* (New York: Simon & Schuster).

1982   *What Was Literature? Class Culture and Mass Society* (New York: Simon & Schuster).

Fields, K.E.
1989   'To Embrace Dead Strangers: Toni Morrison's *Beloved*', in M. Pearlman (ed.), *Mother Puzzles: Daughters and Mothers in Contemporary American Literature* (New York: Greenwood): 159-70.

Figuerola, C.
1996   'The Robinson Myth in Jean-Richard Bloch's *Le Robinson juif*', in L. Spaas and B. Stimpson (eds.), *Robinson Crusoe: Myths and* Metamorphoses (London: Macmillan): 157-64.

Finley, M.I.
1968   *Aspects of Antiquity: Discoveries and Controversies* (Harmondsworth: Penguin Books).
1980   *Ancient Slavery and Modern Ideology* (London: Chatto & Windus).

Finley, M.I. (ed.)
1960   *Slavery in Classical Antiquity: Views and Controversies* (Cambridge: W. Heffer and Sons).

Fisch, H.
1986   'The Hermeneutic Quest in *Robinson Crusoe*', in G.H. Hartman and S. Budick (eds.), *Midrash and Literature* (New Haven: Yale University Press): 213-35.

Fisher, P.
1985   *Hard Facts: Setting and Form in the American Novel* (Oxford: Oxford University Press).

Fitzgerald, J.T.
1988   *Cracks in an Earthen Vessel: An Examination of the Catalogues of Hardship in the Corinthian Correspondence* (Atlanta: Scholars Press).

Fitzmyer, J.A.
1989   *Luke the Theologian: Aspects of his Teaching* (New York: Paulist Press).

Fleischner, J.
1991   'Hawthorne and the Politics of Slavery', *SN* 23: 96-106.

Flint, C.
1988   'Orphaning the Family: The Role of Kinship in *Robinson Crusoe*', *ELH* 55: 381-491.

Fluck, W.
1992   'The Power and Failure of Representation in Harriet Beecher Stowe's *Uncle Tom's Cabin*', *NLH* 23: 319-38.

Flynn, J.P.
1969   'Booker T. Washington: Uncle Tom or Wooden Horse?', *JNH* 54: 262-74.

Forbes, C.
1986   'Comparison, Self-Praise and Irony: Paul's Boasting and the Conventions of Hellenistic Rhetoric', *NTS* 32: 1-30.

Forster, E.M.
1990   *Aspects of the Novel* (London: Penguin Books).

Foster, J.O.
1992   '*Robinson Crusoe* and the Uses of the Imagination', *JEGP* 91: 179-202.

France, R.T.
    1986   'Liberation in the New Testament', *EvQ* 58: 1-17.
Fraser, P.
    1998   *Images of the Passion: The Sacramental Mode in Film* (Trowbridge: Flicks Books).
Fry, C.L.
    1972   'Fictional Conventions and Sexuality in *Dracula*', *VN* 42: 20-22.
Fry, S.
    1997   'Introduction', in Julian Mitchell, *Wilde: The Screenplay* (London: Orion Media): 8-23.
Furbank, P.N., and W.R. Owens
    1988   *The Canonization of Daniel Defoe* (New Haven: Yale University Press).
Furnas, J.C.
    1956   *Goodbye to Uncle Tom* (New York: William Sloane Associates).
Furnish, V.P.
    1984   *2 Corinthians* (AB, 32A; Garden City, NY: Doubleday).
Gagnier, R.
    1986   *Idylls of the Marketplace: Oscar Wilde and the Victorian Public* (Aldershot: Scolar Press).
    1997   'Wilde and the Victorians', in P. Raby (ed.), *The Cambridge Companion to Oscar Wilde* (Cambridge: Cambridge University Press): 18-334.
Gall, J.
    1992   'The Pregnant Death of Dorian Gray', *VN* 82: 55-58.
Ganzel, D.
    1961   'Chronology in Robinson Crusoe', *PQ* 40: 495-512.
Gardiner, J.
    1978   'The Assault on Uncle Tom: Attempts of Pro-Slavery Novelists to Answer *Uncle Tom's Cabin*', *SHR* 12: 313-24.
Gardner, J.F.
    1991   *Women in Roman Law and Society* (Bloomington, IN: University of Indiana Press).
Garlan, Y.
    1988   *Slavery in Ancient Greece* (London: Gerald Duckworth).
Garnsey, P.
    1996   *Ideas of Slavery from Aristotle to Augustine* (Cambridge: Cambridge University Press).
Gauthier, M.
    1996–97   'The Intersection of the Postmodern and the Postcolonial in J.M. Coetzee's *Foe*', *ELN* 34: 52-71.
Gayer, R.
    1976   *Die Stellung des Sklaven in den paulinischen Gemeinden und bei Paulus* (Frankfurt: Peter Lang).
Gerould, D.C.
    1980   'Uncle Tom's Cabin', in D.C. Gerould (ed.), *American Melodrama* (New York: Performing Arts Journal Publications): 14-18.
Gerson, N.B.
    1976   *Harriet Beecher Stowe: A Biography* (New York: Praeger Publishers).

Gerster, P., and N. Cords
    1977   'The Northern Origins of Southern Mythology', *JSH* 43: 568-69.
Gilbert, S.M., and S. Gubar
    1979   *The Madwoman in the Attic: The Woman Writer and the Nineteenth-Century Literary Imagination* (New Haven: Yale University Press).
Gildon, C.
    1719   *The Life and Strange Surprising Adventures of Mr. D—— De F——, Hosier* (London: J. Roberts).
Giles, K.
    1994   'The Biblical Argument for Slavery: Can the Bible Mislead? A Case Study in Hermeneutics', *EvQ* 66: 3-17.
Gill, A.
    1997   *The Devil's Mariner: William Dampier, Pirate and Explorer* (London: Michael Joseph).
Gillespie, M.P.
    1992   'Picturing Dorian Gray: Resistant Readings in Wilde's Novel', *ELT* 35: 7-25.
    1994   'Ethics and Aesthetics in *The Picture of Dorian Gray*', in C.G. Sandulescu (ed.), *Rediscovering Oscar Wilde* (Gerrards Cross: Colin Smythe): 127-55.
    1995   *The Picture of Dorian Gray: 'What the World Thinks of Me'* (New York: Twayne Publishers).
Girdler, L.
    1953   'Defoe's Education at Newington Green Academy', *SP* 50: 573-91.
Gold, B.J.
    1997   'The Domination of Dorian Gray', *VN* 91: 27-30.
Goldknopf, D.
    1972   *The Life of the Novel* (Chicago: University of Chicago Press).
González, A.B.
    1994   'The Mirror of Narcissus in *The Picture of Dorian Gray*', in C.G. Sandulescu (ed.), *Rediscovering Oscar Wilde* (Gerrards Cross: Colin Smythe): 1-12.
Gordon, J.B
    1967   ' "Parody as Initiation": The Sad Education of "Dorian Gray" ', *Criticism* 9: 355-71.
Gossett, T.F.
    1985   *Uncle Tom's Cabin and American Culture* (Dallas: Southern Methodist University Press).
    1994   'Anti-Uncle Tom Literature', in E. Ammons (ed.), *Harriet Beecher Stowe's Uncle Tom's Cabin* (Norton Critical Edition; New York: W.W. Norton): 442-53.
Graham, T.
    1973   'Harriet Beecher Stowe and the Question of Race', *NEQ* 46: 614-22.
Green, M.
    1990   *The Robinson Crusoe Story* (London: Pennsylvania State University Press).
Grief, M.J
    1966   'The Conversion of Robinson Crusoe', *SEL* 6: 551-74.

Griffin, G.
    1980   ' "Your Girls That You All Love Are Mine" ', *Dracula* and the Victorian Male Sexual Imagination', *IJWS* 3: 454-65.

Grinstein, A.
    1983   'Uncle Tom's Cabin and Harriet Beecher Stowe: Beating Fantasies and Thoughts of Dying', *AI* 40: 115-44.

Haenchen, E.
    1964   'Acta 27', in E. Dinkler (ed.), *Zeit und Geschichte: Dankesgabe an Rudolf Bultmann zum 80. Geburtstag* (Tübingen: J.C.B. Mohr [Paul Siebeck]): 235-54.
    1965   ' "We" in Acts and the Itinerary', *JTC* 1: 65-99.
    1971   *The Acts of the Apostles* (Oxford: Basil Blackwell).

Haining, P. (ed.)
    1995   *The Vampire Omnibus* (London: Orion Books).

Halberstam, J.
    1993   'Technologies of Monstrosity: Bram Stoker's *Dracula*', *VS* 36: 333-52.

Halewood, W.H.
    1964   'Religion and Invention in *Robinson Crusoe*', *EC* 14: 339-51.

Haley, B.
    1985   'Wilde's "Decadence" and the Positivist Tradition', *VS* 28: 25-29.

Hall, B.
    1993   'The Mutilated Tongue: Symbol of Communication in J.M. Coetzee's *Foe*', *UES* 31: 16-22.

Halttunen, K.
    1986   'Gothic Imagination and Social Reform: The Haunted Houses of Lyman Beecher, Henry Ward Beecher, and Harriet Beecher Stowe', in E.J. Sundquist (ed.), *New Essays on Uncle Tom's Cabin* (Cambridge: Cambridge University Press): 107-134.

Hamm, J.-J.
    1996   'Caliban, Friday and their Masters', in L. Spaas and B. Stimpson (eds.), *Robinson Crusoe: Myths and Metamorphoses* (London: Macmillan): 110-24.

Hammond, J.R.
    1993   *A Defoe Companion* (London: Macmillan).

Harrill, J.A.
    1993   'Ignatius, *Ad Polycarp*. 4.3 and the Corporate Manumission of Christian Slaves', *JECS* 1: 107-42.
    1994   'Paul and Slavery: The Problem of 1 Corinthians 7.21', *BibRes* 39: 5-28.

Hart-Davis, R. (ed.)
    1962   *Selected Letters of Oscar Wilde* (Oxford: Oxford University Press).

Hasseler, T.A.
    1993   'The Physiological Determinism Debate in Oscar Wilde's *The Picture of Dorian Gray*', *VN* 84: 31-35.

Hastings, W.
    1912   'Errors and Inconsistencies in Defoe's *Robinson Crusoe*', *MLN* 27: 161-66.

Hatlen, B.
  1980   'The Return of the Repressed/Oppressed in Bram Stoker's *Dracula*', *MR*
            15: 80-97.
Häusermann, H.W.
  1935   'Aspects of Life and Thought in *Robinson Crusoe*', *RES* 2: 299-12, 439-
            56.
Hayden, L.K.
  1981   'The Black Presence in Eighteenth-Century Novels', *CLAJ* 24: 400-415.
Hayne, B.
  1968   'Yankee in the Patriarchy: T.B. Thorpe's Reply to *Uncle Tom's Cabin*',
            AQ 20: 180-95.
Hays, R.B.
  1997   *First Corinthians* (IC; Louisville: John Knox Press).
Hearne, J.
  1967   'The Naked Footprint: An Inquiry into Crusoe's Island', *REL* 8: 97-107.
Hedrick, C.W.
  1981   'Paul's Conversion/Call: A Comparative Analysis of the Three Reports in
            Acts', *JBL* 100: 415-32.
Hedrick, J.D.
  1988   ' "Peacable Fruits": The Ministry of Harriet Beecher Stowe', *AQ* 40: 307-
            32.
  1994   *Harriet Beecher Stowe: A Life* (Oxford: Oxford University Press).
Hemer, C.J.
  1975   'Euraquilo and Melita', *JTS* 26: 100-111.
  1985   'First Person Narrative in Acts 27-28', *TynBul* 36: 79-109.
  1989   *The Book of Acts in the Setting of Hellenistic History* (WUNT, 49;
            Tübingen: J.C.B. Mohr [Paul Siebeck]).
Henderson, M.C.
  1994   'Tom-Shows', in E. Ammons (ed.), *Harriet Beecher Stowe's Uncle
            Tom's Cabin* (Norton Critical Edition; New York: W.W. Norton): 454-
            55.
Henderson, M.G.
  1991   'Toni Morrison's *Beloved*: Re-Membering the Body as Historical Text',
            in H.J. Spillers (ed.), *Comparative American Identities: Race, Sex, and
            Nationality in the Modern Text* (London: Routledge): 62-86.
Henderson, R.M.
  1972   *D.W. Griffith: His Life and Work* (Oxford: Oxford University Press).
Hennelly, M.M., Jr
  1977   '*Dracula*: The Gnostic Quest and Victorian Wasteland', *ELT* 20: 13-26.
Henson, J.
  1994   'Life of Josiah Henson', in E. Ammons (ed.), *Harriet Beecher Stowe's
            Uncle Tom's Cabin* (Norton Critical Edition; New York: W.W. Norton):
            398-405.
Hentzi, G.
  1992   'Sublime Moments and Social Authority in *Robinson Crusoe* and *A Jour-
            nal of the Plague Year*', *ECS* 26: 419-34.

Heston, C.
  1995   *In the Arena* (London: HarperCollins).
Higgins, A.J.B.
  1952   *The Lord's Supper in the New Testament* (SBT, 6; London: SCM Press).
Hindle, M.
  1993   'Introduction', in *Bram Stoker's Dracula* (London: Penguin Books): vii-
              xxx.
Hirsch, S.A.
  1978   'Uncle Tomitudes: The Popular Reaction to *Uncle Tom's Cabin*', in
              J. Myerson (ed.), *Studies in the American Renaissance* (Boston: Twayne
              Publishers): 303-30.
Hoare, P.
  1997   *Wilde's Last Stand: Decadence, Conspiracy & the First World War*
              (London: Gerald Duckworth).
Hodgson, J.A.
  1996–97   'An Allusion to Arthur Conan Doyle's *A Study in Scarlet* in *The Picture
              of Dorian Gray*', *ELN* 34: 41-44.
Hodgson, R.
  1983   'Paul the Apostle and First-Century Tribulation Lists', *ZNW* 74: 59-80.
Hogan, D.J.
  1988   *Dark Romance: Sex and Death in the Horror Film* (Wellingborough:
              Thorsons Publishing Group).
Hogan, M.
  1997   'Built on the Ashes: The Fall of the House of Sutpen and the Rise of the
              House of Seth', in C.A. Kolmerton, S.M. Ross and J.B. Wittenberg (eds.),
              Unflinching Gaze: Morrison and Faulkner Re-Envisioned (Jackson, MI:
              University of Mississippi Press): 167-80.
Holland, G.
  1993   'Speaking Like a Fool: Irony in 2 Corinthians 10-13', in S.E. Porter and
              T.H. Olbricht (eds.), *Rhetoric and the New Testament: Essays from the
              1992 Heidelberg Conference* (JSNTSup, 90; Sheffield: Sheffield Aca-
              demic Press): 250-64.
Holland, M.
  1997   'Biography and the Art of Lying', in P. Raby (ed.), *The Cambridge Com-
              panion to Oscar Wilde* (Cambridge: Cambridge University Press): 3-17.
Holland, V.
  1954   *Son of Oscar Wilde* (New York: E.P. Dutton & Co.).
  1966   *Oscar Wilde* (London: Thames & Hudson).
Hollinger, V.
  1997   'Fantasies of Absence: The Postmodern Vampire', in J. Gordon and
              V. Hollinger (eds.), *Blood Red: The Vampire as Metaphor in Contempo-
              rary Culture* (Philadelphia: University of Pennsylvania Press): 199-212.
Holmes, A.F.
  1972   'Crusoe, Friday and God', *PF* 11: 319-39.
Holmes, G.F.
  1994   'Review of *Uncle Tom's Cabin*', in E. Ammons (ed.), *Harriet Beecher
              Stowe's Uncle Tom's Cabin* (Norton Critical Edition; New York: W.W.
              Norton): 467-77.

Hopes, J.
    1996   'Real and Imagined Stories: *Robinson Crusoe* and the *Serious Reflections*', *ECF* 8: 313-28.
Hopkins, K.
    1978   *Conquerors and Slaves* (Cambridge: Cambridge University Press).
Horrell, D.G.
    1996   *The Social Ethos of the Corinthian Correspondence: Interests and Ideology from 1 Corinthians to 1 Clement* (Edinburgh: T. & T. Clark).
Horvitz, D.
    1989   'Nameless Ghosts: Possession and Dispossession in *Beloved*', *SAF* 17: 157-67.
Hovet, R.
    1981   'Modernization and the American Fall into Slavery', *NEQ* 54: 499-518.
Hovet, T.R.
    1979   'Principles of the Hidden Life: *Uncle Tom's Cabin* and the Myth of the Inward Quest in Nineteenth-Century American Culture', *JACult* 2: 265-70.
    1979–80   'Mrs. Thomas C. Upham's "Happy Phebe": A Feminine Source for Uncle Tom', *AL* 51: 267-70.
Howard, J.K.
    1969   ' "Christ our Passover": A Study of the Passover-Exodus Theme in 1 Corinthians', *EvQ* 41: 97-108.
Howes, M.
    1988   The Mediation of the Feminine: Bisexuality, Homoerotic Desire, and Self-Expression in Bram Stoker's *Dracula*', *TSLL* 30: 104-119.
Hudson, B.F.
    1963   'Another View of "Uncle Tom" ', *Phylon* 24: 79-87.
Hudson, N.
    1988   ' "Why God No Kill the Devil?": The Diabolical Disruption of Order in *Robinson Crusoe*', *RES* 39: 494-501.
Hunter, A.M.
    1961   *Paul and his Predecessors* (London: SCM Press, rev. edn).
Hunter, J.P.
    1963   'Friday as a Convert: Defoe and the Accounts of Indian Missionaries', *RES* 14: 243-48.
    1966   *The Reluctant Pilgrim: Defoe's Emblematic Method and Quest for Form in 'Robinson Crusoe'* (Baltimore: The Johns Hopkins University Press).
Hutchings, P.
    1993   *Hammer and Beyond: The British Horror Film* (Manchester: Manchester University Press).
Hutchins, H.C.
    1925   *Robinson Crusoe and its Printings (1719–1731)* (New York: Columbia University Press).
Huxley, A.
    1962   *Island* (London: Chatto & Windus).
Hyde, H.M.
    1973   *The Trials of Oscar Wilde* (New York: Dover Publications [1948]).
    1976   *Oscar Wilde* (London: Eyre Methuen).

Irvine, L.
　1983　　　*Castaway* (London: Victor Gollancz).
Jager, E.
　1987–88　'The Parrot's Voice: Language and the Self in *Robinson Crusoe*', *ECS* 21: 316-33.
James, E.A.
　1972　　　*Daniel Defoe's Many Voices: A Rhetorical Study of Prose Style and Literary Method* (Amsterdam: Rodopi NV).
Jancovich, M.
　1992　　　*Horror* (London: Batsford).
Jann, R.
　1989　　　'Saved by Science? The Mixed Messages of Stoker's *Dracula*', *TSLL* 31: 271-87.
Jehlen, M.
　1989　　　'The Family Militant: Domesticity versus Slavery in *Uncle Tom's Cabin*', *Criticism* 31: 383-400.
Jenkins, C.
　1908　　　'Origen on 1 Corinthians, III', *JTS* 9: 507-508.
Jenkins, J.L.
　1992　　　'Failed Mothers and Fallen Houses: The Crisis of Domesticity in *Uncle Tom's Cabin*', *ESQ* 38: 161-87.
Jeremias, J.
　1969　　　*Jerusalem in the Time of Jesus* (London: SCM Press).
　1977　　　*The Eucharistic Words of Jesus* (Philadelphia: Fortress Press).
Johnson, A.A.
　1973　　　'Old Bones Uncovered: A Reconsideration of *Robinson Crusoe*', *CLAJ* 17: 271-78.
Johnson, A.
　1984a　　'Dual Life: The Status of Women in *Dracula*', *TSL* 27: 20-39.
　1984b　　'Bent and Broken Necks: Signs of Design in Stoker's *Dracula*', *VN* 67: 17-24.
Johnson, L.T.
　1992　　　*The Acts of the Apostles* (SPC, 5; Collegeville, MN: Liturgical Press).
Jones, F.S.
　1987　　　*'Freiheit' in den Briefen des Apostels Paulus: Eine historische, exegetische und religionsgeschichtliche Studie* (Göttingen: Vandenhoeck & Ruprecht).
Jones, S.
　1993　　　*The Illustrated Vampire Movie Guide* (London: Titan Books).
Joseph, G.
　1987　　　'Framing Wilde', *VN* 72: 61-63.
Joswick, T.P.
　1984　　　' "The Crown without the Conflict": Religious Values and Moral Reasoning in *Uncle Tom's Cabin*', *NCF* 39: 253-74.
Joyce, J.
　1964　　　'Daniel Defoe', *BS* 1: 1-25.
　1994　　　'Daniel Defoe', in M. Shinagel (ed.), *Daniel Defoe's Robinson Crusoe* (Norton Critical Edition; New York: W.W. Norton): 320-23.

Julian, P.
    1988   'Oscar Wilde', in D.L. Lawler (ed.), *Oscar Wilde's The Picture of Dorian Gray* (Norton Critical Edition; London: W.W. Norton): 405-412.
Käsemann, E.
    1964   *Essays on New Testament Themes* (London: SCM Press).
Kavanaugh, T.M.
    1978   'Unraveling Robinson: The Divided Self in Defoe's *Robinson Crusoe*', *TSLL* 20: 416-32.
Kazin, A.
    1997   *God & the American Writer* (New York: Alfred A. Knopf).
Keck, L.E.
    1979   *Paul and his Letters* (PC; Philadelphia: Fortress Press).
Keefe, R.
    1973   'Artist and Model in *The Picture of Dorian Gray*', *SN* 5: 63-70.
Keenan, S.
    1993   ' "Four Hundred Years of Silence": Myth, History, and Motherhood in Toni Morrison's *Beloved*', in J. White (ed.), *Recasting the World: Writing after Colonialism* (Baltimore: The Johns Hopkins University Press): 45-81.
Kiberd, D.
    1996   *Inventing Ireland* (Cambridge, MA: Harvard University Press).
Kimball, G.
    1982   *The Religious Ideas of Harriet Beecher Stowe: Her Gospel of Womanhood* (Lewiston, NY: The Edwin Mellen Press).
Kirschenbaum, A.
    1987   *Sons, Slaves and Freedmen in Roman Commerce* (Jerusalem: Magnes Press).
Kistemaker, S.J.
    1993   *1 Corinthians* (NTC; Grand Rapids: Baker Book House).
Kisthardt, M.J.
    1994   'Flirting with Patriarchy: Feminist Dialogics', in M.I. Lowance, Jr, E.E. Westbrook and R.C. De Prospo (eds.), *The Stowe Debate: Rhetorical Strategies in Uncle Tom's Cabin* (Amherst: University of Massachusetts Press): 37-56.
Kittel, G.
    1964   'αἴνιγμα (ἔσοπτρον)', *TDNT*, I: 178-80.
Klauck, H.-J.
    1992   'Lord's Supper', *ABD*, IV: 362-72.
Knox, M.
    1994   *Oscar Wilde: A Long and Lovely Suicide* (New Haven: Yale University Press).
Kohl, N.
    1989   *Oscar Wilde: The Works of a Conformist Rebel* (Cambridge: Cambridge University Press).
Korg, C.E.
    1990   'Women, Slaves, and Family in *Uncle Tom's Cabin*: Symbolic Battleground in Antebellum America', *MQ* 31: 252-69.

Korg, J.
    1967–68   'The Rage of Caliban', *UTC* 37: 75-89.

Kreitzer, L.J.
    1993   *The New Testament in Fiction and Film: On Reversing the Hermeneutical Flow* (BS, 17; Sheffield: Sheffield Academic Press).
    1994   *The Old Testament in Fiction and Film: On Reversing the Hermeneutical Flow* (BS, 24; Sheffield: Sheffield Academic Press).
    1996   *2 Corinthians* (NTG; Sheffield: Sheffield Academic Press).
    1997   'The Scandal of the Cross: Crucifixion Imagery and Bram Stoker's *Dracula*', in G. Aichele and T. Pippin (eds.), *The Monstrous and the Unspeakable: The Bible as Fantastic Literature* (PTT, 1; Sheffield: Sheffield Academic Press): 181-219.

Krumholz, L.
    1992   'The Ghosts of Slavery: Historical Recovery in Toni Morrison's *Beloved*', *AAR* 26: 395-408.

Krumm, P.
    1995   'Metamorphosis as Metaphor in Bram Stoker's *Dracula*', *VN* 88: 5-11.

Kurz, W.S.
    1987   'Narrative Approaches to Luke–Acts', *Biblica* 68: 195-220.

Kyrtatas, D.J.
    1987   *The Social Structure of the Early Christian Communities* (London: Verso Books).

Ladouceur, D.
    1980   'Hellenistic Preconceptions of Shipwreck and Pollution as a Concept for Acts 27-28', *HTR* 73: 435-49.

Lake, K., and H.J. Cadbury
    1933   'Note XXVII: The Winds', in F.J. Foakes Jackson and K. Lake (eds.), *The Beginnings of Christianity: Part 1. The Acts of the Apostles*, V (London: Macmillan): 338-44.

Lane, C.
    1994   'Framing Fears, Reading Designs: The Homosexual Art of Painting in James, Wilde, and Beerbohm', *ELH* 61: 923-54.

Lang, A.S.
    1986   'Slavery and Sentimentalism: The Strange Case of Augustine St. Clare', *WS* 12: 31-54.
    1987   *Prophetic Women: Anne Hutchinson and the Problem of Dissent in the Literature of New England* (Berkeley: University of California Press).

Lang, R. (ed.)
    1994   *The Birth of a Nation: D.W. Griffith, Director* (New Brunswick, NJ: Rutgers University Press).

Lange, B.S.
    1983   'Toni Morrison's Rainbow Code', *Critique* 34: 173-81.

Latham, R.
    1997   'Consuming Youth: The Lost Boys Cruise Mallworld', in J. Gordon and V. Hollinger (eds.), *Blood Red: The Vampire as Metaphor in Contemporary Culture* (Philadelphia: University of Pennsylvania Press): 129-47.

Lawler, D.L

1972   'Oscar Wilde's First Manuscript of *The Picture of Dorian Gray*', *SB* 25: 125-35.

1974   'The Revisions of *Dorian Gray*', *VIJ* 3: 21-36.

1988a   'A Note on the Texts', in D.L. Lawler (ed.), *Oscar Wilde's The Picture of Dorian Gray* (Norton Critical Edition; London: W.W. Norton, 1988): x-xiii.

1988b   'Keys to the Upstairs Room: A Centennial Essay on Allegorical Performance in *Dorian Gray*', in D.L. Lawler (ed.), *Oscar Wilde's The Picture of Dorian Gray* (Norton Critical Edition; London: W.W. Norton): 431-57.

1994   'The Gothic Wilde', in C.G. Sandulescu (ed.), *Rediscovering Oscar Wilde* (Gerrards Cross: Colin Smythe): 249-68.

Lawler, D.L., and C.E. Knott

1975–76   'The Context of Invention: Suggested Origins of *Dorian Gray*', *MP* 73: 389-98.

Leatherdale, C.

1993   *Dracula: The Novel and the Legend* (Brighton: Desert Island Books).

Lebedun, J.

1974–75   'Harriet Beecher Stowe's Interest in Sojourner Truth, Black Feminist', *AL* 46: 359-63.

Leverenz, D.

1989   *Manhood and the American Renaissance* (New York: Cornell University Press).

Levine, L.W.

1979   'Slave Songs and Slave Consciousness: An Exploration in Neglected Sources', in A. Weinstein, F.O. Gatell and D. Sarasohn (eds.), *American Negro Slavery: A Modern Reader* (Oxford: Oxford University Press, 3rd edn): 143-72.

Levine, R.S.

1992   '*Uncle Tom's Cabin* in *Frederick Douglass' Paper*: An Analysis of Reception', *AL* 64: 71-93.

Levy, D.W.

1970   'Racial Stereotypes in Antislavery Fiction', *Phylon* 31: 265-79.

Lowance, M.I., Jr

1994   'Biblical Typology and the Allegorical Mode: The Prophetic Strain', in M.I. Lowance, Jr, E.E. Westbrook and R.C. De Prospo (eds.), *The Stowe Debate: Rhetorical Strategies in Uncle Tom's Cabin* (Amherst: The University of Massachusetts Press): 159-84.

Lüdemann, G.

1989   *Early Christianity According to the Acts of the Apostles: A Commentary* (London: SCM Press).

Ludlam, H.

1962   *A Biography of Dracula: The Life Story of Bram Stoker* (London: Foulsham).

Lyall, F.

1970–71   'Roman Law in the Writings of Paul—The Slave and the Freedman', *NTS* 17: 73-79.

1984   *Slaves, Citizens, Sons: Legal Metaphors in the Epistles* (Grand Rapids: Eerdmans).

Mabee, C.

1997   'Review of Larry Kreitzer's *The Old Testament in Fiction and Film: On Reversing the Hermeneutical Flow*', *JBL* 51: 88.

Macaskill, B., and J. Colleran

1992   'Reading History, Writing Heresy: The Resistance of Representation and the Representation of Resistance in J.M. Coetzee's *Foe*', *CL* 33: 432-57.

Maccoby, H.

1991   'Paul and the Eucharist', *NTS* 37: 247-67.

MacDonald, J.I.H.

1998   *The Crucible of Christian Morality* (London: Routledge).

MacDonald, R.H.

1976   'The Creation of an Ordered World in *Robinson Crusoe*', *DR* 56: 23-34.

MacFarlane, L.W.

1990   '"If Ever I Get to Where I Can": The Competing Rhetorics of Social Reform in *Uncle Tom's Cabin*', *ATQ* 4: 135-47.

MacLaine, A.H.

1955   '*Robinson Crusoe* and the Cyclops', *SP* 52: 599-604.

Maddox, Jr., J.H.

1984   'Interpreter Crusoe', *ELH* 51: 33-52.

Malan, F.S.

1981   'Bound to Do Right', *Neotestamentica* 15: 118-38.

Malmgren, C.D.

1995   'Mixed Genres and the Logic of Slavery in Toni Morrison's *Beloved*', *Critique* 36: 96-106.

Mare, W. de la

1930   *Desert Islands and Robinson Crusoe* (London: Faber & Faber).

Marez, C.

1997   'The Other Addict: Reflections on Colonialism and Oscar Wilde's Opium Smoke Screen', *ELH* 64: 257-87.

Marsh, C., and G. Ortiz (eds.)

1997   *Explorations in Theology and Film: Movies and Meaning* (Oxford: Basil Blackwell, 1997).

Marsh, C.

1997   'Did You Say "Grace"? Eating in Community in *Babette's Feast*', in C. Marsh and G. Ortiz (eds.), *Explorations in Theology and Film: Movies and Meaning* (Oxford: Basil Blackwell): 207-218.

Marshall, I.H.

1980a   *Acts* (TNTC; Leicester: IVP).

1980b   *Lord's Supper & Last Supper* (Exeter: Paternoster Press).

1993   'Lord's Supper', in R.P. Martin (ed.), *Dictionary of Paul and his Letters* (Leicester: IVP): 569-75.

Marshall, P.

1987   *Enmity in Corinth: Social Conventions in Paul's Relations with the Corinthians* (WUNT, 2.23; Tübingen: J.C.B. Mohr [Paul Siebeck]).

Martin, D.B.
    1990   *Slavery as Salvation: The Metaphor of Slavery in Pauline Christianity* (New Haven: Yale University Press).

Martin, J.W., and Conrad E. Ostwalt, Jr (eds.)
    1995   *Screening the Sacred: Religion, Myth, and Ideology in Popular American Film* (Boulder, CO: Westview Press).

Martin, R.K.
    1983   'Parody and Homage: The Presence of Pater in Dorian Gray', *VN* 63: 15-18.

Martin, R.P.
    1974   *Worship in the Early Church* (London: Marshall, Morgan & Scott).
    1986   *2 Corinthians* (WBC, 40; Waco, TX: Word Books).

Marx, K.
    1994   'Crusoe and Capitalism', in M. Shinagel (ed.), *Daniel Defoe's Robinson Crusoe* (Norton Critical Edition; New York: W.W. Norton): 274-77.

Marxsen, W.
    1970   *The Lord's Supper as a Christological Problem* (Philadelphia: Fortress Press).

Massey, M., and P. Moreland
    1978   *Slavery in Ancient Rome* (London: Macmillan).

Matheson, R.
    1991   *I Am Legend* (Forestville, CA: Eclipse Books [1954]; a four-part graphic comic-book version of the novel adapted by Steve Niles and illustrated by Elman Brown).

McCormack, J.
    1997   'Wilde's Fiction(s)', in P. Raby (ed.), *The Cambridge Companion to Oscar Wilde* (Cambridge: Cambridge University Press): 96-117.

McDonald, J.
    1993   ' "The Devil is Beautiful" *Dracula*: Freudian Novel and Feminist Drama', in P. Reynolds (ed.), *Novel Images: Literature in Performance* (London: Routledge): 80-104.

McKeon, M.
    1987   *The Origins of the English Novel (1600–1740)* (Baltimore: The Johns Hopkins University Press, 1987).

McNally, R., and R. Florescu
    1975   *In Search of Dracula: A True History of Dracula and the Vampire Legends* (London: New English Library).

McPherson, J.M.
    1965   'Abolitionist and Negro Opposition to Colonization during the Civil War', *Phylon* 26: 391-99.

Meagher, S.
    1996   'Resisting Robinson Crusoe in Dechanel's Film', in L. Spaas and B. Stimpson (eds.), *Robinson Crusoe: Myths and Metamorphoses* (London: Macmillan, 1996): 148-56.

Meeks, W.A.
    1983   *The First Urban Christians: The Social World of the Apostle Paul* (New Haven: Yale University Press).

1996   'The "Haustafeln" and American Slavery: A Hermeneutical Challenge',
              in E.H. Lovereing, Jr and J.L. Sumney (eds.), *Theology and Ethics in
              Paul and his Interpreters: Essays in Honor of Victor Paul Furnish*
              (Nashville: Abingdon Press, 1996): 232-53.

Meggitt, J.J.
1998   *Paul, Poverty and Survival* (Edinburgh: T. & T. Clark).

Mégroz, R.L.
1939   *The Real Robinson Crusoe* (London: Cresset Books).

Meinardus, O.F.A.
1976   'St. Paul Shipwrecked in Dalmatia', *BA* 39: 145-47.

Merrett, R.J.
1989   'Narrative Continuities as Signs in Defoe's Fiction', *ECF* 1: 171-85.

Meyer, M.J.
1994   'Toward a Rhetoric of Equality: Reflective and Refractive Images in
              Stowe's Language', in M.I. Lowance, Jr, E.E. Westbrook and R.C. De
              Prospo (eds.), *The Stowe Debate: Rhetorical Strategies in Uncle Tom's
              Cabin* (Amherst: University of Massachusetts Press, 1994): 236-54.

Middleton, S.
1987   'The Fugitive Slave Crisis in Cincinnati, 1850–1860: Resistance,
              Enforcement, and Black Refugees', *JNH* 72 (1987): 20-32.

Miles, G.B., and G. Trompf
1976   'Luke and Antiphon: The Theology of Acts 27-28 in the Light of Beliefs
              about Divine Retribution, Pollution, and Shipwreck', *HTR* 69: 259-67.

Milgrom, J.
1991   *Leviticus 1–16* (AB, 3; New York: Doubleday).

Miller, E.
1994   '*Dracula*: The Narrative Patchwork', *Udolpho* 18: 27-30.

Milne, L.
1996   'Myth as Microscope: Michel Tournier's *Vendredi ou les limbes du
              Pacifique*', in L. Spaas and B. Stimpson (eds.), *Robinson Crusoe: Myths
              and Metamorphoses* (London: Macmillan): 157-81.

Minto, W.
1879   *Daniel Defoe* (London: Macmillan).

Mitchell, A.
1974   *Man Friday: A Play* (London: Methuen).

Mitchell, M.M.
1992   *Paul and the Rhetoric of Reconciliation: An Exegetical Investigation of
              the Language and Composition of 1 Corinthians* (Louisville, KY: West-
              minster/John Knox Press).

Moers, E.
1976   *Literary Women: The Great Writers* (Garden City, NY: Doubleday).

Moffatt, J.
1919   'The Religion of Robinson Crusoe', *Contemporary Review* 115: 664-69.

Moore, J.R.
1939   *Defoe in the Pillory and Other Studies* (Bloomington, IN: Indiana Uni-
              versity Publications).
1941   'Defoe's Religious Sect', *RES* 18: 461-67.

| 1945 | '*The Tempest* and *Robinson Crusoe*', *RES* 21: 52-56. |

1958   *Daniel Defoe: Citizen of the Modern World* (Chicago: University of Chicago Press).

1970–71   'Daniel Defoe: King William's Pamphleteer and Intelligence Agent', *HLQ* 34: 251-60.

1972–73   'A Footnote to a Charge of Scandal Against Defoe', *HLQ* 36: 159-62.

Moretti, F.

1983   *Signs Taken for Wonders: Essays in the Sociology of Literary Forms* (London: Verso Press, 1983).

Morrison, R.D.

1994   'Reading Barthes and Reading *Dracula*: Between Work and Text', *KPR* 9: 23-28.

Morrison, T.

1988   *Beloved* (London: Plume Books).

Moule, C.F.D.

1957   *The Epistles to the Colossians and to Philemon* (CGTC; Cambridge: Cambridge University Press).

Murphy-O'Connor, J.

1996   *Paul: A Critical Life* (Oxford: Oxford University Press).

Murray, I.

1972   'Some Elements in the Composition of *The Picture of Dorian Gray*', *Durham University Journal* 64 (June): 220-31.

1974   'Introduction', in Oscar Wilde, *The Picture of Dorian Gray* (London: Oxford University Press): vii-xxvi.

1994   'Oscar Wilde in his Literary Element: Yet Another Source for *Dorian Gray*?', in C.G. Sandulescu (ed.), *Rediscovering Oscar Wilde* (Gerrards Cross: Colin Smythe): 283-96.

Nandris, G.

1966   'The Historical Dracula: The Theme of his Legend in the Western and Eastern Literatures of Europe', *CLS* 3: 367-96.

Nelsen, A.K., and H.M. Nelsen

1970   'The Prejudicial Film: Progress and Stalemate, 1915–1967', *Phylon* 31: 142-47.

Nethercot, A.H.

1944   'Oscar Wilde and the Devil's Advocate', *PMLA* 59: 833-50.

Nichols, C.

1954   'The Origins of *Uncle Tom's Cabin*', *Phylon* 19: 328-34.

Nixon, N.

1997   'When Hollywood Sucks, or, Hungry Girls, Lost Boys, and Vampirism in the Age of Reagan', in J. Gordon and V. Hollinger (eds.), *Blood Red: The Vampire as Metaphor in Contemporary Culture* (Philadelphia: University of Pennsylvania Press): 115-28.

Nolan, S.

1998   'The Books of the Films: Trends in Religious Film-Analysis', *LT* 12: 1-15.

Novak, M.E.

1961   'Robinson Crusoe's Fear and the Search for the Natural Man', *MP* 58: 238-45.

1962 'Crusoe the King and the Political Evolution of his Island', *SEL* 2: 337-50.

1963 *Defoe and the Nature of Man* (Oxford: Oxford University Press).

1964 'Defoe's Theory of Fiction', *SP* 61: 650-68.

1966 *Economics and the Fiction of Daniel Defoe* (Berkeley: University of California Press).

1970–71 'A Whiff of Scandal in the Life of Daniel Defoe', *HLQ* 34: 35-42.

1974 'Imaginary Islands and Real Beasts: The Imaginary Genius of *Robinson Crusoe*', *TSL* 19: 57-78.

Nuernberg, S.M.
1994 'The Rhetoric of Race', in M.I. Lowance, Jr, E.E. Westbrook and R.C. De Prospo (eds.), *The Stowe Debate: Rhetorical Strategies in Uncle Tom's Cabin* (Amherst: University of Massachusetts Press): 255-70.

Nunokawa, J.
1992 'Homosexual Desire and the Effacement of the Self in *The Picture of Dorian Gray*', *AI* 49: 311-21.

Oates, J.C.
1988 '*The Picture of Dorian Gray*: Wilde's Parable of the Fall', in D.L. Lawler (ed.), *Oscar Wilde's The Picture of Dorian Gray* (Norton Critical Edition; London: W.W. Norton): 422-31.

O'Connell, C.E.
1994 '"The Magic of the Real Presence of Distress": Sentimentality and Competing Rhetorics of Authority', in M.I. Lowance, Jr, E.E. Westbrook and R.C. De Prospo (eds.), *The Stowe Debate: Rhetorical Strategies in Uncle Tom's Cabin* (Amherst: University of Massachusetts Press): 13-36.

Ogilvie, R.M.
1958 'Phoenix', *JTS* 9: 308-314.

Otten, T.
1989 *The Crime of Innocence in the Fiction of Toni Morrison* (Columbia, MT: University of Missouri Press).

Paglia, C.
1991 *Sexual Personae: Art and Decadence from Nefertiti to Emily Dickinson* (New York: Vintage Books).

Pappas, J.J.
1972 'The Flower and the Beast: A Study of Oscar Wilde's Antithetical Attitudes toward Nature and Man in *The Picture of Dorian Gray*', *ELT* 25: 37-48.

Parker, G.
1925 'The Allegory of *Robinson Crusoe*', *History* 10: 11-25.

Parrish, T.L.
1997 'Imagining Slavery: Toni Morrison and Charles Johnson', *SAF* 25: 81-100.

Peck, H. D.
1973 '*Robinson Crusoe*: The Moral Geography of Limitation', *JNT* 3: 20-31.

Perlman, E.H.
1976–77 'Robinson Crusoe and the Cannibals', *Mosaic* 10: 39-55.

Plate, S.B.
    1998   'Religion/Literature/Film: Towards a Religious Visuality of Film', *LT* 12:
                16-38.
Poe, E.A.
    1994   'Defoe's Faculty of Identification', in M. Shinagel (ed.), *Daniel Defoe's
                Robinson Crusoe* (Norton Critical Edition; New York: W.W. Norton):
                270-71.
Pokorný, P.
    1973   'Die Romfahrt des Paulus und der antike Roman', *ZNW* 64: 233-44.
Porter, R.
    1992   'The Historical Dracula' (a 12-page article posted on the Internet dated
                30 April).
Porter, S.E.
    1994   'The "We" Passages', in D.W.J. Gill and C. Gempf (eds.), *The Book of
                Acts in its Graeco-Roman Setting* (BAFCS, 2; Carlisle: Paternoster
                Press): 545-74.
Portnoy, W.E.
    1974   'Wilde's Debt to Tennyson in *Dorian Gray*', *ELT* 17: 75-89.
Post, R.M.
    1989   'The Noise of Freedom: J.M. Coetzee's *Foe*', *Critique* 30: 143-54.
Poteet, L.J.
    1971   '*Dorian Gray* and the Gothic Novel', *MFS* 27: 239-48.
Powell, K.
    1978–79   'Massinger, Wilde, and *The Picture of Dorian Gray*', *ELN* 16: 312-15.
    1980   'Hawthorne, Arlo Bates, and *Dorian Gray*', *PLL* 16: 403-416.
    1983   'Tom, Dick, and Dorian Gray: Magic-Picture Mania in Late Victorian
                Fiction', *PQ* 62: 147-70.
    1984   'The Mesmerizing of Dorian Gray', *VN* 65: 10-15.
    1986–87   'Who Was Basil Hallward?', *ELN* 24: 84-91.
    1997   'A Verdict of Death: Oscar Wilde, Actresses and Victorian Women', in
                P. Raby (ed.), *The Cambridge Companion to Oscar Wilde* (Cambridge:
                Cambridge University Press): 181-94.
Praeder, S.M.
    1984   'Acts 27.1-28.16: Sea Voyages in Ancient Literature and the Theology of
                Luke–Acts', *CBQ* 46: 683-706.
Prior, D.
    1985   *The Message of 1 Corinthians* (BST; Leicester: IVP).
Punter, D.
    1980   *The Literature of Terror: A History of Gothic Fiction from 1765 to the
                Present Day* (London: Longman).
Purdy, A.
    1996   ' "Skilful in the Usury of Time": Michel Tournier and the Critique of
                Economism', in L. Spaas and B. Stimpson (eds.), *Robinson Crusoe:
                Myths and Metamorphoses* (London: Macmillan): 182-98.
Railton, S.
    1984   'Mothers, Husbands, and Uncle Tom', *GR* 38: 129-44.

Rapske, B.M.

1994 'Acts, Travel and Shipwreck', in D.W.J. Gill and C. Gempf (eds.), *The Book of Acts in its Graeco-Roman Setting* (BAFCS, 2; Carlisle: Paternoster Press): 1-47.

Rawson, B. (ed.)

1986 *The Family in Ancient Rome: New Perspectives* (London: Croom Helm).

Reed, K.T.

1968 '*Uncle Tom's Cabin* and the Heavenly City', *CLAJ* 12: 150-54.

Richardson, H.

1971 *The Sexual Life of Robinson Crusoe* (London: Olympia Press).

Richetti, J.J.

1975 *Defoe's Narratives: Situations and Structures* (Oxford: Clarendon Press,).

1987 *Daniel Defoe* (Boston: Twayne Publishers).

Richman, M.

1997 'Uncle Tom's Montgomery County Cabin', *The Washington Post* (10 December), Section H: 5.

Ridderbos, H.N.

1974 'The Earliest Confession of the Atonement in Paul', in R. Banks (ed.), *Reconciliation and Hope: New Testament Essays on Atonement and Eschatology Presented to L.L. Morris on his 60th Birthday* (Grand Rapids: Eerdmanns): 76-89.

Ridgely, J.V.

1959–60 'Woodcraft: Simms's First Answer to *Uncle Tom's Cabin*', *AL* 31: 421-33.

Riggio, T.P.

1976 '*Uncle Tom* Reconstructed: A Neglected Chapter in the History of a Book', *AQ* 28: 56-70.

Riss, A.

1994 'Racial Essentialism and Family Values in Uncle Tom's Cabin', *AQ* 46: 513-44.

Robbins, S.

1997 'Gendering the History of the Antislavery Narrative: Juxtaposing *Uncle Tom's Cabin* and *Benito Cereno*, *Beloved* and *Middle Passage*', *AQ* 49: 531-73.

Robbins, V.K.

1978 'By Land and by Sea: The We-Passages and Ancient Sea Voyages', in C.H. Talbert (ed.), *Perspectives on Luke–Acts* (Edinburgh: T. & T. Clark, 1978): 215-42.

Roberson, S.L.

1994 'Matriarchy and the Rhetoric of Domesticity', in M.I. Lowance, Jr, E.E. Westbrook and R.C. De Prospo (eds.), *The Stowe Debate: Rhetorical Strategies in Uncle Tom's Cabin* (Amherst: University of Massachusetts Press): 116-37.

Roberts, D.

1994 *The Myth of Aunt Jemima: Representations of Race and Region* (London: Routledge Press).

Roberts S.
   1991   ' "Post-Colonialism: Or, the House of Friday"—J.M. Coetzee's *Foe*',
             WLWE 31: 87-92.
Robins, H.F.
   1952   'How Smart Was Robinson Crusoe?', *PMLA* 57: 782-89.
Roditi, E.
   1969   'Fiction as Allegory: The Picture of Dorian Gray,' in R. Ellmann (ed.),
             Oscar Wilde: A Collection of Critical Essays (Englewood Cliffs, NJ:
             Prentice–Hall): 47-55.
Rody, C.
   1995   'Toni Morrison's *Beloved*: History, "Rememory," and a "Clamour for a
             Kiss" ', *ALH* 7: 92-119.
Rogers, P.
   1974   'Crusoe's Home', *EC* 24: 375-90.
   1979   *Robinson Crusoe* (London: Allen & Unwin).
Rollins, W.G.
   1987   'Greco-Roman Slave Terminology and Pauline Metaphors for Salvation',
             in K.H. Richards (ed.), *Society of Biblical Literature 1987 Seminar
             Papers* (Atlanta: Scholars Press): 100-110.
Romero, L.
   1989   'Bio-Political Resistance in Domestic Ideology in *Uncle Tom's Cabin*',
             ALH 1: 715-34.
Rosen, G.
   1998   ' "Amistad" and the Abuse of History', *Commentary* 105: 46-51.
Ross, A.
   1985   'Appendix: Alexander Selkirk', in *idem*, *Daniel Defoe's Robinson
             Crusoe* (Harmondsworth: Penguin): 301-310.
Rossi, D.
   1969   'Parallels in Wilde's "The Picture of Dorian Gray" and Goethe's
             "Faust" ', *CLAJ* 13: 188-91.
Roth, J.
   1977   'Suddenly Sexual Women in Bram Stoker's *Dracula*', *LP* 27: 113-21.
Rousseau, J.-J.
   1994   'A Treatise on Natural Education', in M. Shinagel (ed.), *Daniel Defoe's
             Robinson Crusoe* (Norton Critical Edition; New York: W.W. Norton):
             262-64.
Rowland, C.
   1985   *Christian Origins: An Account of the Setting and Character of the Most
             Important Messianic Sect of Judaism* (London: SPCK).
Rushdy, A.H.A.
   1992   'Daughters Signifyin(g) History: The Example of Toni Morrison's
             Beloved', *AL* 64: 567-97.
Ryder, A. (ed.)
   1987   *The Penguin Book of Vampire Stories* (Harmondsworth: Penguin Books).
Saberhagen, F.
   1992   *Bram Stoker's Dracula* (New York: Signet Books).

Saller, R.
    1987   'Slavery and the Roman Family', in M.I. Finley (ed.), *Classical Slavery*
               (London: Frank Cass & Co.): 65-87.
Sampley, J.P.
    1988   'Paul, his Opponents in 2 Corinthians 10-13, and the Rhetorical Hand-
               books', in J. Neusner, E.S. Frerichs, P. Borgen and R. Horsley (eds.), *The
               Social World of Formative Christianity and Judaism* (Philadelphia:
               Fortress Press): 162-77.
Sánchez-Eppler, K.
    1988   'Bodily Bonds: The Intersecting Rhetorics of Feminism and Abolition-
               ism', *Representations* 24: 28-59.
Saxton, A.
    1996   'Female Castaways', in L. Spaas and B. Stimpson (eds.), *Robinson
               Crusoe: Myths and Metamorphoses* (London: Macmillan): 141-47.
Scarpa, G.
    1991–92   'Narrative Possibilities at Play in Toni Morrison's *Beloved*', *Melus* 17:
               91-103.
Schaffer, T.
    1994   ' "A Wilde Desire Took Me": The Homoerotic History of *Dracula*', *ELH*
               61: 381-425.
Schonhorn, M.
    1991   *Defoe's Politics: Parliament, Power, Kingship, and Robinson Crusoe*
               (Cambridge: Cambridge University Press).
Schweizer, E.
    1967   *The Lord's Supper According to the New Testament* (Philadelphia:
               Fortress Press).
Scott, W.
    1972   'Scott on Defoe's Life and Works', in P. Rogers (ed.), *Defoe: The Criti-
               cal Heritage* (London: Routledge & Kegan Paul): 78.
Seaford, R.
    1984   '1 Corinthians XIII.12', *JTS* 35: 117-20.
Secord, A.
    1951   'Defoe in Stoke Newington', *PMLA* 66: 211-25.
Sedgwick, E.K.
    1985   *Between Men: English Literature and Male Homosocial Desire* (New
               York: Columbia University Press).
    1990   *Epistemology of the Closet* (Berkeley: University of California Press).
Seed, D.
    1985   'The Narrative Method of *Dracula*', *NCF* 40: 61-75.
Seidel, M.
    1981   'Crusoe in Exile', *PMLA* 96: 363-74.
    1991   *Robinson Crusoe: Island Myths and the Novel* (Boston: Twayne Pub-
               lishers).
Senf, C.A.
    1979   'The Unseen Face in the Mirror', *JNT* 9: 160-70.
    1982   ' "*Dracula*": Stoker's Response to the New Woman,' *VS* 26: 33-49.

Shaw, G.
   1983   *The Cost of Authority: Manipulation and Freedom in the New Testament*
              (London: SCM Press).
Shaw, S.B.
   1994   'The Pliable Rhetoric of Domesticity', in M.I. Lowance, Jr, E.E. West-
              brook and R.C. De Prospo (eds.), *The Stowe Debate: Rhetorical Strate-
              gies in Uncle Tom's Cabin* (Amherst: University of Massachusetts Press):
              73-98.
Sheeley, S.M.
   1992   *Narrative Asides in Luke–Acts* (JSNTSup, 72; Sheffield: Sheffield Aca-
              demic Press).
Shewan, R.
   1977   *Oscar Wilde: Art and Egotism* (New York: Barnes & Noble).
Shinagel, M.
   1968   *Defoe and Middle-Class Gentility* (Cambridge, MA: Harvard University
              Press).
   1994   'A Note on the Text', in M. Shinagel (ed.), *Daniel Defoe's Robinson
              Crusoe* (Norton Critical Edition; New York: W.W. Norton & Co.): 221-
              24.
Shinagel, M. (ed.)
   1994   *Daniel Defoe's Robinson Crusoe* (Norton Critical Edition; New York:
              W.W. Norton).
Showalter, E.
   1991   *Sister's Choice: Tradition and Change in American Women's Writing*
              (Oxford: Clarendon Press).
Sill, G.M.
   1983   *Defoe and the Idea of Fiction (1713–1719)* (London: Associated Uni-
              versity Presses).
   1994   'Crusoe in the Cave: Defoe and the Semiotics of Desire', *ECF* 6: 215-32.
   1994–95   'A Source for Crusoe's Tobacco Cure', *ELN* 32: 46-48.
Silver, A., and J. Ursini
   1993   *The Vampire Film: From Nosferatu to Bram Stoker's Dracula* (New
              York: Limelight Editions, 2nd edn).
Sim, S.
   1987   'Interrogating an Ideology: Defoe's *Robinson Crusoe*', *BJECS* 10: 163-
              73.
Skal, D.J.
   1990   *Hollywood Gothic: The Tangled Web of Dracula from Novel to Stage to
              Screen* (London: Andre Deutsch).
Slout, W.L.
   1973   '*Uncle Tom's Cabin* in American Film History', *JPFT* 2: 137-51.
Smith, D.E.
   1981   'Meals and Morality in Paul and his World', in K.H. Richards (ed.),
              Society of Biblical Literature 1981 Seminar Papers (Chico, CA: Scholars
              Press): 319-39.
Smith, J.
   1848   *The Voyage and Shipwreck of St Paul* (London: Longmans, Green).

Smith, J.H.
    1925   'The Theology of *Robinson Crusoe*', *HR* 16: 37-47.
Smith, P.E., and M.S. Helfand (eds.)
    1989   *Wilde's Oxford Notebooks: A Portrait of Mind in the Making* (Oxford: Oxford University Press).
Smith, R.J.
    1997   'Those Who Go Before: Ancestors of Eva St. Clare', *NEQ* 30: 314-18.
Smith-Rosenberg, C.
    1977   'Beauty, the Beast and the Militant Woman: A Case Study in Sex Roles and Social Stress in Jacksonian America', *AQ* 23: 562-84.
Smylie, J.H.
    1973   '*Uncle Tom's Cabin* Revisited', *Interpretation* 27: 67-85.
Snowden, F.M., Jr
    1983   *Before Color Prejudice: The Ancient View of Blacks* (Cambridge, MA: Harvard University Press, 1983).
Spaas, L.
    1996   'Narcissus and Friday: From Classical to Anthropological Myth', in L. Spaas and B. Stimpson (eds.), *Robinson Crusoe: Myths and Metamorphoses* (London: Macmillan): 98-109.
Spark, M.
    1958   *Robinson* (London: Macmillan).
Spencer, A.B.
    1981   'The Wise Fool (and the Foolish Wise): A Study of Irony in Paul', *NovT* 23: 349-60.
Spivak, G.C.
    1991   'Theory in the Margin: Coetzee's *Foe* Reading Defoe's *Crusoe/Roxana*', in J. Arac and B. Johnson (eds.), *Consequences of Theory* (Baltimore: The Johns Hopkins University Press): 154-80.
Spivey, T.R.
    1960   'Damnation and Salvation in *The Picture of Dorian Gray*', *BUSE* 4: 162-70.
Stamm, R.
    1936   'Daniel Defoe: An Artist in the Puritan Tradition', *PQ* 15: 225-46.
Starr, G.A.
    1965   *Defoe and Spiritual Autobiography* (Princeton, NJ: Princeton University Press).
    1969   '*Robinson Crusoe* and the Myth of Mammon', in F.H. Ellis (ed.), *Twentieth Century Interpretations of Robinson Crusoe: A Collection of Critical Essays* (Englewood Cliffs, NJ: Prentice–Hall): 102-106.
    1973–74   'Defoe's Prose Style: 1. The Language of Interpretation', *MP* 71: 277-94.
Ste Croix, G.E.M. de
    1975   'Early Christian Attitudes to Poverty and Slavery', *SCH* 12: 1-38.
    1983   *The Class Struggle in the Ancient Greek World: From the Archaic Age to the Arab Conquests* (London: Gerald Duckworth, rev. edn).
    1988   'Slavery and Other Forms of Unfree Labour', in L.J. Archer (ed.), *Slavery and Other Forms of Unfree Labour* (London: Routledge): 19-32.

Steele, T.F.
     1972   'Tom and Eva: Mrs. Stowe's Two Dying Christs?', *NALF* 6: 85-90.
Stein, R.H.
     1992   'Last Supper', in J.B. Green and S. McKnight (eds.), *Dictionary of Jesus and the Gospels* (Leicester: IVP): 444-50.
Stein, W.B.
     1965   'Robinson Crusoe: The Trickster Tricked', *CenR* 9: 271-88.
Stepto, R.B.
     1986   'Sharing the Thunder: The Literary Exchanges of Harriet Beecher Stowe, Henry Bibb, and Frederick Douglass', in E.J. Sundquist (ed.), *New Essays on Uncle Tom's Cabin* (Cambridge: Cambridge University Press): 135-53.
Stevenson, J.A.
     1988   'A Vampire in the Mirror: The Sexuality of *Dracula*', *PMLA* 103: 139-49.
Stevenson, R.L.
     1882   'A Gossip on Romance', *Longman's Magazine* (November).
Stewart, G.
     1995   'Film's Victorian Retrofit', *VS* 38: 153-98.
Stoker, B.
     1993   *Dracula* (ed. Maurice Hindle; London: Penguin Books [1897]).
Stokes, J.
     1978   *Oscar Wilde* (Writers and their Works; Harlow: Longman).
Stone, H.
     1957   'Charles Dickens and Harriet Beecher Stowe', *NCF* 12: 188-202.
Stowe, C.E.
     1889   *The Life of Harriet Beecher Stowe Compiled from her Letters and Journals* (New York: Houghton, Mifflin & Company).
Stowe, H.B.
     1869   'The True Story of Lady Byron's Life', *Atlantic Monthly* 24 (September): 295-313.
     1982   *Uncle Tom's Cabin, or, Life among the Lowly* (ed. A. Douglas; London: Penguin Books [1852]).
     1994   'From The Key to "Uncle Tom's Cabin"', in E. Ammons (ed.), *Harriet Beecher Stowe's Uncle Tom's Cabin* (Norton Critical Edition; New York: W.W. Norton & Co.): 415-26.
Strout, C.
     1968   'Uncle Tom's Cabin and the Portent of the Millennium', *YR* 57: 375-85.
Sullivan, K.
     1972   *Oscar Wilde* (New York: Columbia University Press).
Sundquist, E.J.
     1985   'Slavery, Revolution and the American Renaissance', in W.B. Michaels and D. Pease (eds.), *The American Renaissance Reconsidered* (Baltimore: The Johns Hopkins University Press): 1-33.
     1986   'Introduction', in E.J. Sundquist (ed.), *New Essays on Uncle Tom's Cabin* (Cambridge: Cambridge University Press): 1-44.
Sutherland, James
     1938   *Defoe* (New York: J.B. Lippincott Co.).

Sutherland, John
    1997   *Can Jane Eyre Be Happy? More Puzzles in Classic Fiction* (Oxford: Oxford University Press).

Swartley, W.M.
    1983   *Slavery, Sabbath, War and Women: Case Studies in Biblical Interpretation* (Scottdale, PA: Herald Press).

Szczesiul, A.E.
    1996   'The Canonization of Tom and Eva: Catholic Hagiography and *Uncle Tom's Cabin*', *ATQ* 10: 59-72.

Talbert, C.H.
    1987   *Reading Corinthians: A Literary and Theological Commentary on 1 and 2 Corinthians* (New York: Crossroad).

Tandy, J.R.
    1922   'Pro-Slavery Propaganda in American Fiction of the Fifties', *SAQ* 21: 41-58, 170-78.

Taylor, W.R.
    1979   *Cavalier and Yankee: The Old South and American National Character* (Cambridge, MA: Harvard University Press).

Theissen, G.
    1982   *The Social Setting of Pauline Christianity* (Edinburgh: T. & T. Clark).

Thurman, J.
    1987   'A House Divided', *NY* (9 November): 175-80.

Tompkins, J.P.
    1994   'Sentimental Power: *Uncle Tom's Cabin* and the Politics of Literary History', in E. Ammons (ed.), *Harriet Beecher Stowe's Uncle Tom's Cabin* (Norton Critical Edition; New York: W.W. Norton & Co.): 501-522.

Tournier, M.
    1967   *Vendredi ou les limbes du Pacifique* (Paris: Gallimard).

Travis, S.H.
    1973   'Paul's Boasting in 2 Corinthians 10-12', *SE* 6: 527-32.
    1994   'Christ as Bearer of Divine Judgment in Paul's Thought about the Atonement', in J.B. Green and M. Turner (eds.), *Jesus of Nazareth Lord and Christ: Essays on the Historical Jesus and New Testament Christology* (Grand Rapids: Eerdmans, 1994): 332-45.

Trummer, P.
    1975   'Die Chance der Freiheit: Zur Interpretation des μᾶλλον χρῆσαι in 1 Kor 7,21', *Biblica* 56: 344-68.

Twitchell, J.B.
    1981   *The Living Dead: A Study of the Vampire in Romantic Literature* (Durham, NC: Duke University Press).
    1985   *Dreadful Pleasures: An Anatomy of Modern Horror* (Oxford: Oxford University Press).

Tyler, P.
    1947   *Magic and Myth of the Movies* (New York: Simon & Schuster).

Urbach, E.E.
    1964   'The Laws Regarding Slavery as a Source for Social History of the Period of the Second Temple, the Mishnah, and Talmud', in J.G. Weiss

(ed.), *Papers of the Institute of Jewish Studies* (Jerusalem: Magnes Press): 1-94.

Van Buren, J.
    1986   '*Uncle Tom's Cabin*: A Myth of Familial Relations', *JP* 13: 251-76.
Van Hoy, M.S.
    1973   'Two Allusions to Hungary in *Uncle Tom's Cabin*', *Phylon* 34: 433-35.
Vickers, I.
    1996   *Defoe and the New Sciences* (Cambridge: Cambridge University Press).
Vogt, J.
    1974   *Ancient Slavery and the Ideal of Man* (Oxford: Basil Blackwell).
Walaskay, P.W.
    1983   '*And so we came to Rome*': The Political Perspective of St Luke* (SNTSMS, 49; Cambridge: Cambridge University Press).
Waldrep, S.
    1996   'The Aesthetic Realism of Oscar Wilde's *Dorian Gray*', *SLI* 29: 103-112.
Wallace, R., and W. Williams
    1998   *The Three Worlds of Paul of Tarsus* (London: Routledge).
Wardley, L.
    1992   'Relic, Fetish, Femmage: The Aesthetics of Sentiment in the Work of Stowe', *YJC* 5: 165-91.
Warhol, R.R.
    1986   'Toward a Theory of the Engaging Narrator: Earnest Interventions in Gaskell, Stowe, and Eliot', *PMLA* 101: 811-18.
Wasson, R.
    1966   'The Politics of *Dracula*', *VN* 9: 24-27.
Watson, A.
    1987   *Roman Slave Law* (Baltimore: The Johns Hopkins University Press).
Watson, C.S.
    1976–77   'Simms's Review of *Uncle Tom's Cabin*', *AL* 48: 365-68.
Watson, F.
    1959   'Robinson Crusoe: An Englishman of the Age', *HT* 9: 760-66.
Watson, N.
    1992   *The First Epistle to the Corinthians* (EC; London: Epworth Press).
Watt, I.
    1951   'Robinson Crusoe as a Myth', *EC* 1: 95-119.
    1952   'Defoe and Richardson on Homer: A Study of the Relation of Novel and Epic in the Early Eighteenth Century', *RES* 3: 325-40.
    1957a   'Defoe as Novelist', in B. Ford (ed.), *From Dryden to Johnson* (The Pelican Guide to English Literature, 4; Harmondsworth: Penguin Books): 203-216.
    1957b   *The Rise of the Novel: Studies in Defoe, Richardson and Fielding* (Harmondsworth: Penguin Books).
Weinstein, P.M.
    1996   *What Else But Love? The Ordeal of Race in Faulkner and Morrison* (New York: Columbia University Press).
Weissman, J.
    1977   'Women and Vampires: *Dracula* as Victorian Novel', *MQ* 18: 392-405.

Welter, B.
1966   'The Cult of True Womanhood: 1820–1860', *AQ* 18: 151-74.
West, R.
1997   *The Life and Strange Surprising Adventures of Daniel Defoe* (London: HarperCollins).
Westermann, W.L.
1955   *The Slave Systems of Greek and Roman Antiquity* (Philadelphia: American Philosophical Society).
Westra, H.P.
1994   'Confronting Antichrist: The Influence of Jonathan Edwards's Millennial Vision', in M.I. Lowance, Jr, E.E. Westbrook and R.C. De Prospo (eds.), *The Stowe Debate: Rhetorical Strategies in Uncle Tom's Cabin* (Amherst: University of Massachusetts Press): 141-58.
Wheeler, R.
1995   '"My Savage", "My Man": Racial Multiplicity in *Robinson Crusoe*', *ELH* 62: 821-61.
White, D.G.
1987   'The Nature of Female Slavery', in L.K. Kerber and J. De Hart-Mathews (eds.), *Women's America: Refocusing the Past* (Oxford: Oxford University Press, 2nd edn): 100-116.
White, I.
1994   'Sentimentality and the Uses of Death', in M.I. Lowance, Jr, E.E. Westbrook and R.C. De Prospo (eds.), *The Stowe Debate: Rhetorical Strategies in Uncle Tom's Cabin* (Amherst: University of Massachusetts Press): 99-115.
Whitney, L.
1993   'In the Shadow of *Uncle Tom's Cabin*: Stowe's Vision of Slavery from the Great Dismal Swamp', *NEQ* 66: 552-69.
Wicke, J.
1992   'Vampiric Typewriting: *Dracula* and its Media', *ELH* 59 (1992): 467-93.
Wiedemann, T.E.J.
1981   *Greek and Roman Slavery* (London: Croom Helm).
1985   'The Regularity of Manumission at Rome', *ClQ* 35: 162-75.
1997   *Slavery* (*Greece & Rome*, New Surveys in the Classics No. 19; Oxford: Oxford University Press).
Wilde, O.
1985   *The Picture of Dorian Gray* (ed. Peter Ackroyd; London: Penguin Books [1891]).
Williams, A.
1991   '*Dracula*: Si(g)ns of the Fathers', *TSLL* 33: 445-63.
Williams, L.
1996   'Versions of Uncle Tom: Race and Gender in American Melodrama', in C. McCabe and D. Petrie (eds.), *New Scholarship from BFI Research* (London: British Film Institute): 111-39.
Williams, R.R.
1953   *The Acts of the Apostles* (TBC; London: SCM Press).

Willimon, W.H.
    1988   *Acts* (IC; Atlanta: John Knox Press).
Wilson, A.N.
    1983   'Introduction', in Bram Stoker, *Dracula* (Oxford: Oxford University Press): vii-xix.
Wilson, Edmund
    1962   *Patriotic Gore: Studies in the Literature of the American Civil War* (Oxford: Oxford University Press).
Wilson, E.
    1996   '*Vendredi ou les limbes du Pacifique*: Tournier, Seduction and Paternity', in L. Spaas and B. Stimpson (eds.), *Robinson Crusoe: Myths and Metamorphoses* (London: Macmillan): 199-209.
Wilson, R.F.
    1942   *Crusader in Crinoline: The Life of Harriet Beecher Stowe* (London: Hutchinson).
Winter, B.W.
    1978   'The Lord's Supper at Corinth: An Alternative Reconstruction', *RTR* 37: 73-82.
Wiodat, C.M.
    1993   'Talking Back to Schoolteacher: Morrison's Confrontation with Hawthorne in *Beloved*', *MFS* 39: 527-46.
Witherington III, B.
    1995   *Conflict & Community in Corinth: A Socio-Rhetorical Commentary on 1 and 2 Corinthians* (Carlisle: Paternoster Press).
    1998   *The Acts of the Apostles: A Socio-Rhetorical Commentary* (Carlisle: Paternoster Press).
Wolf, L.
    1993   *The Essential Dracula: The Definitive Annotated Edition of Bram Stoker's Classic Novel* (London: Plume Books).
Wolff, C.G.
    1995   '"Masculinity in *Uncle Tom's Cabin*', *AQ* 47: 595-618.
Wood, R.
    1979   'The Dark Mirror: Murnau's *Nosferatu*', in R. Lippe and R. Wood (eds.), *The American Nightmare* (Ottowa: University of Toronto): 43-49.
    1983   'Burying the Undead: The Use and Obsolescence of Count Dracula', *Mosaic* 16: 175-87.
Yarborough, R.
    1986   'Strategies of Black Characterization in *Uncle Tom's Cabin* and the Early Afro-American Novel', in E.J. Sundquist (ed.), *New Essays on Uncle Tom's Cabin* (Cambridge: Cambridge University Press): 45-84.
Yavetz, Z.
    1988   *Slaves and Slavery in Ancient Rome* (New Brunswick: Transaction).
Yellin, J.F.
    1986   'Doing it Herself: *Uncle Tom's Cabin* and Woman's Role in the Slavery Crisis', in E.J. Sundquist (ed.), *New Essays on Uncle Tom's Cabin* (Cambridge: Cambridge University Press): 85-105.

| 1989 | 'Hawthorne and the American National Sin,' in H.D. Peck (ed.), *The Green American Tradition: Essays and Poems for Sherman Paul* (Baton Rouge: Louisiana State University Press): 75-97. |

Zanger, J.

| 1997 | 'Metaphor into Metonymy: The Vampire Next Door', in J. Gordon and V. Hollinger (eds.), *Blood Red: The Vampire as Metaphor in Contemporary Culture* (Philadelphia: University of Pennsylvania Press): 17-26. |

Zeender, M.-N.

| 1994 | 'John Melmoth and Dorian Gray: The Two-Faced Mirror', in C.G. Sandulescu (ed.), *Rediscovering Oscar Wilde* (Gerrards Cross: Colin Smythe): 432-40. |

Zeitlin, S.

| 1962–63 | 'Slavery during the Second Commonwealth and the Tannaitic Period', *JQR* 53: 185-218. |

Zimmerman, E.

| 1971 | 'Defoe and Crusoe', *JELH* 38: 377-96. |
| 1975 | *Defoe and the Novel* (Berkeley: University of California Press). |

Zwarg, C.

| 1994 | 'Fathering and Blackface in *Uncle Tom's Cabin*', in E. Ammons (ed.), *Harriet Beecher Stowe's Uncle Tom's Cabin* (Norton Critical Edition; New York: W.W. Norton): 568-84. |

INDEXES

INDEX OF REFERENCES

Biblical References

Old Testament

Genesis
2.23-24	125
3.19	51
4	127
5.24	122
5.27	123
8.8-12	123

Exodus
2.22	123
20	153
40.34-38	123

Leviticus
13.45-46	125
17.10-12	116

Numbers
12.6	83
12.8	83

Deuteronomy
12.23	114, 124

Joshua
1.5	61

1 Samuel
28.15	64

1 Kings
17.4-6	55

Psalms
50.15	56
68.22	123
78.19	57

Isaiah
62.5	122

Jeremiah
18.2-6	51
31.31	116

Jonah
1	52
1.5	52

Zechariah
13.1	113, 141

New Testament

Matthew
4.9	123
10.29-31	122
13.1-9	122
14.13-21	125
25.1-10	122
25.31-46	158
26.26-29	115
26.39	123
27.46	135

Mark
4.1-9	122
6.32-44	125

8.24	122
14.22-25	115
14.24	116
14.36	123
15.34	135

Luke
4.7	123
7.1-10	38
8.4-8	122
9.10-17	125
12.6-7	122
15.11-32	52
16.19-31	61
22.15-20	115
22.42	123
23.46	124
23.47	38
24.30	115

John
3.29	122
6.1-15	125
12.24-25	55
19.30	135
19.34	124

Acts
2.42	115
2.46	115
9.30	37
10.1-48	38
11.25-26	37
13.4	37

13.13	37	8.12-17	149		95, 101,
14.25-26	37	8.21-23	149		192
16.10-17	37	8.35	35	4.8-9	35
16.11	37	9.21	51	6.4-5	35
17.14-15	37	16.20	51	6.8-10	35
18.18-22	37			10–13	36
18.27	37	*1 Corinthians*		11.1–12.13	35
20.5-15	37	4.9-13	35	11.17-18	36
20.7	115	5.1-13	117	11.22-28	35, 192
20.11	115	5.7	23, 117,	11.25-26	18, 34,
21.1-18	37		192		77
22.25-26	38	7	144, 148,	11.25	35
23.23-24	38		149	11.26	35
25.12	39	7.17-24	192	12.10	35
27–28	34	7.17	148		
27	37	7.20-24	23, 144,	*Galatians*	
27.1–28.16	37, 38,		145, 150,	1.10	151
	77, 78,		159, 160,	3.28	26, 145
	192		164, 170,	4.1-9	149
			189	4.24-25	149
27.1-44	18, 38,	7.20	148, 189	5.1	149
	53	7.21	27, 147-		
27.1	39		49, 189	*Ephesians*	
27.6	37	7.22-23	150	1.17	116
27.8	37	7.22	26, 148	2.13	116
27.9	75	7.24	148, 189	5.31	125
27.14-17	38	9	23, 150,	6.5-8	189
27.18	52		159, 160,		
27.21-26	39		189, 192	*Philippians*	
27.24	39	9.16-18	151	1.1	151
27.26	38	9.19-23	150, 151	4.11	167
27.27-44	36	9.19	191	4.12	35
27.30	18	10.16	116		
27.33-38	60	10.17	116	*Colossians*	
27.35-36	38	11.20	115	1.20	116
27.35	38, 115	11.23-26	23, 115,	3.22-24	189
27.37	39		192		
27.44	38, 40	12.13	145	*1 Timothy*	
		13.11	85	2.13	153
Romans		13.12	21, 82-	6.1-2	189
1.1	151		84, 94,		
2.14-16	51		95, 101,	*Philemon*	
3.25	116		102, 192	10-19	145, 164
5.1-21	51			16	26
5.9	116	*2 Corinthians*			
6.6-9	149	3.18	21, 82,	*Jude*	
6.16-23	149		83, 94,	12	115
7.7-8	51				

Other Ancient References

Didache
9.1   115

Philo
Quaest. in Gen.
2.3.101-103   83

Josephus
Life
14–15   36

Christian Authors
Ignatius
Letter to the Smyrnaeans
8.1   115

Justin Martyr
Apology to the Jews
66.1   115

Classical
Aeschylus
Agamemnon
1112   84

Apollodorus
The Library
3.5.8   85

Diodorus Siculus
Library of History
4.64.3   85

Sophocles
Oedipus the Tyrant
391   85

INDEX OF AUTHORS

Ackroyd, P. 80, 89
Acworth, A. 36
Adkinson, R. 129
Albert, J. 92
Alcott, L.M. 87
Alexander, L. 37
Alkon, P.K. 44
Allen, W. 46
Ammons, E. 159, 160
Anderson, B.A. 168
Arac, J. 165
Arata, S.D. 121
Armstrong, D. 44
Armstrong, K.A. 44
Askeland, L. 165
Austen, J. 143
Ayers, R.W. 52

Babington, B. 193
Bach, A. 193
Backscheider, P.R. 40, 46, 48, 52
Baker, H.A. 93
Bakhtin, M. 93
Baldwin, J. 155
Banks, M. 152
Barrett, C.K. 37, 115, 150
Barrow, R.H. 146
Bartchy, S.S. 24, 147-49, 173
Barton, S. 114
Bassett, S.E. 82
Bastian, F. 40
Baumert, N. 149
Baym, N. 155
Beckson, K. 89, 95
Begam, R. 33
Belford, B. 118, 120

Bell, I.A. 44, 49
Bellin, J.D. 26, 187
Bender, J. 45
Benjamin, E.B. 56
Bentley, C.F. 121
Bergson, K. 89
Berne, E. 44
Bierman, J.S. 118
Birdsall, V.O. 44
Blackburn, T.C. 44
Blewett, D. 33, 49, 63
Blinderman, C.S. 125
Bloch, J.-R. 34
Boardman, M.M. 44, 78
Bogle, D. 25
Boreham, F.W. 55
Bradley, K.R. 146, 148
Bradley, L.R. 145
Brandstadter, E. 26, 153
Brauch, M. 149
Braverman, R. 44
Brînzeu, P. 90
Bristow, J. 87
Brodhead, R.H. 170
Bronfen, E. 127, 155
Brown, D.S. 167
Brown, G. 159, 160
Brown, H.O. 54
Brown, J.P. 93
Budgen, F. 31
Bultmann, R. 116
Buñel, L. 66
Bunyan, J. 43, 73
Burgess, A. 26
Burnett, P. 33

Cadbury, H.J. 37, 38
Camfield, G. 164
Camus, A. 49
Canady, N. Jr 153
Cannon, K.G. 145
Carroll, J.T. 117
Carter, E. 25
Cartledge, P.A. 87, 146
Case, S.E. 120
Cassara, E. 156
Cervo, N. 19
Chaput, D. 156
Charlesworth, B. 90
Coetzee, J.M. 32, 33
Cohen, W.A. 87
Coleridge, S.T. 33
Colleran, J. 33
Conan Doyle, A. 87
Conzelmann, H. 36, 82, 151
Coppola, F.F. 134
Corcoran, P. 33
Cords, N. 143
Corey, S. 166
Cottom, D. 44
Cowper, W. 9, 47, 113, 141
Cox, J.M. 164
Craft, C. 120
Crane, G.D. 164
Crouch, J.E. 149
Crouch, S. 166
Crozier, A.C. 158
Crumpacker, L. 159
Curtis, L.A. 41

Dale, P.A. 88
Dalzell, F. 23, 92
Damrosch, L. Jr 43
Danker, F.W. 82
Danson, L. 87, 89
Davis, L.J. 46
Dawes, G.W. 148
Defoe, D. 8, 17-19, 31-34, 40-53, 58,
    59, 62-66, 68, 71, 72, 75-79, 192
Dellamora, R. 89
Demetrakopoulos, S. 121
Deming, W. 149
Demos, J. 163
Dibelius, M. 37

Dickens, C. 25, 143
Dickson, D.R. 81, 107
Disraeli, B. 87
Dixon, T. 25
Dodd, C.H. 147
Donovan, J. 156
Doody, M.A. 46
Dottin, P. 40
Douglas, A. 143, 155, 159
Ducksworth, S.S. 156
Dunn, J.D.G. 37, 117, 149
Duvall, S.P.C. 153

Earle, P. 40, 41
Edwards, O.D. 85
Egan, J. 62
Elliott, N. 149
Ellis, F.H. 44, 46, 50, 63
Ellmann, R. 86, 89
Emerton, J.A. 116
Engelibert, J.-P. 33
Erickson, R.A. 49
Espey, J. 86
Evans, P.W. 193
Eyles, A. 129

Fanu, J.S. le 119
Farson, D. 21, 118
Fee, G.D. 82, 149
Ferguson, R. 166
Fiedler, L.A. 25, 159, 161, 169
Fields, K.E. 166
Figuerola, C. 34
Finley, M.I. 24, 146, 148
Fisch, H. 52
Fisher, P. 159
Fitzgerald, J.T. 35
Fitzmyer, J.A. 37
Fleischner, J. 165
Flint, C. 52
Florescu, R. 118
Fluck, W. 155
Flynn, J.P. 190
Forbes, C. 35
Forster, E.M. 41
Foster, J.O. 44
France, R.T. 26, 27
Fraser, P. 193

Fry, C.L. 120
Fry, N. 129
Fry, S. 20
Furbank, P.N. 40
Furnas, J.C. 156, 173
Furnish, V.P. 35

Gagnier, R. 89, 91, 93
Gall, J. 93
Ganzel, D. 58
Gardiner, J. 153
Gardner, J.F. 148
Garlan, Y. 146
Garnsey, P. 146
Gauthier, M. 33
Gautier, T. 87
Gay, J. 19
Gayer, R. 150
Gerould, D.C. 174
Gerson, N.B. 25
Gerster, P. 143
Gilbert, S.M. 161
Gildon, C. 46
Giles, K. 145
Gill, A. 46
Gillespie, M.P. 81, 86, 90, 93
Girdler, L. 40
Goethe, J.W. von 87
Gogol, N. 88
Gold, B.J. 89
Golding, W. 62
Goldknopf, D. 46
González, A.B. 95
Gordon, J.B. 88
Gossett, T.F. 26, 153, 155, 156, 158,
    166, 173, 188, 190
Graham, T. 156
Green, J.B. 117
Green, M. 32
Grief, M.J. 56
Griffin, G. 120, 127
Grinstein, A. 156
Gubar, S. 161

Haenchen, E. 37
Haining, P. 119
Halberstam, J. 121
Halewood, W.H. 47

Haley, B. 93
Hall, B. 33
Hammond, J.R. 63, 167
Hare, D. 19
Harrill, J.A. 147, 148
Hart, J.V. 134, 136
Hart-Davis, R. 90
Hastings, W. 58
Hatlen, B. 121
Häusermann, H.W. 40
Hawthorne, N. 88, 127
Hayne, B. 153
Hays, R.B. 82, 149
Hearne, J. 48
Hedrick, J.D. 25, 55, 154, 157, 158, 161,
    163
Helfand, M.S. 93
Hemer, C.J. 36, 37
Henderson, M.C. 173
Henderson, M.G. 166
Henderson, R.M. 25, 39
Hennelly, M.M. Jr 121
Henson, J. 153
Hentzi, G. 44
Heron-Allen, E. 87
Heston, C. 138, 141
Higgins, A.J.B. 115, 116
Hindle, M. 120
Hirsch, S.A. 153
Hoare, P. 19
Hodgson, J.A. 87
Hodgson, R. 35
Hogan, D.J. 120
Hogan, M. 166
Holland, G. 35
Holland, M. 89
Holland, V. 85, 97
Hollinger, V. 117
Holmes, A.F. 44
Holmes, G.F. 153
Hopes, J. 44
Hopkins, K. 146
Horrell, D.G. 149
Horvitz, D. 166
Hovet, T.R. 153, 160, 163
Howard, J.K. 117
Howes, M. 22, 120
Hudson, B.F. 24, 156

Hudson, N. 44
Hunter, A.M. 115
Hunter, J.P. 45, 52, 62
Hutchings, P. 129
Hutchins, H.C. 43
Huxley, A. 113
Huxley, T.H. 88
Huysman, K. 87
Hyde, H.M. 20, 86, 89

Irvine, L. 17

Jager, E. 44
James, E.A. 47, 58
Jancovich, M. 121
Jann, R. 121
Jehlen, M. 159
Jenkins, C. 148
Jenkins, J.L. 159
Jeremias, J. 115, 116, 146
Johnson, A. 120, 121
Johnson, L.T. 36
Jones, F.S. 148
Jones, S. 129
Joseph, G. 87
Joswick, T.P. 155, 165, 170, 172
Joyce, J. 31, 33, 65, 89
Julian, P. 87

Kafka, F. 7
Käsemann, E. 116
Kaufmann, M. 19
Kavanaugh, T.M. 44
Kazin, A. 158
Keck, L.E. 150
Keefe, R. 91, 95
Keenan, S. 166
Kiberd, D. 85
Kimball, G. 158
King, M.L. Jr 190
Kirschenbaum, A. 146
Kistemaker, S.J. 149
Kisthardt, M.J. 160
Kittell, G. 83
Klauck, H.-J. 115
Knott, C.E. 88
Knox, M. 89
Kohl, N. 87

Korg, C.E. 159
Korg, J. 88
Kreitzer, L.J. 7-11, 22, 28, 35, 83, 124
Krumholz, L. 166
Krumm, P. 120
Kurz, W.S. 37
Kyrtatas, D.J. 148, 150

Ladouceur, D. 37
Lake, K. 38
Lane, C. 87
Lang, A.S. 159
Lange, B.S. 166
Latham, R. 136
Lawler, D.L. 86, 88
Leatherdale, C. 118, 120
Leverenz, D. 160
Levine, L.W. 152, 175
Levy, D.W. 156
Locke, J. 44
Lounsbery, G.C. 98
Lowance, M.I. Jr 158, 167, 187
Lüdemann, G. 36, 39
Ludlam, H. 118
Lyall, F. 148

Mabee, C. 29
Macaskill, B. 33
Maccoby, H. 116
MacDonald, J.I.H. 44, 150
MacFarlane, L.W. 169, 187
MacLaine, A.H. 31
Maddox, J.H. Jr 44
Malan, F.S. 150
Malmgren, C.D. 166
Mare, W. de la 42
Marez, C. 85
Marsh, C. 128, 193
Marshall, I.H. 18, 19, 115
Marshall, P. 35
Martin, D.B. 147, 149, 151, 152, 173
Martin, J.W. 193
Martin, R.K. 87
Martin, R.P. 35, 115
Marx, K. 43, 190
Marxsen, W. 115
Massey, M. 148
Matheson, R. 9, 138, 139

Maturin, C.R. 87
McCormack, J. 87
McDonald, J. 121
McKeon, M. 44, 46, 49, 57
McNally, R. 118
McPherson, J.M. 156
Meagher, S. 73
Meeks, W.A. 145, 151
Meggitt, J.J. 149
Mégroz, R.L. 46
Meindarus, O.F.A. 36
Merrett, R.J. 44
Meyer, M.J. 155, 156
Middleton, S. 157
Miles, G.B. 37
Milgrom, J. 80
Miller, E. 120
Miller, M.M. 98
Milne, L. 32
Minto, W. 46
Mitchell, A. 32, 66
Mitchell, M.M. 150
Moers, E. 143
Moffatt, J. 47
Moore, J.R. 40-42
Moreland, P. 148
Moretti, F. 121
Morrison, R.D. 121, 166
Morrison, T. 165
Murphy-O'Connor, J. 37
Murray, I. 86, 87

Nandris, G. 118
Nelsen, A.K. 25
Nelsen, H.M. 25
Nethercot, A.H. 90
Nichols, C. 153
Nixon, N. 131, 137
Nolan, S. 28, 29
Novak, M.E. 42, 44, 46, 52, 64
Nozière, M. 98
Nuernberg, S.M. 156
Nunokawa, J. 87

Oates, J.C. 88
O'Connell, C.E. 164
Ogilvie, R.M. 38
Ortiz, G. 193

Osborne, J. 98
Ostwalt, C.E. Jr 193
Otten, T. 166
Owens, W.R. 40

Paglia, C. 88, 92
Pappas, J.J. 93
Parker, G. 45
Parrish, T.L. 166
Pater, W. 87
Peck, H.D. 44
Perlman, E.H. 44
Plate, S.B. 194
Poe, E.A. 79, 87, 88
Pokorný, P. 37
Porter, R. 118
Porter, S.E. 37
Portnoy, W.E. 87
Post, R.M. 33
Poteet, L.J. 88
Powell, K. 87, 88, 91, 97
Praeder, S.M. 37
Prior, D. 149
Prynne, H. 127
Punter, D. 119
Purdy, A. 32

Railton, S. 159
Rapske, B.M. 37
Rawson, B. 24
Reed, K.T. 187
Richardson, H. 44
Richetti, J.J. 40, 44, 47
Richman, M. 153
Ridderbos, H.N. 117
Ridgely, J.V. 153
Riggio, T.P. 25
Riss, A. 156
Robbins, S. 165
Robbins, V.K. 37
Roberson, S.L. 159
Roberts, D. 153, 161
Roberts, S. 33
Robins, H.F. 50
Roditi, E. 87
Rody, C. 166
Rogers, P. 44, 49
Rollins, W.G. 150

Romero, L. 154
Rosen, G. 23
Ross, A. 31, 46
Rossi, D. 87
Roth, J. 121
Rousseau, J.-J. 43
Rowland, C. 189
Rushdy, A.H.A. 166
Ryder, A. 119

Saller, R. 24
Sampley, J.P. 35
Sánchez-Eppler, K. 154
Saxton, A. 17
Scarpa, G. 166
Schaffer, T. 22
Schonhorn, M. 44
Schweizer, E. 115
Scott, W. 31
Seaford, R. 82
Secord, A. 42, 46
Sedgwick, E.K. 87, 88
Seed, D. 120
Seidel, M. 41, 46, 55
Senf, C.A. 120, 121
Shaw, G. 36, 165
Shaw, S.B. 159, 187
Sheeley, S.M. 40
Shewan, R. 90
Shinagel, M. 41, 43-46
Showalter, E. 161
Sill, G.M. 44, 55
Sim, S. 44
Simms, W.G. 153
Skal, D.J. 129, 134
Slout, W.L. 174
Smith, D.E. 115
Smith, J. 36
Smith, J.H. 47
Smith, P.E. 93
Smith, R.J. 155
Smith-Rosenberg, C. 159
Smylie, J.H. 158
Spaas, L. 31
Spark, M. 32
Spencer, A.B. 35
Spivak, G.C. 33

Spivey, T.R. 91
Stamm, R. 41
Starr, G.A. 44, 45
Ste Croix, G.E.M. de 27, 150
Steele, T.F. 167
Stein, R.H. 115
Stein, W.B. 44
Stepto, R.B. 153
Stevenson, J.A. 120
Stevenson, R.L. 65, 87, 143
Stewart, G. 131
Stoker, B. 9, 21-23, 114, 117-19, 121,
    124, 126, 129-32, 134, 135, 137,
    140, 141, 192
Stokes, J. 112
Stone, H. 26
Stowe, H.B. 10, 23-27, 143-45, 152,
    153, 155-61, 163, 167, 169, 173,
    175, 177, 182, 187-92
Strout, C. 155, 187
Sullivan, K. 21
Sundquist, E.J. 154, 155, 164
Sutherland, James 46
Sutherland, John 64
Swartley, W.M. 145
Szczesiul, A.E. 158

Talbert, C.H. 149
Tandy, J.R. 153
Taylor, W.R. 143
Tennyson, A. 87
Theissen, G. 114, 151, 152
Thurman, J. 166
Tompkins, J.P. 155, 159, 187
Tournier, M. 32
Travis, S.H. 35, 117
Trompf, G. 37
Trummer, P. 149
Twitchell, J.B. 119, 126
Tyler, P. 104

Urbach, E.E. 146

Van Buren, J. 159
Van Hoy, M.S. 165
Vickers, I. 44
Vogt, J. 146

Walaskay, P.W. 38
Waldrep, S. 93
Wallace, R. 149
Wardley, L. 159
Warhol, R.R. 177
Washington, B.T. 190
Wasson, R. 121
Watson, A. 148
Watson, C.S. 153
Watson, F. 44
Watson, N. 149
Watt, I. 31, 44, 46, 47
Weinstein, P.M. 166
Weissman, J. 120
Welter, B. 159
West, R. 40
Westermann, W.L. 146
Westra, H.P. 187
Wheeler, R. 34
White, D.G. 157
White, I. 155
Whitney, L. 164
Wicke, J. 121
Wiedemann, T.E.J. 146, 148
Wilde, O. 8, 9, 19-22, 80-82, 85-95, 97-99, 104, 105, 107, 110-12, 192

Williams, A. 121
Williams, L. 25, 174
Williams, R.R. 52
Williams, W. 149
Willimon, W.H. 38
Wilson, A.N. 119
Wilson, E. 32
Wilson, Edmund 158
Wilson, R.F. 25, 158
Winter, B.W. 114
Wiodat, C.M. 165
Witherington, B. III 35, 37, 114, 149
Wolf, L. 124
Wolff, C.G. 159
Wood, R. 120, 129
Woolf, V. 143

Yarborough, R. 153, 156, 166
Yavetz, Z. 146
Yellin, J.F. 154, 165

Zanger, J. 137
Zeender, M.-N. 87
Zeitlin, S. 146
Zimmerman, E. 49, 56
Zwarg, C. 160